QUESTIONING FINANCIAL GOVERNANCE FROM A FEMINIST PERSPECTIVE

Questioning Financial Governance from a Feminist Perspective brings together feminist economists and political economists from different countries located in North America and Europe to analyse the 'strategic silence' about gender in fiscal and monetary policy, and financial regulation. This silence reflects a set of assumptions that the key instruments of financial governance are gender neutral. This often masks the ways in which financial governance operates to the disadvantage of women and reinforces gender inequality.

This book examines both the transformations in the governance of finance that predate the financial crisis, as well as some dimension of the crisis itself. An important aspect of the transformations has been the creation of policy rules (often enacted in laws) that limit the discretion of national policy makers with respect to fiscal, monetary and financial sector policies. These policy rules tend to have inscribed in them a series of biases that have gender (as well as class and race-based) outcomes. The biases identified by the authors in the various chapters are the deflationary bias, male breadwinner bias, and commodification bias, adding two new biases: risk bias and creditor bias.

The originality of the book is that its primary focus is on macroeconomic policies (fiscal and monetary) and financial governance from a feminist perspective with a focus on the gross domestic product and its fluctuations and growth, paid employment and inflation, the budget surplus/deficit, levels of government expenditure and tax revenue, and supply of money. The central findings are that the key instruments of financial governance are gender neutral. Each chapter considers examples of financial governance, and how it relates to the gender order, including divisions of labour, and relations of power and privilege.

This book is key reading for anyone studying feminist economics, and should also be of interest to those researching macroeconomics, political economics and women's studies.

Brigitte Young is Professor of International Political Economy at the Institute of Political Science, University of Münster, Germany.

Isabella Bakker is Professor of Political Science and Political Economy at York University, Toronto, Canada.

Diane Elson is Professor of Sociology at the University of Essex, UK.

Routledge IAFFE Advances in Feminist Economics

IAFFE aims to increase the visibility and range of economic research on gender; facilitate communication among scholars, policymakers and activists concerned with women's well-being and empowerment; promote discussions among policy makers about interventions which serve women's needs; educate economists, policy makers, and the general public about feminist perspectives on economic issues; foster feminist evaluations of economics as a discipline; expose the gender blindness characteristic of much social science and the ways in which this impoverishes all research, even research that does not explicitly concern women's issues; help expand opportunities for women, especially women from underrepresented groups, within economics; and, encourage the inclusion of feminist perspectives in the teaching of economics. The IAFFE book series pursues the aims of the organization by providing a forum in which scholars have space to develop their ideas at length and in detail. The series exemplifies the value of feminist research and the high standard of IAFFE sponsored scholarship.

1 **Living Wages, Equal Wages**
Gender and labor market policies in the United States
Deborah M. Figart, Ellen Mutari and Marilyn Power

2 **Family Time**
The social organization of care
Edited by Nancy Folbre and Michael Bittman

3 **Feminist Economics and the World Bank**
History, theory and policy
Edited by Edith Kuiper and Drucilla K. Barker

4 **Sexual Orientation Discrimination**
An international perspective
Edited by M. V. Lee Badgett and Jefferson Frank

5 **The Feminist Economics of Trade**
Edited by Irene van Staveren, Diane Elson, Caren Grown, and Nilufer Cagatay

6 **Sex Markets**
A denied industry
Marina Della Giusta, Maria Di Tommaso and Steinar Strøm

7 **Gender and Chinese Development**
Towards an equitable society
Lanyan Chen

8 **Gender and the Contours of Precarious Employment**
Leah Vosko, Martha MacDonald and Iain Campbell

9 **Questioning Financial Governance from a Feminist Perspective**
Edited by Brigitte Young, Isabella Bakker and Diane Elson

QUESTIONING FINANCIAL GOVERNANCE FROM A FEMINIST PERSPECTIVE

Edited by Brigitte Young, Isabella Bakker and Diane Elson

Routledge
Taylor & Francis Group
LONDON AND NEW YORK

First published 2011
by Routledge
2 Park Square, Milton Park, Abingdon, Oxon, OX14 4RN

Simultaneously published in the USA and Canada
by Routledge
711 Third Avenue, New York, NY 10017

Routledge is an imprint of the Taylor & Francis Group, an informa business

British Library Cataloguing in Publication Data
A catalogue record for this book is available from the British Library

Library of Congress Cataloging in Publication Data
Questioning financial governance from a feminist perspective/edited by Brigitte Young, Isabella Bakker and Diane Elson.
p. cm.
Includes bibliographical references and index.
1. Feminist economics. 2. Monetary policy. 3. Fiscal policy. 4. Finance—Government policy. I. Young, Brigitte, 1946- II. Bakker, Isabella, 1956- III. Elson, Diane.
HQ1381.Q47 2011
339.5'2082--dc22 2011003934

ISBN: 978-0-415-67669-4 (hbk)
ISBN: 978-0-415-67670-0 (pbk)
ISBN: 978-0-203-80730-9 (ebk)

Typeset in Bembo by Sunrise Setting Ltd, Torquay, UK

CONTENTS

LIST OF ILLUSTRATIONS

List of figures

List of tables

LIST OF CONTRIBUTORS

Isabella Bakker is Professor of Political Science and Political Economy at York University, Toronto, Canada. Her published works include: *The Strategic Silence: Gender and Economic Policy*; *Rethinking Restructuring: Gender and Change in Canada; Power, Production and Social Reproduction: Human In/security in the Global Political Economy* (with Stephen Gill) and *Beyond States and Markets: The Challenges of Social Reproduction* (with Rachel Silvey). She has worked extensively on gender and macroeconomic issues with Status of Women Canada, with the United Nations on two of its Human Development Reports, with UNIFEM and with the Division for the Advancement of Women. She is currently a Trudeau Fellow.

Elissa Braunstein is Associate Professor in the Department of Economics at Colorado State University. She gained her PhD in economics from the University of Massachusetts Amherst, and a Master of Pacific International Affairs from the School of International Relations and Pacific Studies at the University of California San Diego. Prior to joining CSU, Dr Braunstein was Assistant Research Professor at the Political Economy Research Institute at UMASS Amherst. Her research focuses on feminist analyses of macroeconomics and international economics. Current work involves developing a macroeconomic model of the care economy, and gaining a better understanding of the empirical relationship between patriarchal institutions and economic growth.

Diane Elson is Professor of Sociology at the University of Essex, UK. She has been Visiting Professor at Carleton, Ruhr and Rutgers universities. She is a former Vice-President of the International Association for Feminist Economics, and has published widely on gender and development. Her recent publications include: 'Gender issues in development', in A.K. Dutt and J. Ros (eds) *International Handbook of Development Economics*, (Edward Elgar, Cheltenham, 2008); 'Gender equality and economic growth in the World Bank *World Development Report* 2006', *Feminist Economics* 15(3) 2009; 'Gender and the global economic crisis in developing countries: a framework for analysis', *Gender and Development*, 18(2) (pp. 201–212), 2010. A chapter on her work is included in *Fifty Key Thinkers on Development* (edited by D. Simon, Routledge, 2006).

Stephen Gill is Distinguished Research Professor of Political Science at York University, Toronto. He has been a Visiting Professor at Warwick, Tokyo, Meiji Gakuin, UCLA, New York University, UCSB and the University of Helsinki. A former Vice-President and Distinguished Scholar of the International Studies Association, his books include: *The Global Political Economy* (with David Law, Johns Hopkins, 1988); *American Hegemony and the Trilateral Commission* (Cambridge 1991, 2009); *Gramsci, Historical Materialism and International Relations* (editor, Cambridge 1993); *Globalization, Democratization and Multilateralism* (editor, UN University Press and Macmillan, 1997); *Innovation and Transformation in International Studies* (co-editor, Cambridge 1997); *Power, Production and Social Reproduction: Human In/security in the Global Political Economy* (co-editor with Isabella Bakker, Palgrave 2003); and *Power and Resistance in the New World Order* (Palgrave 2003, 2008) which won the *Choice* Outstanding Academic Title Award. In 2009 he was named one of the top 50 all-time thinkers in international relations in Martin Griffiths *et al.*, *Fifty Key Thinkers in International Relations* (New York, Routledge 2009).

Caren Grown is Economist-in-Residence at the American University, where she also co-directs the Program on Gender Analysis in Economics. Her recent books include *Taxation and Gender Equity*, (co-edited with Imraan Valodia, Routledge 2010) and *The Feminist Economics of Trade*, (co-edited with Irene Van Staveren, Diane Elson and Nilufer Cagatay, Routledge 2007). Her articles have appeared in *World Development*, *Journal of International Development*, *Feminist Economics*, *Health Policy and Planning*, and *The Lancet*. Dr Grown is an Associate Editor of *Feminist Economics*, a member of the External Gender Forum of the Asian Development Bank, and a founding member of the International Working Group on Gender and Macroeconomics (GEM-IWG). She holds a PhD in Economics from the New School for Social Research (1992).

James Heintz is Associate Research Professor and Associate Director of the Political Economy Research Institute, University of Massachusetts, Amherst. His research focuses on global employment, egalitarian development and economic and social rights. He has collaborated with numerous UN agencies, including ILO, UNDP, UNIFEM, UNRISD, DAW (of UN DESA) and UNECA. Recent publications with a gender focus include: 'Women's employment, economic risk, and poverty' (in Sylvia Chant, (ed.) *International Handbook of Gender and Poverty*) and, with Francoise Carré, 'Dimensions of employment "precarity" in the United States' (in L. Vosko, M. MacDonald, and I. Campbell, (eds) *Cross-National Perspectives on Precarious Employment: Developing Common Understandings Across Space, Scale, and Social Location*). At the time of publication, he is co-editing, with Sakiko Fukuda-Parr and

Stephanie Seguino, a special edition of the journal *Feminist Economics: Critical and Feminist Perspectives on Economic and Financial Crises.*

Elisabeth Klatzer is a Political Economist, lecturer at Vienna University of Economics and Business, Austria and works freelance in research, consultancy and as an activist to promote gender-sensitive economic and budgetary policies. Her research interests include feminist analysis of economic institutions and economic policy arrangements, public finance, gender-responsive budgeting and European economic policies.

Friederike Maier is Professor of Economics at the Berlin School of Economics and Law (Hochschule für Wirtschaft und Recht Berlin). She is head of the School's Harriet Taylor Mill-Institute for Gender and Economic Research and the German member of the European Commission's Network of Experts on Gender, Employment and Equality. Her research fields are labour market and employment policies, macroeconomic developments and social inclusion. Recent publications are: 'Re-cession or He-cession – gender dimensions of economic crisis and economic policy', (in Andreas Botsch/Andrew Watt, (eds) *After the Crisis: Towards a Sustainable Growth Model.* ETUI Brüssel 2010, pp. 79–83); Die wirtschaftspolitischen Leitlinien der Europäischen Union – eine feministische Kritik', (in Christine Bauhardt/Gülay Caglar (Hrsg.), *Gender and Economics. Feministische Kritik der politischen Ökonomie*, VS Verlag Wiesbaden 2010, pp. 233–257); 'Gender mainstreaming in employment policies in Germany', Discussion Paper des Harriet Taylor Mill-Instituts 08, 12/2009, (with Elisabeth Botsch).

Adrienne Roberts is a Post-Doctoral Fellow in the Department of Political Studies at Queen's University, Kingston, Ontario. She received her PhD from York University, Toronto, Ontario in 2010. Her dissertation was entitled 'Governing social marginality: towards a feminist political economy of poverty, crime and punishment'. Recent publications include: 'Toward a feminist political economy of capitalism and carcerality', *Signs: Journal of Women in Culture and Society*, 36(1), 2010 (co-written with Genevieve LeBaron), and 'Privatizing social reproduction: the primitive accumulation of water in an era of neoliberalism', *Antipode* 40(4): 535–560, 2008.

Christa Schlager studied economics and business administration at the Vienna University of Economics and Business and at the Copenhagen Business School. Since 1999, she has worked as an economist in the Chamber of Labour Vienna, Department of Economic Statistics. Her research interests focus on income distribution and public and feminist economics. She is a member of the editorial board of the quarterly journal *Kurswechsel* and a member of the Austrian Government Debt Committee.

Helene Schuberth is senior adviser at the National Bank of Austria. In 2007 and 2008 she served as an economic policy adviser to the prime minister of Austria. She studied economics and social sciences at the University of Vienna and Harvard. Her research interests include monetary and fiscal policies, structural and labour market policies, financial governance and macroeconomic coordination, which is documented in several publications. In 2006, she co-edited the book *The Political Economy of Financial Market Regulation: The Dynamics of Inclusion and Exclusion* (Edward Elgar). She is also co-editor of *Economic Policy Under Uncertainty: The Role of Truth and Accountability in Policy Advice* (Edward Elgar, 2004).

Tonia Warnecke is Assistant Professor of Economics and Research Associate of the China Center at Rollins College, Florida (USA). Her primary research interests include economic development, the economics of gender, globalization, labour markets, social welfare regimes and international financial institutions. She has been published in several journals including the *Journal of Economic Issues*, the *Journal of Industrial Relations*, the *International Journal of Business and Globalisation*, and the *International Journal of Pluralism and Economics Education*, along with a chapter in *Ethics and the Market: Insights from Social Economics* (Routledge, 2006). She is currently working with Deborah M. Figart on an edited volume, *Research Handbook on Gender and Economic Life*, to be published by Edward Elgar.

Brigitte Young has been Professor of International Political Economy, Institute of Political Science, University of Münster, Germany since 1999 and has held guest professorships at several universities, the most recent being at the Science-Politique/CERI in Paris 2008/2009. She was Expert Adviser to the Enquete-Commission of the German Parliament on Globalization of the World Economy, and is a senior member of the research project, funded by the EU-6th Framework Program, Global Governance, Regionalisation, and Regulation: The Role of the EU (GARNET). She chairs the sections on Gender in Political Economy (GIPE). Dr Young was also a member of the Warwick Commission on The Multilateral Trade Regime (2007), and is presently a German Delegate to the EU-Cost Project: Systemic Risks, Financial Crisis and Credit. Her research areas include: economic globalization; global governance, financial market governance and financial regulatory reforms in the EU; multilateral trade regime; and feminist political economy. Her most recent book is *Gender Knowledge and Knowledge Networks in International Political Economy*, Baden-Baden: NOMOS (with Christoph Scherrer, 2010).

ACKNOWLEDGEMENTS

This book is an outcome of activities that are part of the EU-Network of Excellence GARNET, *Global Governance, Regionalisation and Regulation: The Role of the EU* (funded by the 6th Framework 2005–2010), comprising some 42 research centres in Western and Eastern Europe. GARNET has challenged traditional understandings of governance and recognized that these understandings have remained largely gender-blind, formulated without consideration for asymmetrical relations of power based on gender.

One of the 17 subthemes of the Jointly Executed Research Activities focused on *Gender in International Political Economy (GIPE)*, coordinated by Brigitte Young, University of Münster, with about 20 members from different research centres in the Network. An important aim of GIPE was to clarify theoretically and empirically what it means to adopt gender as a central analytical category in debates and analyses in International Political Economy and to make the resulting insights more visible in EU research and policy making. This book, *Questioning Financial Governance from a Feminist Perspective*, is a collaboration of some of the members of GARNET, bringing together feminist economists and feminist political economists from different countries located in North America and Europe to analyse financial governance, a field in which women researchers, and also women practitioners in key regulatory institutions, central banks, and financial sector networks, are largely absent. We aimed to provide multidisciplinary perspectives covering a variety of countries and regions, both at the meso- and macro-levels, using a combination of qualitative and quantitative methods of analysis. The intent was to present an innovative approach to the topic of financial governance, a topic which has increased in importance since the financial crisis started in the USA in 2007 and went on to engulf the entire Eurozone in a sovereign debt crisis. More than ever, the financial crisis and its impact on the real economy has demonstrated that the traditional paradigms in economics do not have an answer on how to put the global and highly mobile financial sector at the service of the real economy, and the improvement of equality and well-being.

This book has benefited substantially from many sources. First, we wish to thank GARNET for the generous financial support for organizing conferences and workshops. A special note of appreciation goes to Richard Higgott, Director of GARNET and Pro-Vice Chancellor at the University of Warwick, who has been a staunch supporter of the research activities of GIPE from its inception. We also want to express our appreciation to Teresa Ghilarducci, Director of the Schwartz Center for Economic Policy Analysis (SCEPA), and Willi Semmler, then Dean of the Economics Department, New School, New York, for hosting a GIPE workshop to discuss the drafts of our papers in September 2008, and for organizing a public event on financial governance from a feminist perspective.

Isabella Bakker would like to thank the Trudeau Foundation; the Social Science and Humanities Research Council; Robert Drummond, former Dean, Faculty of Arts, York University; Kate Pendakis; and Adrienne Roberts.

Diane Elson would like to thank the University of Essex and Rutgers University for providing facilities to assist in the editing of this book.

Most importantly, we want to thank each of the authors of the chapters for their excellent contributions, their patience in responding to comments and for making this project such an enjoyable and stimulating experience. Finally, we also appreciate the excellent insights and comments from the three anonymous reviewers.

Brigitte Young, Isabella Bakker, Diane Elson

INTRODUCTION

Brigitte Young, Isabella Bakker and Diane Elson

Minsters of Finance, Governors of Central Banks, boards of public and private financial institutions, and the economists that advise them, all maintain a 'strategic silence' (Bakker 1994) about gender. That silence reflects a set of assumptions that fiscal and monetary policy and financial regulation, the key instruments of financial governance, are gender-neutral. These policies focus on the economy as an aggregation of monetized stocks and flows: gross domestic product and its fluctuations and growth; paid employment and inflation; the budget surplus/deficit; levels of government expenditure and tax revenue; and the supply of money. The silence about gender is 'strategic' in the sense that this silence obscures the ways in which financial governance interacts with, and reinforces, or restructures, the social organization of gender relations, the gender orders[1] that prevail at different times and places. This often masks the ways in which financial governance operates to the disadvantage of women and reinforces gender inequality.

The 'strategic silence' prevails not only because women are not well-represented in the institutions that make macroeconomic policy and govern finance, but also because the discourses through which governance is framed, and the empirical evidence that is deemed relevant, obliterate gender. It is not enough to inquire into how women are represented in decision making, it is also important to understand what tacit assumptions about gender orders underpin scientific knowledge claims in policy processes (Young and Scherrer 2010).

Feminist political economists have been challenging this silence (see for example, Bakker and Gill 2003), as have feminist economists (for example, Cagatay *et al.* 1995; Grown *et al.* 2000). This book brings together – for the first time – contributors from both disciplines, to break this silence, in the context of the massive meltdown of the global financial markets in 2008, which triggered a worldwide decline in growth rates, and a serious recession in developed countries.

This book examines both the transformations in the governance of finance that pre-date the financial crisis, as well as some dimensions of the crisis itself. These transformations increasingly involved private as well as public forms of power, along with institutions of state and civil society, operating at the local, national, regional and global levels. What is at stake in transforming regimes of governance are ideas and norms that justify or legitimize political power and influence, the institutions that regulate and reproduce these ideas and systems of incentives and sanctions that support this framework of ideas, institutions and dominant social forces (Bakker and Gill 2003: 5).

An important aspect of these transformations has been the creation of policy rules (often enacted in laws) that limit the discretion of national policy makers with respect to fiscal, monetary and financial sector policies. Examples of specific policy rules related to these key areas include laws requiring balanced budgets (such as in Canada); regional treaties prescribing limits to government borrowing (such as the Maastricht treaty for the EU countries); independent central banks pursuing inflation (but not employment) targets (in many developed and developing countries); policy conditions attached to loans from international financial institutions, such as the IMF and World Bank; laws that prescribe financial liberalization, allowing much more freedom for banks, insurance companies and hedge funds to move money around the world and create new financial instruments.

These policy rules tend to have inscribed in them a series of biases that have gender (as well as class and race-based) outcomes. Three such biases were identified by Elson and Cagatay (2000): *deflationary bias, male breadwinner bias* and *commodification bias*. Deflationary bias refers to the priority given to low inflation and fiscal restraint compared to public spending to create and sustain full employment. Deflationary bias has a disproportionately negative effect on women and ties governments' hands in dealing with recession and in promoting economic growth and improvements in health and education. Examples of this kind of bias are provided in this book by Braunstein and Heintz (Chapter 5), and Elson and Warnecke (Chapter 6).

Male breadwinner bias comes from assuming that 'the nonmarket sphere of social reproduction is articulated with the market economy of commodity production through a wage which is paid to a male breadwinner and which largely provides for the cash needs of a set of dependents' (Elson and Cagatay 2000: 1335). Examples of male breadwinner bias can be found in the chapters by Maier (Chapter 1) and Klatzer and Schlager (Chapter 3), which illustrate how macroeconomic policy regimes that seek to make more use of women's labour, nevertheless integrate women into labour markets largely as 'secondary workers', in low paid, part-time and/or precarious jobs.

Commodification (or marketization) bias occurs 'when macroeconomic policy is designed to minimize the role of public provision' (Elson and Cagatay 2000: 1356). This bias occurs when reduction of budget deficits, or achievement of balanced budgets, takes place primarily via reductions in public expenditure rather than through increases in tax revenue. As a result, more and more of the work of social reproduction is absorbed into the unpaid sphere of families and communities, where it is (largely) women's work; or, in the case of more affluent women, marketized via the hiring of domestic workers who are often migrant women. The chapters by Bakker (Chapter 2) and Klatzer and Schlager (Chapter 3) examine the operation of commodification bias in Canada and Austria respectively.

We might add two more biases: *risk bias* and *creditor bias*. Risk bias is defined as forms of governance that reduce the extent to which risk is pooled, and measures to protect against it are shared, and instead individualizes risk. As the chapter by Schuberth and Young (Chapter 7) illustrates, existing economic institutions, including those within the state, embed gendered assumptions about risk. With few if any savings, and limited ownership of real wealth, women are affected in a particularly negative way by the individualization of risk. They are often seen as more risky borrowers than are men, and, as the chapter by Gill and Roberts (Chapter 8) argues, many women in the US are integrated into credit markets on terms that are more disadvantageous than the terms open to men. Housing is a good example of risk bias. The provision of social housing by the state at low cost to people with low and/or uncertain incomes, has been cut back and more and more emphasis has been placed on people buying their own homes. Rules that required women to have a male guarantor for loans have been scrapped and more women have taken loans to buy houses. Gill and Roberts point to evidence that women in general, and black women in particular, pay higher rates of interest on mortgages than men and are subject to greater surveillance with respect to their economic situation. While there is a progressive aspect to increased numbers of women owning their own homes, it takes many years to pay off a mortgage and the immediate effect is that women become integrated into financial markets primarily as debtors. Here women come up against creditor bias in financial governance (Young 2010). The increasing power of financial capital on a global scale has meant that the relationship between creditors and debtors has become highly asymmetrical. When black women in the US are unable to service their debts, their homes are taken from them. When important lending institutions, such as big banks, get into difficulty, they are bailed out.

Our discussion of the biases of contemporary financial governance has only touched on one facet of the rich analysis provided in each chapter. Here we explain further how the contributors to this book consider examples of financial governance, and how it relates to the gender order, including divisions of labour, and relations of power and privilege.

In Chapter 1, Maier considers the central role of mainstream macroeconomic theory in decisions on financial governance in EU and OECD member countries, showing how gender issues (and indeed all equality issues) are relegated to the micro level. She identifies the main elements of the dominant policy consensus, which downplays the role of fiscal and monetary policy in employment creation[2] and discusses the institutional structures that govern macroeconomic policy and promote this consensus, the strength of which varies between countries. She also compares medium-term economic performance (from mid-1990s to mid-2000s) of different countries, finding considerable variations between economic growth and employment growth, with two very different models of success – the 'Nordic' model and the 'Anglo-Saxon' model. Maier breaks new ground by asking how macroeconomic performance interacts with gender orders; and finds that both 'successful' models emphasize the integration of women in the labour markets, and have high employment rates for both men and women. However, a substantial gender wage gap remains, though it is lower in Nordic countries than in Anglo-Saxon countries. Moreover, the two models have major differences in the way they organize the relation between paid work and care. While the Nordic model uses the public sector to provide care services (largely employing women), the Anglo-Saxon model relies much more on the private sector (again largely employing women). In other western European countries and Japan, economic and employment growth have not been as high, nor has so much attention been paid to reconciliation of work and family life, whether through the public sector or the market. Only the Nordic countries have begun to challenge men's roles by providing incentives for men to play a greater role in unpaid work. Thus, in OECD and EU countries, while higher levels of integration of women into labour markets appears to be associated with better macroeconomic performance, it is only in the Nordic countries where this is associated with a more egalitarian gender order.

In Chapter 2, Bakker examines both the changing and continuing aspects of the Canadian gender order through a consideration of the macroeconomics of fiscal austerity that has marked the last 20 years or so. She argues that macroeconomic policy rules related to 'sound' policies and the resultant social policy regime in Canada (one of the countries in Maier's 'Anglo-Saxon' model) reflect the increasing labour force participation of women and the shift to a male wage earner model. Here provisions for care remain privatized, and women continue to perform the bulk of social reproduction work. This may signal an 'undoing of gender' if women experience an increase in financial autonomy and independence. On the other hand, the prevalence of transnational mothering – care work provided by women from other countries who are hired privately in the home – implies a continuity of the boundaries around productive and reproductive work and the gender divisions of labour that mark this division. In a sense, this continuity is hidden, since it conceals not just the complexities of migrant domestic workers' own social reproduction but also that of their employers – middle-class women whose citizenship rights are mediated on the condition they participate in the labour markets as if they were men. Bakker focuses on two key aspects of economic governance and regulation: the macroeconomic framing through national budgets of sound economic policies and the resultant social policy regime with its diverse range of policies and programmes (including health care, education, training, housing, income support, unemployment insurance and care). She concludes that both the economic regime and the social policy regime are contributing to a shift in gender arrangements towards a single earner model that places both responsibility for well-being and risk on the individual irrespective of their structural inequalities (e.g. gendered division of care labour) and, that this is also leading to the gradual disappearance of the gendered subject – both in discourse and practice – from Canadian policy making.

Chapter 3, by Klatzer and Schlager, considers the gender implications of recent changes in European financial governance. Through an examination of three regulatory instruments – the Treaty of Maastricht, the Stability and Growth Pact, and Quality of Public Finance discourse – the authors reveal a system of governance that privileges fiscal sustainability and the reduction of national debts and deficits over other economic targets, such as growth, employment and distributive justice. Drawing from the case of Austria, the authors demonstrate that these forms of governance have in fact aggravated the economic downturn, as the capacity of member states to pursue anti-cyclical fiscal policies has been reduced. The governance system is shown to be gendered, as women are negatively and disproportionally affected by the privatization of public goods and services, the reduction in public expenditures, increased unemployment, stagnating wages, the rise of precarious work forms and the restructuring of state benefits. Specifically, women are more likely to experience unemployment and poverty and thus are increasingly dependent on state welfare programmes. Moreover, given the fact that women are more likely to be employed in precarious work forms, they are negatively impacted by the restructured unemployment and pension architectures that assume full-time and uninterrupted employment trajectories. The authors conclude that in the context of changing macroeconomic policy systems, there are significant structural exclusions and inclusions along gender lines. They call for 'gender-sensitive budget analysis' in macroeconomic policy making and governance.

Chapter 4, by Braunstein and Grown, uses quantitative methods to explore the gendered relationship between state taxes and employment in the US, in the context of well-documented gender differences in employment and economic activity and the persistence of significant occupational segregation by sex. Taking into consideration the *level*, *composition* and *competitiveness* of state taxes, the authors ask whether tax levels create or detract from employment in gender-specific ways and whether financing a greater proportion of tax revenues by corporate income taxes has gender-differentiated employment effects. In addition, they examine the potential gendered effects of inter state tax competition on the relationship between taxation and employment. Statistical analysis of these variables reveals that there is a positive relationship between state tax levels and employment for both women and men and that women's employment is much more (positively) sensitive to corporate income taxes than men's. It is further shown that both men and women experience employment losses as a result of interstate tax competition, with women's employment more vulnerable when faced with *corporate* income tax competition in particular. On the basis of these findings, the authors challenge the mainstream policy claim that increased taxes harm employment and argue that women's employment would be most secure if all states have a high share of corporate tax in total tax revenue. The primary contribution of this study to our understanding of the relationship between financial governance and gender orders is the finding that taxation, a key instrument of fiscal policy, is not gender-neutral, thus formulation of tax policies must incorporate gender into the analysis.

In Chapter 5, Braunstein and Heintz focus on the policies of central banks in developing countries, and especially on the gendered implications of their emphasis on targeting very low inflation rates. While there is little evidence that maintaining low inflation rates raises economic growth, this strategy remains a key feature of the neoliberal monetary policies of most central banks. Here, the authors focus on the gendered employment costs of polices to reduce inflation. Distinguishing between contractionary inflation reduction and expansionary inflation reduction, the authors find that during periods of the former, costs to women's employment are disproportionately negative, whereas during the latter, no clear pattern of gendered employment effects are evident. Drawing on empirical data and statistical testing, they show that countries that respond to inflation by increasing interest rates are more likely to experience contractionary periods, with the costs shouldered disproportionately by women. In contrast, those countries that maintain competitive real exchange rates tend to reverse the negative impact of contractionary inflation reduction, on women's employment, relative to men's. This is likely to happen because a real depreciation of the exchange rate favours tradable sectors, in which female labour is concentrated. Braunstein and Heintz provide an important challenge to the dominant policy position of central banks by emphasizing that their policies are not gender-neutral in their impact.

Chapter 6, by Elson and Warnecke, discusses a type of financial governance produced by the IMF, in the form of the policy conditions attached to loans under the Poverty Reduction and Growth Facility (PRGF) (established in 1997). The authors provide three ways of integrating gender into examinations of the PRGF. The first involves sex-disaggregated impact analysis in order to determine the extent to which costs and benefits of the PRGF are equally distributed among women and girls, on the one hand, and men and boys, on the other. The second incorporates a gender analysis of the extent of fiscal space (the space that developing countries have for expanding public expenditures without compromising IMF economic stability targets). The authors argue that the supply response to expansion of public expenditure is structured by the gender order. A gendered division of labour underpins both the market economy (the focus of the IMF) and the non-market, unpaid domestic economy. Looking at the case of sub-Saharan Africa, the authors argue that an appropriately designed expansion of public expenditure could increase supply, as well as demand, and thus would not lead to unsustainable increases in inflation. An example would be a balanced expansion of public investment to support women farmers, both in their work as farmers, and also in their work as carers, supplying them with inputs and services to improve the productivity of their food production, and to reduce their unpaid care burdens. Importantly, against the common IMF assumption that enhancing public expenditure threatens economic stability, they conclude that investment of this kind would actually result in a significant pay-off in terms of growth in food supply and reductions in poverty. The third method of integrating gender into programme analysis is to identify the gendered inscriptions that are implicitly woven into the PRGF rules. A set of gendered norms and values and laws support the assumption that the impact of macroeconomic policies on social stability can be ignored. Specifically, it is tacitly assumed that women will continue to shoulder the burden of social reproduction through their unpaid work. As the authors show, however, the rapid increase in food prices in 2008 called into question the ability and willingness of women to do this. As food prices have started to increase since 2010, there is likely to be continued tension between the forms of financial governance promoted by the IMF and the gender order.

In Chapter 7, Schuberth and Young contribute to the discussion of relations between financial governance and gender orders in two ways: first, through a comprehensive examination of women's exclusion from the global financial architecture; second, through an analysis of the gendered impact of emerging financial arrangements that shift regulatory competence to private institutions. The authors highlight what they refer to as *financial governance without women* in the top decision-making positions in US and EU financial governance institutions and networks, intergovernmental private and global regulatory institutions, and regulatory reform initiatives. Corresponding with the mainstream macroeconomic framework that is centred on the 'efficient market hypothesis' and a conception of social actors premised on the utilitarian model of a 'rational man', the authors reveal a masculine epistemic community within the financial sector that both physically excludes women and ideologically excludes alternative perspectives and values deemed feminine, irrational and non-scientific. Taking the position that the 2008 financial crisis was rooted in masculine conceptualizations of risk, the authors ask us to reflect on what kinds of financial regulation alternatives might emerge from this excluded 'feminine' territory. On the question of the gendered impact of the global financial architecture, the authors note that there are two channels through which men and women are disproportionately affected: first, through corporate governance of resource allocation among stakeholders and shareholders (because the majority of women are stakeholders, they are more directly impacted by recessions and also bear the brunt of budget consolidations and fiscal retrenchments following severe financial crisis); second, through the individualizing of risk that is a consequence of financial governance (with little savings and limited ownership of financial and real wealth, women – especially single mothers and the working poor – are particularly vulnerable to the individualization of risk). Taking the position that any decision-making process must include the voices of those most affected by reforms, Schuberth and Young call for the participation of women and other marginalized groups in financial governance institutions and processes.

In the context of the 2008/9 economic crisis Gill and Roberts consider in Chapter 8, some of the emergent tensions of what the authors term 'disciplinary neoliberalism', which refers to both a discourse of political economy and punitive policies of social reform and state restructuring geared towards the extension of capitalist markets. The authors demonstrate, on the one hand, a move towards the socialization of risk for wealthy financiers and corporations, and on the other hand, increased privatized risk for the majority of the population. In contrast to the massive government handouts to corporations, we have seen the emergence of privatized risks and costs associated with cuts to social services, and what the authors term the 'reprivatization of social reproduction',[3] evidenced in the increased reliance on private healthcare and childcare. Moreover, the authors show that while economic theory and policy making have been dominated by the 'efficient market hypothesis', which assumes that the market functions best with the least intervention, and thus advocates for self-regulation, there has been a heightened surveillance and disciplining of those who rely on social and welfare services. Women are shown to be disproportionately affected by these disciplinary practices, as they are more likely to experience poverty and rely on state provisions. Indeed, against the neoliberal conception of the abstract rational individual, who engages with full knowledge and on equal footing with others on the market, the authors show that a regime of market citizenship exists that differentially allocates risk and resources along gendered, classed and racialized lines. The authors draw on the case of US subprime mortgage lending to show how gender and race structurally determine one's position in markets and the disciplinary neoliberal project.

After the crisis: reinforcement of biases in the governance of finance

At first, the financial crisis appeared to open a window of opportunity to challenge the 'strategic silence' about the gender neutrality of financial governance and produce new ideas about reforming the structure of global, regional and national financial governance. For the first time since the neoliberal restructuring of the world economy began in the 1970s, an intellectual debate started on the merits of economic orthodoxy, the *Efficient Market Hypothesis*, the cornerstone of neoclassical economics, was shown to be a myth (Stiglitz *et al.* 2006).

It was important that the crisis hit the very epicentre of the global financial system, in Wall Street, and not the peripheries, unlike the crises in Latin America and Asia in the 1980s and 1990s. As long as the crisis occurred in the periphery, orthodox economists could safely argue that financial instability was not systemic, but was the result of shortcomings in the affected countries. A sign of the weakening of the old order was the expansion of the G7/8 to the G20 starting with the Washington Summit in November 2008, followed by the London Summit in April 2009, the Pittsburgh Summit in September 2009 and the Toronto Summit in June 2010, to include 'emerging' countries, such as India and China, in discussions of how to reform the global financial architecture. However, the G20 meetings have been disappointing. Three years into the crisis the initial urge to restructure the system has weakened, banks are back in profit, and huge bonuses for bankers have again become the norm. Despite the intellectual uncertainties and lingering global economic risks, the power of financial capital has risen from the ashes of the phoenix faster than had been expected.

This was evident at the last G20 meeting in Toronto in June 2010, where the world leaders agreed with the German Chancellor, Angela Merkel, that it was a top priority for developed countries to cut public expenditure in order to reduce the high levels of public debt and budget deficits incurred as a result of bailing out the banks.

It is likely that women will have to bear the brunt of the expenditure cuts, which will reduce availability of the public services and welfare benefits that have been important in supporting a more equal gender order. For example, a study by Queens University Law Professor Kathleen Lahey found that the most recent Canadian federal budget only channelled approximately 7 to 22 percent of federal infrastructure spending towards women. As women are underrepresented in the construction, manufacturing and engineering industries and since increased spending in social infrastructure was lacking in the government's stimulus spending, a male breadwinner bias was reinforced (the *Toronto Star*, 3 March 2010). In the UK, it is estimated by researchers at the House of Commons library, that women will pay over £6 billion (72 percent) of the 8 billions 'saved' by cuts in welfare benefits and changes to direct taxes in the budget introduced in June 2010 by the new Conservative/Liberal Democrat coalition government (the *Guardian*, 4 July 2010). The budget combined and reinforced deflationary, male breadwinner and commodification bias. The UK coalition government itself has not published any estimate of the gender impact of its budget. Like most governments, it maintains a 'strategic silence' on public finance and gender equality. Other European countries are also cutting expenditure and raising taxes, with likely similar results. It is vital to conduct research on the gender impact of expenditure cuts across the OECD countries. These cuts will results in major loss of jobs, and since women tend disproportionately to be employed by the public sector in countries with welfare states, women will be hit harder than men. Gender norms may make it harder for them to find new jobs. A global survey conducted in 2005 found that almost 40 percent of those interviewed agreed with the statement that when jobs are scarce, men have more of a right to a job than women (Seguino 2009).

Some reform in governance of the banks is still under discussion. There is still a small chance for policy makers to reduce risk and creditor bias, and create a system to govern banks in ways that put them at the service of production and social reproduction, and offer support to a more equitable gender order. Feminist researchers must continue to engage with the intricacies of financial governance. There is still much work that needs to be done in order to break the 'strategic silence'.

Notes

1 Many definitions of 'gender order' exist. The concept derives from R.W. Connell, who uses the term to describe the social organization of gender relations at different levels of social life. For Connell, modern gender orders are constituted and reconstituted through intersecting processes of industrialization, urbanization and globalization. The term as it is used here reflects this understanding and incorporates the broader institutionalized relations of power and privilege, and divisions of labour that are organized around gender difference.

2 After a brief fracturing of this consensus in the aftermath of the 2008 financial crisis, it has been fully restored by summer 2010.

3 'Reprivatization' is similar to 'commodification'.

Bibliography

Bakker, I. (1994) *The Strategic Silence: Gender and Economic Policy,* London: Zed Books.

Bakker, I. and Gill, S. (eds) (2003) *Power, Production and Social Reproduction,* New York: Palgrave Macmillan.

Cagatay, N., Elson, D. and Grown, C. (eds) (1995) 'Gender, Adjustment and Macroeconomics', Special Issue, *World Development,* 23(11).

Elson, D. and Cagatay, N. (2000) 'The Social Content of Macroeconomic Policies', *World Development,* 28(7): 1347–1364.

Grown, C., Elson, D. and Cagatay, N. (eds) (2000) 'Growth, Trade, Finance and Gender Inequality', Special Issue, *World Development,* 28(7): 1347–1364.

Seguino, S. (2009) The Global Economic Crisis, its Gender Implications, and Policy Responses. Paper prepared for presentation to the Commission on the Status of Women, 53rd Session, United Nations, New York, 2–13 March 2009.

Stiglitz, Joseph E., Ocampo, J. A., Spiegel, S., French-Davis, R., Nayyar, D. (2006) *Stability with Growth. Macroeconomics, Liberalization, and Development,* Oxford: Oxford University Press.

Young, B. (2010) 'The Gendered Dimension of Money, Finance and the Subprime Crisis', in C. Bauhardt and G. Caglar (eds), *Gender and Economics. Feministische Kritik der politischen Ökonomie.* Wiesbaden: VS Verlag für Sozialwissenschaft, pp. 203–218.

Young, B. and Scherrer, C. (2010) 'Introduction: Gender Knowledge and Knowledge Networks', in B. Young and C. Scherrer, *Gender Knowledge and Knowledge Networks in International Political Economy,* Baden-Baden: Nomos.

Young, B. and Schuberth, H. (2010) The Global Financial Meltdown and the Impact of Financial Governance on Gender, *GARNET Policy Brief,* No.10, January 2010, Paris: Science Politique/CERI, www.garnet-eu.org.

1

MACROECONOMIC REGIMES IN OECD COUNTRIES AND THE INTERRELATION WITH GENDER ORDERS

Friederike Maier

What is macroeconomics about? An introduction

Macroeconomics is a broad field of study, which is comprised of many areas of research. Key concerns of the discipline include the attempt to understand the causes and consequences of short-run fluctuations in economic activity (the business cycle), the attempt to understand the level of demand and supply in various markets (especially the product market, the labor market, and the capital market), the attempt to understand the interrelation between these markets, and the behavior of different agents in the aggregate markets (such as households, firms, governments, unions, central banks, and others). Another important field of study examines the determinants of long-run economic growth (defined as increases in national income).

Macroeconomic theories are closely related to macroeconomic policy and policy targets. The major objectives of macroeconomic policy include full employment, low inflation rates, and economic growth (expressed in terms of gross domestic product (GDP)). In order to achieve these goals, attention is focused on government fiscal policies, central bank monetary and exchange rate policies, and wage policies. On an aggregate level, policies may be concentrated on the aggregate supply side; that is, the conditions and factors associated with production (e.g. the cost of input factors such as energy, materials, wages, taxes, and financial capital), the aggregate demand side (determined largely by private households, investment of private firms, and government demand), or both (in which case a mixed approach is used). Narrowly defined, macroeconomics considers factors influencing the aggregate demand or supply, whereas questions of income distribution, economic welfare, and the provision of public goods and services, are relegated to "microeconomic" policy concerns (Burda and Wyplosz 2005: 363; Arestis and Sawyer 2007: 331). This division appears to be quite arbitrary and artificial however, when we consider the interrelation between the micro- and macroeconomic levels, and the fact that policies and regulations concerning income distribution may exert an influence on the aggregate demand of private households or the aggregate supply of labor. Moreover, macroeconomic policies may have an impact on the distribution of income and on individual behavior, and these impacts may in turn increase or decrease the effect of the macroeconomic policy (Heine *et al.* 2006: 19). Thus, the interrelation of individual behavior and aggregate outcomes requires further inquiry and should be integrated into economic analyses.

The study of gender orders is not an integral part of macroeconomics, and questions as to whether macroeconomic policies differently influence men and women or the extent to which gender orders influence the outcomes of macroeconomic policies or the choice of instruments and tools of macroeconomic policies are not taken into consideration. When the impacts of macroeconomic policies on men's and women's economic and social positions are studied, this is perceived to be a concern of micro analysis. The interrelation of gender and macroeconomic orders has been investigated only to a limited degree. The literature is relatively small, concentrated on specific policy fields, and dominated by a microeconomic approach; for example, if we can show that women and men exhibit different behaviors in key decisions related to markets (such as labor supply, consumption, savings, and investments) gender differences should be taken into account. Stotsky (2006) surveys research of this kind and finds a number of differences in women's and men's behavior using microeconomic models. However, the question of whether macroeconomic policy regimes and gender regimes exert an influence on each other has not been studied in detail. The importance of gender, both in terms of how gender roles impact on macroeconomic outcomes and how macroeconomic policies influence gender orders has been largely ignored.

This chapter is a first step in the examination of how macroeconomic developments and gender orders are related to each other in highly developed countries and is structured as follows: First, I present a short description of contemporary macroeconomic theory and the policy framework of mainstream economists. Second, I show how this consensus has influenced policy making at the European Union (EU) and the Organization for Economic Cooperation and Development (OECD) levels during the last decades. Third, I analyze the macroeconomic policy targets and tools and show how different countries performed in the main macroeconomic fields in the years before the actual economic crises using descriptive empirical findings. Lastly, I relate these macroeconomic performances to gender orders by developing some preliminary arguments on the interrelations between gender and macroeconomic regimes.

Mainstream macroeconomic theory and policy

Since the 1930s there have been controversies within macroeconomic theory and policy discourse about the appropriate goals and tools of macroeconomic policies, especially in relation to the questions of whether low inflation rates and full employment are achievable at the same time, and whether stable economic growth is engendered through supply-oriented policies or those intended to stabilize aggregate demand. The impacts of monetary policy and exchange rate policy on the real development of product and labor markets have been under dispute, along with the role governments should play in the macroeconomic policy. For example, if governments intervene, should they concentrate on supply-side factors, aggregate demand measures, or a combination of demand and supply-oriented measures in order to achieve macroeconomic targets in a given situation and economy? Short-run effects and long-run effects are often studied separately to distinguish between immediate effects and those that are mediated by the changing expectations and behaviors of economic actors in various situations.

In recent years a new consensus in macroeconomics has developed, integrating micro-based neoclassical theories on the rational behavior of economic agents in different markets with macro-based Keynesian theories on the role of macroeconomic policies. This mainstream approach is based on the following assumptions:

- Monetary policy, especially the supply of money and variations in interest rates, is able to stabilize output and employment in the short run, is neutral in respect to output and employment in the long run, and influences inflation rates in the long run. Governments and central banks should "aim to ensure the stability of inflation at a low rate, guarding against the dangers posed both by inflation and deflation. Moreover, by actively changing the interest rate, the central bank should help steer the economy toward the stable inflation equilibrium in the face of short-run disturbances" (Carlin and Soskice 2006: 697).
- Fiscal policy should be handled in such a way as to "ensure long-run fiscal sustainability whilst allowing for short-run stabilization and the achievement of the government's structural objectives" (ibid.).
- Employment and unemployment policies should concentrate on structural problems of the labor market, as the equilibrium unemployment rate is determined by structural characteristics such as dismissal regulations, wage bargaining institutions, and the social benefits system. Wages determine employment levels in the long run, while monetary policy may help to stabilize unemployment rates at the equilibrium level in the short run.
- Inflation and unemployment are no longer seen as targets that have to be balanced, rather, they seem to coexist in a new context which is called the Non-Accelerating Inflation Rate of Unemployment (NAIRU). The NAIRU is defined as the rate of unemployment which is neutral for inflation processes. The level of the NAIRU is based on the labor market and its institutions such as dismissal regulations and level of unemployment benefits, whereas inflation rate targets are set by governments and central banks. If the actual unemployment rate is above the NAIRU, nominal wages will not increase because employees are afraid of further job losses (so that wages will not push prices and inflation rates); however, the problem of deflation may occur. If the actual unemployment is below the NAIRU, wages may increase due to scarcities in the labor market and will thus push inflationary processes. In this way, keeping

unemployment around the NAIRU is neutral for inflationary processes. This may include accepting a high level of unemployment to achieve low inflation rates (see Rothschild (2006) for a critical assessment). The NAIRU itself, which is empirically different for all countries (because labor market institutions differ), can only be reduced by means of structural reforms in the labor markets.

- Actual unemployment above the NAIRU may be influenced by aggregate demand and fiscal and monetary policy. As high unemployment leads to decreasing wages and decreasing aggregate demand, deflationary processes may occur. To avoid deflationary processes, demand policies may be implemented by governments in order to reduce the actual unemployment down to the level of the NAIRU. If actual unemployment is below the NAIRU, central banks may raise interest rates and reduce effective demand.
- Supply-side policies, irrespective of the development of aggregate demand, should focus on labor market institutions and – in the broader context – on supply-side conditions in general, therefore helping to increase production and productivity, improving efficiency in product, labor and financial markets, and increasing competition between suppliers. It is widely agreed that the positive impact of supply-side policy is being realized only in the long run. In the short run, supply-side policies may even increase unemployment (for example as a side effect of privatization of public enterprises or reduced subsidies to certain sectors or increased competition).
- Growth policy should enable long-run growth, measured in real GDP per capita, and the sources of growth are identified as growth in quantities and qualities of input factors, such as human capital, public infrastructure, knowledge, technical innovations, stable economic environment, and sound macroeconomic conditions. International trade and globalization are seen as one possible source of economic growth.

As I will show in the following section, these elements of the new macroeconomic model are accepted by a wide community of economists and policy makers. However, in reality, the economic policies and the economic development of OECD countries have not followed all aspects of this model and macroeconomic performance differs substantially.

Consensus in the macroeconomic mainstream: EU and OECD strategies

Within Europe today, macroeconomic policies are formulated and developed by a series of actors and institutions. The model discussed above is widely accepted and incorporated into economic strategies by the major macroeconomic policy authority of the Union, the European Central Bank (ECB), which is independent both in setting its targets and in choosing its policy instruments. The ECB is entrusted with pursuing a monetary policy strategy with a clear commitment to the maintenance of price stability, which is defined by the ECB as inflation below, but near to, 2 percent per annum over the medium term. In order to reach the goal of price stability, the ECB uses interest rates to influence financial markets' demand and supply. All member countries of the Economic and Monetary Union (Eurozone countries) are regulated by this institution, which has the obligation to follow its one-sided target of low inflation without being responsible for other macroeconomic targets such as employment or economic growth. In contrast to the US or UK central banks, the ECB is constrained by the primacy of its price stability objective over business cycle stabilization and it can only respond to developments that affect the entire Eurozone. Given the fact that members of the Eurozone experienced quite different inflation rates during recent years, there are major doubts as to whether a monetary policy isolated from other macroeconomic instruments is able to cope with Europe's economic developments (Arestis and Sawyer 2007; Carlin and Soskice 2006).

All EU member states are also regulated by supply-side policies (labeled as microeconomic policies), which aim to reduce rigidities in all kinds of markets, especially in the labor market and the goods and capital markets. Some of these are highly controversial. Supply-side policies are a major component of the European Strategy for Growth and Jobs (sometimes called the Lisbon Strategy),[1] which follows the line of the new consensus model in nearly all aspects: the target is to increase employment (the Lisbon Strategy defines an overall employment rate of 70 percent, and 60 percent for women (the only point in which women are mentioned is the discussion of employment) and an employment rate of 50 percent for older people (55 to 64 years)). As this target is not related to other macroeconomic targets via the concept of the NAIRU, the instruments to reach such employment rates are all supply-side oriented. The major problems with European labor markets are seen in regulations concerning dismissals, job protection, work-time flexibility, and early retirement regulations, in social benefits systems, which are seen to be too generous (in terms of amount and duration of payments) and in the inflexible system of wage setting via trade unions and employers' organizations, which do not allow for flexible wage moderation. The very influential 1994 OECD Jobs Study pointed out that European unemployment is a result of labor market rigidities and that major elements of the European labor market institutions need more flexibility and liberalization. The components of the Jobs Study policy included reducing the amount and duration of payments for the unemployed, rechanneling spending to job search activities and labor market programs, reducing dismissal and other protective regulations, and cutting early retirement incentives. The influence of collective bargaining was weakened in many countries by imposing legal constraints and the emergence of less protected forms of employment (i.e. part-time and temporary employment). Despite these reforms, we have observed disparities in the European labor markets during the last decade; high unemployment rates persist in some of the bigger countries such as Germany, France, and Spain, and rather low unemployment rates are evident in countries such as the UK, Denmark, and Sweden. Defenders of the Jobs Study strategy might argue that supply-side measures will influence the labor market in the medium term and the positive effects will be shown in the future. However it is more likely that supply-side reforms of the labor market might not be the main explanation for differences in the overall performance of different European economies.

To enable growth, the Job Study strategy puts much emphasis on the development of productivity and innovation, calling for higher investments in education and research and subsidies in order to support newly created businesses, and the development of information and communications technology (ICT) and other technologies.

In terms of market institutions and regulations, the EU has established a system via the Common Market to create an internal single market with the free movement of goods, services, capital, and people. Over a long period, regulations, deregulations, and re-regulations in the markets for goods, services, and capital and in the labor market have had an impact on EU internal trade, which increased dramatically during the last decade, sometimes with positive price effects for the consumers, sometimes with increases in productivity, and sometimes with increased pressure on wages and employment standards. In one of the major supply-side projects, competition increase – especially in markets that supply goods and public services such as electricity, water, transport, or telecommunication through privatization – has had a major impact on European economies, both in terms of quantity and quality of supply, and in terms of employment in these privatized firms. The outcomes are not all positive; while in some cases prices decreased and the quality of services increased, there are many examples of development in the opposite direction, leaving consumers and employees with lowered quality of goods and services, and decreased employment in these sectors. The privatization of public firms was not only a result of policies that aim to increase market competition, but also the narrow definition of the role of governments in the macroeconomic arena. Governments' ability to use public employment and public firms to stabilize employment and the provision of goods has been limited by the overall strategy of the Stability and Growth Pact (SGP) which regulates government deficit spendings.

Fiscal policy, which seeks to stabilize aggregate demand through government spending, is the only instrument that is available to influence the economic development of countries in the short run. Although the EU member states may use fiscal policies according to their own political targets and objectives, they have been subjected to great restraints by the SGP, which is signed by all member states of the Eurozone and is voluntarily self-binding for all other member states. Following the criteria of the Maastricht Treaty, public debt must not exceed 60 percent of GDP and the current budget deficit must not exceed 3 percent of GDP. The current deficits are closely monitored by the European Council and the European Commission, and member states of the Eurozone may be subject to coercive procedures. During periods of weakened economic activity the SGP requires that member states reduce their deficits in the short and medium term, an action that is fundamentally pro-cyclical and increases the intensity of economic downturns. The SGP limits the ability of governments to respond to changes in the business cycle and stands in contrast to the new consensus approach. It has been criticized not only by post-Keynesian authors (Hein and Truger 2008) but also by mainstream economists:

> Counter-productive in application, the "budgetary discipline" formulated in the SGP is also erroneous in principle, as nothing in economic theory or history suggests that EMU countries should adhere to it [...] The priorities of the SGP should be reversed [...] the EU countries should be able to allow the automatic stabilizers full play and never be constrained to austere budgetary policies during a business cycle downturn. They must also be able to implement expansionary discretionary policies through public spending when these stabilizers prove insufficient [...] The desired fiscal policies are those that stimulate demand while, at the same time, carrying the seeds of their own sustainability. Thus, any tax expenditure package should be phased out as the economy recovers, making it possible to return to a satisfactory debt/GDP ratio. Tax reduction, for example, should then focus on the agents, who are most inclined to consume, in other words, those who have the lowest incomes. Next, in addition to its role of stimulating demand, an increase in public spending should allow for increased production capacities and the long-term well-being of European populations.
>
> (*Beffa et al. 2008*)[2]

For a rather long period, monetary policies, fiscal policies, and supply-side policy in the goods, services, financial, and labor markets were coordinated in separate directorates of the European Commission (while the ECB is not coordinated at all, it tried to influence all other agents by putting forward straight statements concerning the SGP or the Lisbon Strategy) (Arestis and Sawyer 2007: 333). The development of strategic goals was outlined in separate documents and decisions were made by different ministries at both national and EU levels. The Council of Ministers for Finance and Economics, Ecofin, followed an economic strategy (Broad Economic Guidelines, or otherwise termed the Maastricht Strategy) that was only loosely coordinated with the ministers for labor and employment and the directorate for employment and social affairs in the European Commission (where the Lisbon Strategy was followed). Although the separation of employment policies from other macroeconomic activities such as monetary and fiscal policy may be justified by the mainstream economic framework, in 2005 the EU tried to bring together both strategies in a paper called "Integrated guidelines for growth and jobs 2005–2008," which covers a broader range of activities than the former guidelines (see European Commission 2008a).

I would like to briefly discuss here the 2005 paper's integrated economic approach. Under the heading of macroeconomic guidelines the following points are mentioned:

(1) Fiscal policy must follow the SGP regulations, and member states should avoid pro-cyclical fiscal policies and ensure prompt action against excessive deficits.

As I mentioned before, these two goals – especially in times of economic crisis – remain contradictory and cannot be fulfilled simultaneously.

(2) Government policy that influences the allocation and distribution of resources (strictly speaking, a microeconomic concern) should be oriented toward the increase of labor supply (especially among women), encourage wage bargaining systems that promote nominal wage and labor cost developments consistent with price stability and trend productivity over the medium term (this avoids inflation processes by wage increases), and increase flexibility, factor mobility, and adjustment capacity in labor and product markets.

The macroeconomic strategy is therefore bound to the concept of strict monetary rules set by the ECB, the budgetary discipline of the member states (even in times of recession), and the policy that regulates wages around the level of productivity growth and contributes to low inflation and unemployment around the equilibrium NAIRU.

Under the heading of microeconomic guidelines the following points are mentioned:

(1) Economic growth should be stimulated by investment in research and development – through a mixture of private and public expenditure – with the overall investment objective of 3 percent of member state GDP by 2010.
(2) All components of technology-oriented growth are mentioned in the document, including innovation policies, ICT use, and industrial policy.
(3) As a result of the intervention of the European Parliament, a guideline concerning the sustainable use of resources and the synergies between environmental protection and growth is included.
(4) Both deepening internal market integration and increasing competition within Europe and globally through open markets – especially in the network industries, such as telecommunication, railways, and other transport systems – are key issues, along with the aim of reducing administrative burdens on enterprises and creating a more entrepreneurial culture.
(5) The development of Europe's infrastructure should give priority to transport, energy, ICT infrastructure, public–private partnership, and a price system that allows for a more efficient and sustainable balance between technology, innovation, environmental costs, and economic growth.

As these guidelines demonstrate, the proposed microeconomic policies are strictly supply-side oriented and directed to increasing the productivity of input factors and competition within Europe and in global markets. Infrastructure investment in Europe prioritizes that which directly impacts the production side; infrastructure that is related to people's well-being (in health, education, social services, and culture) is neglected.

In addition to proposing macroeconomic and microeconomic guidelines, the paper also focuses on a number of key employment targets: (1) with the objective of full employment, a 70 percent employment rate (at least 60 percent for women and 50 percent for older workers, 55 to 64 years) by 2010; (2) a significant reduction of youth unemployment and increased female participation in the labor market, along with reduced gender gaps in employment, unemployment, and pay; (3) reconciliation of work and private life and the provision of accessible and affordable childcare facilities and care for other dependants; (4) development of modern social protection systems with social adequacy, financial sustainability, and responsiveness to social needs; (5) establishment of work pay strategies that support employment – especially for those with low incomes – by strengthening job search systems and benefits/tax systems; (6) development of a "flexicurity system," which combines high factor flexibility with high individual security for the worker; (7) employment-friendly labor-cost developments and wage-setting mechanisms that avoid gender pay gaps; (8) improvements in human capital investment on all levels of the educational system and adaptation of all educational and training systems to new competence requirements in order to raise productivity of workers.

To the extent that employment guidelines are distinguished from macroeconomic guidelines and targets, the mainstream economic approach is supported. In this framework, all increases in employment or reductions of unemployment are based on the labor market structures, and are not outcomes of macroeconomic developments. The labor market is conceptualized in this neoclassical-institutional approach as following rules different from others, as the factors traded in this market are human beings with all their specific characteristics, which make them different from goods in product markets. Thus the labor market includes more elements relating to social distribution and the creation of incentives and disincentives for particular groups. The labor market is defined as the appropriate place to incorporate people into considerations of economic growth, and to prevent poverty through income generation. If people are hindered from taking up employment, either by incentives or disincentives set by wages, benefit systems, employment protection, or other institutional constraints (such as the lack of childcare facilities), policy needs to intervene in order to remove these obstacles. The aim of integrating different groups of inactive or unemployed people into the labor market is based on the premise that a growing supply of labor allows for more economic production and economic growth, irrespective of the development of aggregate demand.[3] Wages should reflect the relative productivity of workers and a gender wage gap is the result of discriminatory structures in the labor market, which allow employers to pay wages below the productivity of the person (or group).

Whereas inflation targets are set by the independent ECB, the targets concerning government spending are part of the SGP and are binding for the Eurozone member states. Most internal single market regulations are part of binding directives of the Commission and cover all member states. However, employment and research and development targets and instruments do not have the same binding commitment. In the so-called open method of coordination the member states are obliged to report on their policies and program outcomes, and the European Commission assesses the programs and develops recommendations. The growth and employment policies and targets are less obligatory and allow for more member state discretion than the other areas of macroeconomic coordination. Nonetheless, there is some room for interpretation and internal goal setting in these other macroeconomic areas, especially in fiscal policy, such that different allocation and distributional effects may be achieved without disturbing the overall targets in public deficits.

Within OECD countries, similar mechanisms of strategic policy formulation exist without being accompanied by the implementation of regulations via the OECD. The OECD provides a setting in which governments can compare policy experiences, seek answers to common problems, identify good practices, and coordinate domestic and international policies. The mandate of the OECD is broad, covering economic, environmental, and social issues. It provides a forum in which peer pressure can act to develop policy and implement "soft law" – non-binding instruments that can occasionally lead to binding treaties. Information and analysis are provided by a secretariat in Paris. The secretariat collects data, monitors trends, and analyzes and forecasts economic developments. It also researches social changes or evolving patterns in trade, environment, agriculture, technology, taxation, and other areas. In the field of macroeconomics, the OECD is a highly influential think-tank, engaged in both theoretical and empirical research and in monitoring common strategies for the OECD member states. As membership of the OECD is broader than the EU, including all highly developed countries (such as the US, Canada, New Zealand, Australia, and Japan) the OECD covers a wider range of economic and social diversity.

As already mentioned, OECD studies are highly influential for the overall development of economic concepts and political strategies. The 1994 OECD Jobs Study is one example of a path-breaking document that influenced all OECD countries in the development of their labor market policies (Blanchard 2006: 26). Another important publication is the annual OECD *Employment Outlook*. In regards to macroeconomic policy, the OECD publishes a series of important studies such as *Going for Growth* (OECD 2007), *Economic Outlook* (OECD 2008), and *Economic Surveys*, which analyze the performance of each member state. Based on a broad set of internationally comparable indicators, the OECD analysis enables countries to assess their economic performance and structural policies in a range of areas. Within the *Going for Growth* strategy the OECD countries have agreed to measure their economic reforms in relation to structural indicators and policy priorities, such as improving labor productivity performance, easing entry controls, and other competition-restraining regulations in product markets (such as network industries, professional services, and retail distribution), reducing the administrative burdens for firms, reforming cooperate governance, and reducing the scope of public ownership. Beyond these reforms, the "de-bureaucratization" of the public sector, which includes strengthening public sector efficiency, plays an important role, as do policies for the reduction of taxes levied on businesses. Moreover, the OECD puts much more emphasis on education at all levels of the educational system – as part of economic development – and initiatives like the Programme for International

Student Assessment (PISA) have influenced the development of educational systems in all OECD countries.

A primary concern of the OECD's labor policies, especially in Europe, is to increase labor utilization, which requires an increase in labor force participation (both for older workers and women), a reduction in unemployment, and an increase in the number of hours worked per annum. Policies should concentrate on removing disincentives to work at older ages, establishing measures to encourage female labor force participation (such as accessible childcare facilities and tax deductions on the return to work following childbirth), reforming disability and sickness benefits so that people are compelled to return to work, general tax and social benefit systems reform to decrease tax wedges on labor income (this reduces the difference between the gross and the net income of employees by reducing taxes and contributions related to the gross earnings).

Another key concern of the OECD policy strategy is the wage formation process. The OECD proposals call for reductions in minimum wage and a more flexible wage formation system with a less centralized bargaining process (as central bargaining, understood within the OECD framework, provides too much power for trade unions and results in wages that are too high). Labor market reforms (primarily legal regulations) are required to allow more flexible and temporary work contracts, to increase hours of work, and to establish work incentives for low-income earners through modifications to the unemployment benefits system. In this sense, the OECD wage policies are more precisely articulated than those of the EU.

Like the EU guidelines, the OECD policy recommendations are based on the new consensus model and focus on the same policy areas and instruments. Compared to the EU strategy, the OECD papers are different in two dimensions. First, the OECD is much more concerned about macroeconomic stabilization, especially in terms of monetary policy and fiscal policy. This is a less restrictive approach, compared to the ECB policy, which I discuss above, and the neglect of aggregate demand in fiscal policy. The OECD policies are more open to the balancing of inflation containment and output stabilization than the EU policies. This may be due to the different targets of central banks in the US and UK, and the ECB.

The second difference lies on the supply side (microeconomic policy), especially with regard to trade unions and wage policy. While in Europe the balance between capital and labor and the social dimensions of the labor market are seen as important factors of economic and social development (and "the European Social Model" is established to handle conflicting aims and strategies), the OECD is much less concerned with these aspects. It is clearly directed to the development of flexible, less regulated, and less protective labor market regulations, ignoring what Blanchard found to be the most important lesson of the previous labor market reforms:

> Modern economies need to constantly reallocate resources, including labour, from old to new products, from bad to good firms. At the same time, workers value security and insurance against major adverse professional events, job loss in particular. While there is a trade-off between efficiency and insurance,

> the experience of the successful European countries suggests it need not be very steep. What is important in essence is to protect workers, not jobs. This means providing unemployment insurance, generous in level, but conditional on the willingness of the unemployed to train for and accept jobs if available. This means employment protection, but in the form of financial costs to firms to make them internalize the social costs of unemployment, including unemployment insurance, rather than through a complex administrative and judicial process.
>
> (*Blanchard 2006: 45*)

Economic performance – empirical findings

Blanchard is referring to findings that indicate that EU and OECD strategies are not implemented in every aspect or in all member states. Depending on the level of discretion in the relevant policy areas, all highly developed countries followed their own agendas when implementing macroeconomic and microeconomic policies, even within fiscal policy and monetary and exchange rate policy (as in the case of the EU members that did not join the Eurozone). The economic performance of the highly developed countries has been analyzed in a series of studies carried out by institutions from different political and paradigmatic backgrounds. Covering a whole business cycle (1995/6 to mid-2005/6 with the slowdown in 2000/1), these studies found that the performance of the highly industrialized countries differs quite substantially.

Figure 1.1 compares the economic growth (measured by growth of real GDP, during the period 1995 to 2006) and shows a clear difference between the countries; the UK and the US have the highest growth rates followed by Sweden and France. Germany has only a modest growth compared to the others.

As the Figure 1.2 shows, employment growth and employment rates vary considerably between the US, Japan, and the EU member states.

During the business cycle, US employment declined sharply in the 2000/1 recession but grew quite substantially after, reaching the highest growth rate of the countries compared in 2006. In Japan, employment decreased since the end of the 1990s, and at the end of the recession (in 2002) increased only very slowly. The development within the EU 15 (covering the members of the Eurozone) was characterized by a long period of modest growth rate during the recession and afterwards, similar to the development of the EU 27. In 2007, employment growth declined in both the US and Japan (a first sign of the recession to come in 2008). Nevertheless, employment rates in both countries were higher (see Figure 1.3) and unemployment was lower (see Figure 1.4) compared to the EU countries.

As a result of the overall economic development, employment rates in 2007 differ substantially between the US, Japan, the EU 15, and the EU 27, with the latter showing the lowest rates.

As shown in Figure 1.5, the EU 27 includes a broad variety of labor market situations, with Denmark, the Netherlands, Sweden, the UK, and Austria having

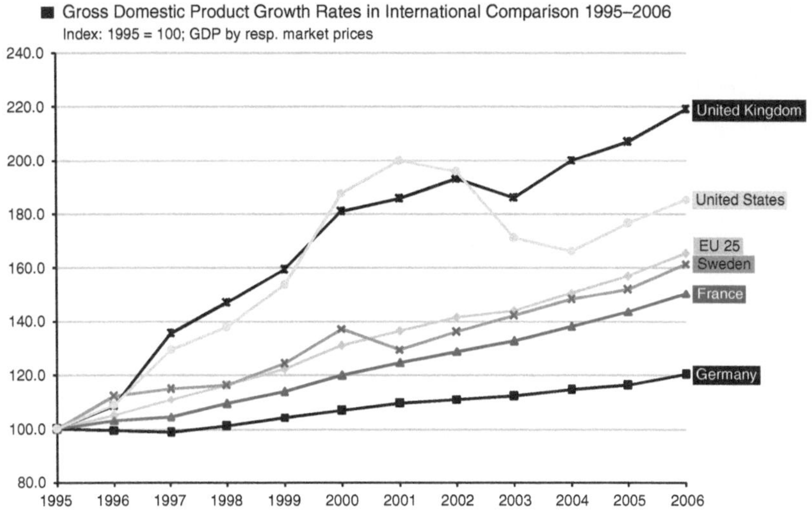

FIGURE 1.1 Growth rates of GDP 1995–2006 (Index: 1995 = 100, GDP in current prices)

Source: Sozialpolitik aktuell 2009.

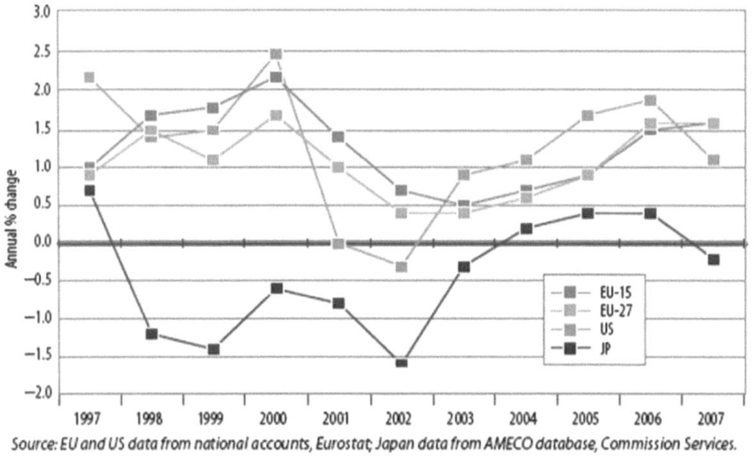

FIGURE 1.2 Employment in growth in the EU, US, and Japan, 1997–2007

Source: European Commission 2008b.

employment rates similar to those of the US and Japan, whereas other EU member states employ less than 60 percent of their working-age population (15 to 64 years old) (this is especially true in the new member states, but also in Italy).

High employment rates and low unemployment rates are macroeconomic targets which should be achieved. In general European countries had consistently

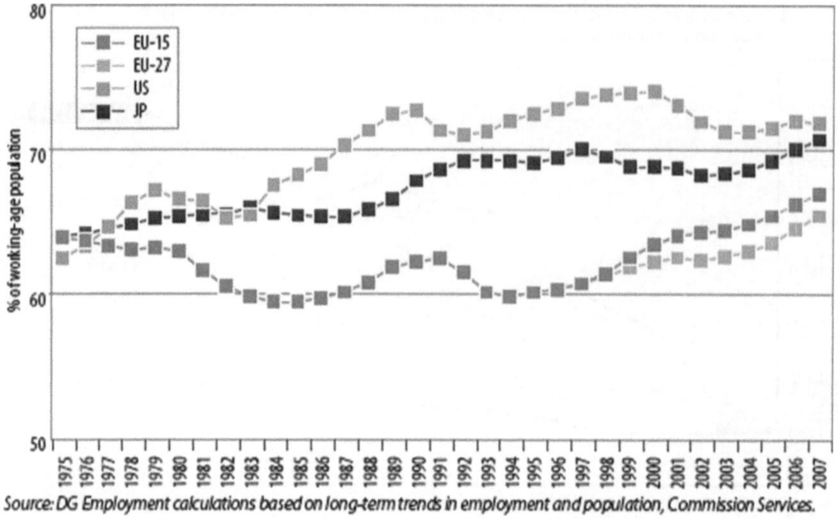

FIGURE 1.3 Employment rates in the EU, US, and Japan, 1975–2007

Source: European Commission 2008b.

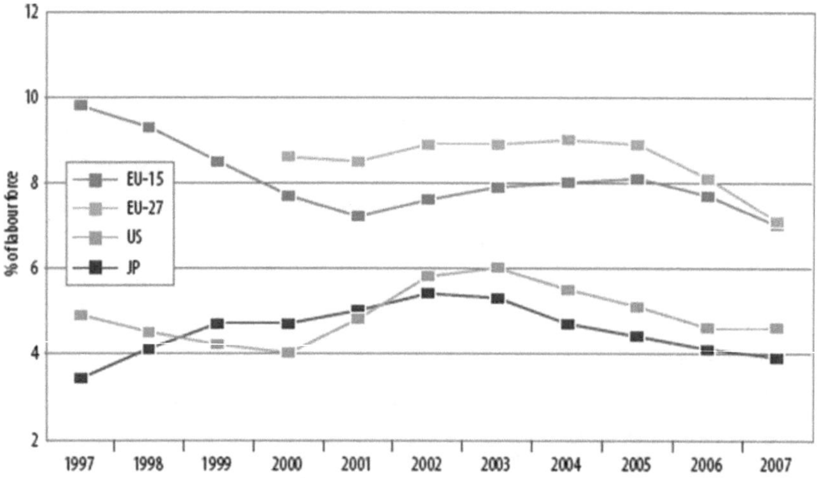

FIGURE 1.4 Unemployment rates in the EU, US, and Japan, 1997–2007

Source: Eurostat, harmonized series on unemployment.

higher unemployment rates than the US and Japan. It must be emphasized, however, that within Europe the differences between high unemployment countries and low unemployment countries are substantial (Figure 1.6). Whereas the Netherlands and Denmark had very low unemployment rates, other EU countries such as Poland and Germany had rates around 8 or 10 percent. In most countries women's unemployment rates were substantially higher than men's; the opposite is

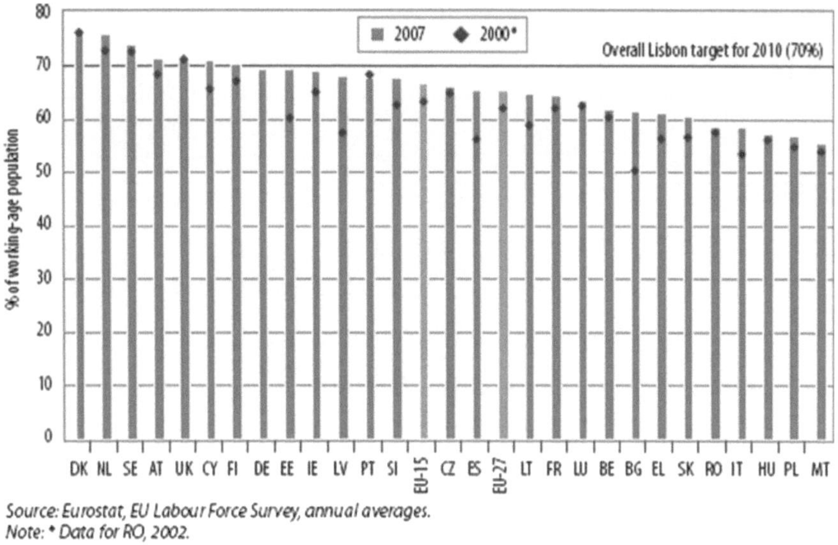

FIGURE 1.5 Overall employment rates for Member States, 2000 and 2007

Source: European Commission 2008b.

true in a few countries, such as the UK and some of the Eastern European transition countries (e.g. Romania, Lithuania, Estonia, and Latvia).

Several studies have analyzed the economic performance of the highly developed countries by using further indicators and different theoretical measures. For example, the German Centre for European Economic Research (ZEW) analyzed performance based on a series of indicators called the "Maastricht-Indikator" and the "Lissabon-Indikator." Maastricht-side indicators included public debt, public expenditure and structure (in terms of investment, infrastructure, education, and research), tax revenues and structure, and social benefits and other transfer systems, such as age related expenses. Lisbon-side indicators included growth rates and factors contributing to potential growth, such as human capital, investment in education, unemployment, duration of unemployment, government expenditure in relation to GDP, distribution of income, openness of financial and commodity markets, Foreign Direct Investment, and age and gender composition of the labor supply. By analyzing the relative strengths and weaknesses of each country, they constructed an indicator for both the Maastricht targets and the Lisbon targets and identified country performances (Figure 1.7).

Figure 1.7 shows good performance (in both dimensions) up to 2006 in the US, Canada, Norway, Finland, Switzerland, Sweden, Denmark, and the UK, a rather weak performance (in both dimensions) in Italy and some of the new member states of the European community, and only modest performances in France, Japan, and Germany. Among the "high performers," the study identifies two quite different social and economical models: the Nordic model of extended welfare states and

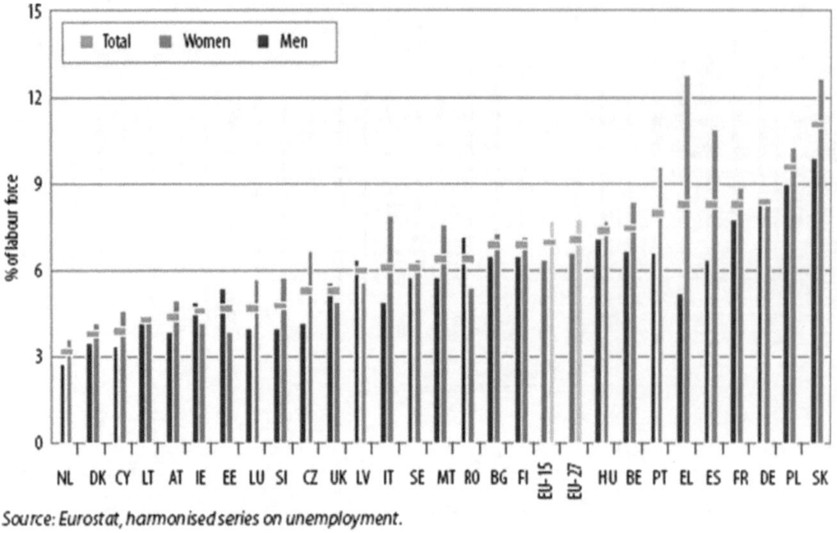

FIGURE 1.6 Unemployment rates for Member States by gender, 2007

Source: European Commission 2008b.

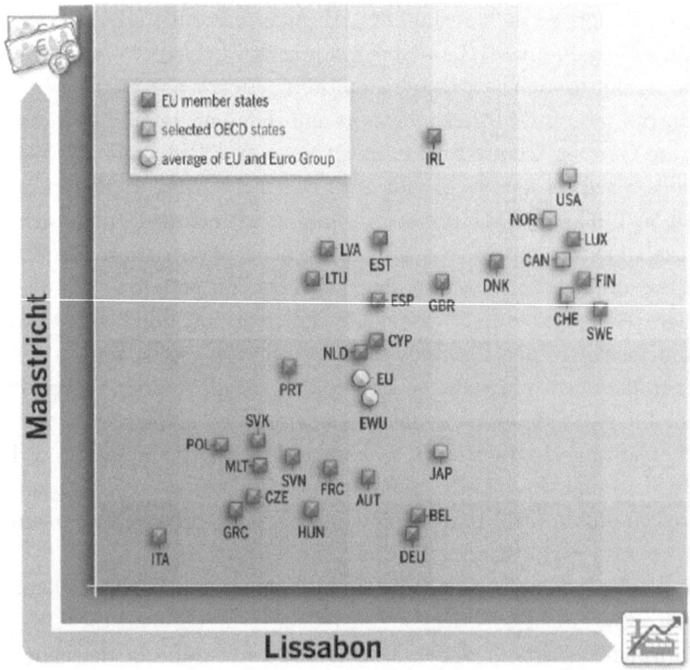

FIGURE 1.7 The Lisbon-Maastricht benchmark

Source: Bertelsmann 2007.

the Anglo-Saxon model of liberal capitalism, which relies on self-responsibility and low government expenditures in social transfers (Bertelsmann 2007: 6).

A study by Hein and Truger (2008) compares the fiscal policies (in the period 1996 to 2005) of France, Germany, the UK, and Sweden. The study thus incorporates two countries within the Eurozone (France and Germany) and two countries that have autonomy over their monetary and fiscal policy (the UK and Sweden). Representing the different models of advanced capitalism discussed above, both the UK and Sweden had better performances than Germany and France. By analyzing different components of the overall macroeconomic strategy, such as monetary policy, exchange rate policy, fiscal policy, and wage policy, the authors come to the conclusion that the strong performances of the UK and Sweden, compared to France and Germany, are not due to structural differences in the labor markets, the social benefit system, or the overall model of capitalism, but rather to the combination of instruments used in macroeconomic policy.

Studies by Heine *et al.* (2006) and Carlin and Soskice (2006) examined the economic performance of selected OECD-member states, including Germany, the UK, the US, and Japan. Although the researchers begin with quite different economic models (Heine *et al.* use a modern Keynesian paradigmatic approach, whereas Carlin and Soskice use the new consensus model), they come to remarkably similar findings. Specifically, monetary policy that is rigidly oriented toward a one-sided target of low inflation (such as the ECB), may increase macroeconomic recessions and act as a restriction to economic stabilization. Whereas the US and the UK central banks do have a dual mandate for price stability and output stabilization, the ECB and the Bank of Japan have been very restrictive. While both studies propose that wage policy should accompany monetary policy, the specific role of wage policy is controversial; whereas Heine *et al.* link wage policy to inflation processes, Carlin and Soskice connect wage policy with the level of unemployment via the NAIRU concept. Nevertheless, both studies find that wage policies that are coordinated and highly centralized fit better into macroeconomic stabilization processes than decentralized and firm-specific regulations. High unemployment combined with the fear of job losses may result in wage increases that are below the level needed to stabilize the economy (as was the case in Japan and Germany). If there are no minimum wage regulations to stabilize the lowest wage levels, deflationary processes may be the result (Heine *et al.* 2006: 200).

Whereas Heine *et al.* are not convinced of the importance of labor market reforms for the macroeconomic performance of the country, Carlin and Soskice argue that the UK labor market reforms of liberalization and increased flexibility contributed to better performance in terms of unemployment and employment rates, but they doubt whether the labor market reforms introduced in Germany have had the same effect:

> A number of UK-type reforms to the labour market and welfare state have been introduced in Germany. Yet the German economy remains much more similar in its institutional arrangements to other continental European

> economies such as the Netherlands [...] An unintended side-effect of the labour market and welfare state reforms that have been implemented in Germany may be to depress household consumption expenditure [...] Germany recorded the largest negative gap between the annual growth in domestic demand and trend growth in GDP amongst eight large OECD countries in the 2000–2003 period.This reflects both weak private consumption and investment, and a highly constrained public sector and stands in sharp contrast to the role that buoyant household and public sector spending have played both in the UK and the USA in sustaining aggregate demand over the past decade.
>
> (*Carlin and Soskice 2006: 762*)

The authors conclude that labor market reforms must be embedded in a macroeconomic policy mix that is consistent with the pre-existing institutional arrangements in order to become coherent and successful. Otherwise, supply-side reforms in the context of a tightly constrained macroeconomic policy may contribute to weak economic performance (as was the case in Germany).

A more recent study by Coats (2006) shows that the correlation between labor market flexibility and unemployment or employment rates is not clear. Countries with "less flexible labor markets" such as Denmark, Sweden, Austria, and the Netherlands performed quite well in the labor market, as did countries such as the US and the UK, in which labor market regulations are more in line with the OECD and EU recommendations.

In concluding this section of the chapter, it should be emphasized that the overall macroeconomic performances of OECD countries cannot be explained only in terms of the strategies written down in the different documents. It seems that the paradigmatic approach, which is formulated in the macroeconomic frameworks of the EU and the OECD, is not followed in all respects by the successful countries. The concept of "one size fits all" is inappropriate for economic realities. However, the success in macroeconomic terms does not mean that the policy chosen ensures that the welfare of all members of society has increased during the last decades. On the contrary: the impact of macroeconomic policies on the well-being of certain groups in society has been negative in some countries, although a discussion of the relation between macroeconomic performance and (microeconomic) distribution of income is beyond the scope of this chapter (see, for example, the 2009 OECD publication on the growing inequality in income distribution). Importantly, it seems that some of the economic instruments used to open financial markets and to decrease the level of regulation within these markets are responsible for the actual deep economic crisis.

The interrelation with gender orders

At first glance, the interrelation between these macroeconomic performances and the gender orders of these countries is certainly not obvious. In regard to the key elements of gender orders (such as access to paid work, organization of care work, distribution of income, regulation of working time and caring time, responsibility for care, and the political empowerment of women) the well performing countries differ quite substantially. The same is true for the countries with weaker macroeconomic development. Across the countries examined here, the relation between the role and responsibilities of private households or individuals in paid employment and care giving, and the role of the state (i.e. welfare institutions) differs quite substantially.

However, in both of the successful "models" (the Nordic and the Anglo-Saxon) addressed here, high priority is placed on women's integration into the labor market, and this is associated with high employment rates for both men and women in the well performing countries (Figure 1.8). We observe higher than average OECD employment rates for women in all the Nordic countries and the major Anglo-Saxon countries (the UK, the US, Canada, Australia, and New Zealand). Lower than average rates are found in Italy, France, and Japan and near average rates are found in Germany.

The integration of women into paid employment may increase the economic power of a country (measured by GDP). As I have already mentioned, the traditional neoclassical view is that the higher the supply of labor, the higher the production of goods (Say's Law). Thus, the higher the level of integration of the potential labor supply, the higher the potential output of production in the country.

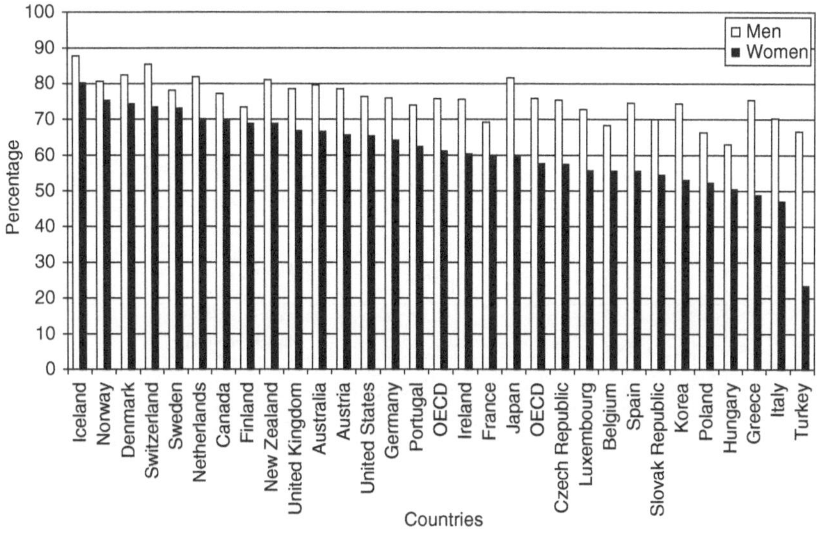

FIGURE 1.8 Employment rates 2008

Source: Own calculations based on OECD Employment database http://www.oecd.org/document/34/0,3343,en_2649_39023495_40917154_1_1_1_1,00.html#avannwage

In other words, integrating more people into the labor market can drive economic growth. As men's employment rates are quite high in nearly all countries, women provide a major source of additional labor supply, an assumption that is widely supported by economists and policy makers, including those at the OECD and the European Commission. In a recent document the OECD states that, "sustainable growth at national and global levels depends on women joining the labor force and fuller use being made of their skills and qualifications" (OECD 2008a: 11). Within both the OECD and the EU papers, the rise of female employment rates is the only gender-specific issue addressed.

The positive relation between economic production and female employment is an empirical fact demonstrated in the data for the EU 27 countries in the year 2006, prior to the economic crises of 2008 (Figure 1.9).

A higher level of labor market integration is associated with both an increase in the GDP (measured in terms of traded goods and services) and an increase in income generated via paid employment. Given the way in which GDP is calculated and measured, the integration of a larger proportion of the population into paid employment leads automatically to an increase in GDP. This accounts, at least partially, for the association between strong macroeconomic performance and high female employment rates.

Having said this, one must add that the causality is not quite clear: is strong economic performance a result of high female employment rates, or are high female employment rates a result of good economic performance? The answer to this question depends on the theoretical point of view; one theory assumes that labor

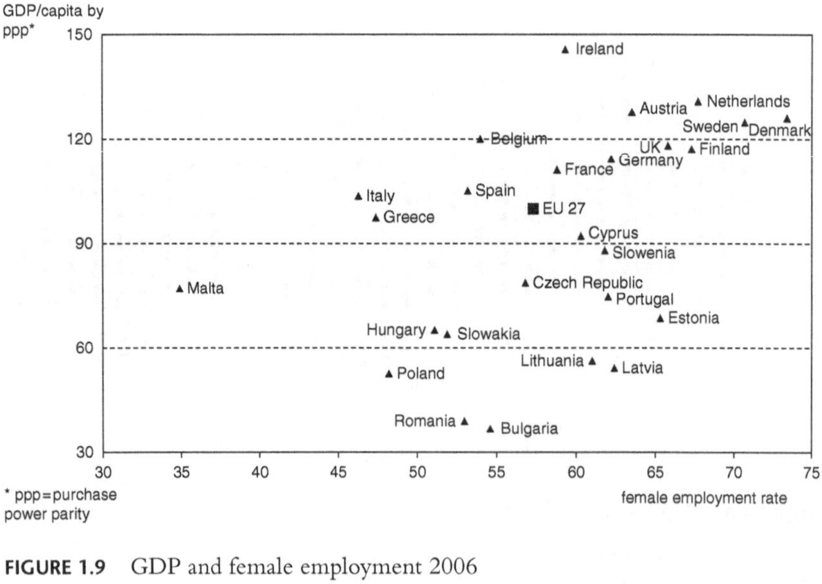

FIGURE 1.9 GDP and female employment 2006

Source: Own calculations based on Eurostat data.

supply generates economic growth (the neoclassical point of view), the other argues that only sufficient aggregate demand creates employment, so women's rising employment is a result of demand in the markets for goods and services. Given the presence of other differences between men and women in employment, such as the gender wage gap, high female participation rates may increase the output of an economy through their lower wages, which leads to lower production costs.

While all highly performing countries do have higher employment rates for women than the lower performing countries, there remains a substantial wage gap between men and women in nearly all countries, but the gap is less pronounced in most of the Nordic countries than in most of the Anglo-Saxon countries (Figure 1.10).

Microeconomic theory, which analyzes household economics and allocation of time within households, would argue that women's integration into the labor market may itself create additional demand in the goods and services market. As women have the responsibility for (unpaid) caring work and other household production, their engagement in paid work depends heavily on the question of whether this unpaid work could be substituted by goods or services provided via the market or public services. Once women have entered the labor market (a move which is constructed as a matter of choice, based on opportunity cost principles), their additional employment creates additional demand in terms of care and household related goods and services. A crucial concern is how societies organize the relation between paid and unpaid work in general (often reduced to the question of how households reconcile paid work and family duties) and what is the gendered nature of these reconciliation policies (see Saam 2003).

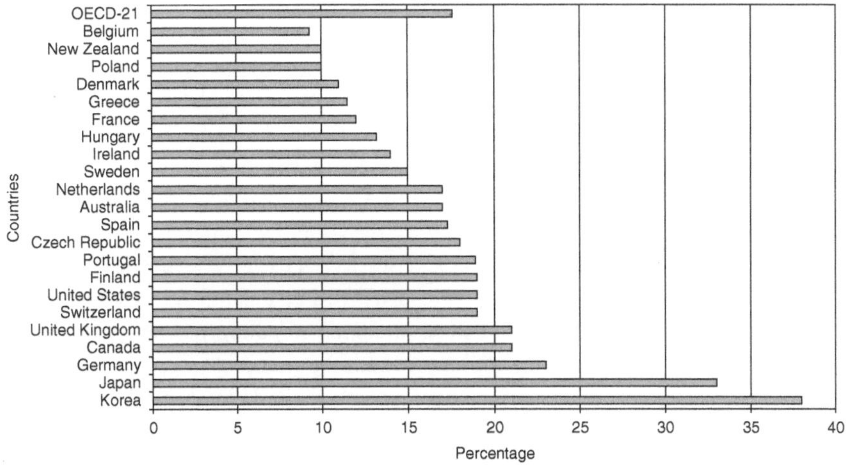

FIGURE 1.10 Gender gap in median earnings 2006 (full-time employees)

Source: Own calculations based on OECD Employment database http://www.oecd.org/document/34/0,3343,en_2649_39023495_40917154_1_1_1_1,00.html#avannwage

To come back to the macroeconomic developments over the last decade, the most successful countries have high female employment rates but they substantially differ in the way the relation between paid and unpaid work and the "reconciliation between work and private life" are organized. Walby (2004) distinguishes between two strategies: (1) the Nordic countries are characterized by a social-democratic (public) service-led route, built on the public sector to create capacities to increase women's employment by offering services related to care and at the same time, employ women in these public services; (2) the Anglo-Saxon strategy organizes the link between employment and unpaid work through the market. This market-led route relies on market mechanisms to create goods and services in the care industry. Both strategies have an immediate positive impact on women's employment opportunities, but result in different outcomes concerning both gender equality and equality between women in the macroeconomic framework.

In the (public) service-led route, women's employment is based on the regulations of the public sector (including wage regulations) and the services are offered at a price that is regulated by government decisions. Therefore, both employment and price regulation are strongly related to the overall development of government policy, which is part of the macroeconomic strategies of fiscal policies. Therefore, women's position in the Nordic countries is much more vulnerable to changes in fiscal policies, especially government policies concerning the allocation of public resources, the priorities of public spending, and tax policies. This means that women's economic position in the Nordic countries is part of the overall political process and is influenced heavily by political campaigns, elections, and the activities both of the state and civil society. Women's involvement in these processes is, therefore, of crucial importance. Their political empowerment is an important precondition to keep the high level of economic integration. In the Nordic model, employment conditions, working times, and workers' representation are quite well organized, leading to a relatively well-protected labor market position (combining a high level of economic security with a high level of equality both between men and women, and between different groups of women). The gender orders of the Nordic countries aim to reduce gender gaps by integrating women into employment and creating new responsibilities both for households and the state. The concept of the dual earner family is supported by a rather generous welfare state, both in terms of services and employment security. However, men's roles in the division of labor have only been modestly challenged by incentives to take parental leave, and are not forced by market dynamics such as falling real wages in male dominated sectors or growing unemployment among men.

In the market-led route, women's employment is linked closely to the development of markets both for goods and services, the latter being a major source of reconciling paid work and private life. In contrast to the employment standards of Nordic countries, employment conditions and wages are less regulated, creating greater wage differentials both between men and women and between different groups of women. The marketization of household related goods and services created a poorly paying labor market segment in which women and other marginalized groups find employment. This has been a major source of economic growth and growth of employment in the US (compared to the continental European economies) (see Freeman and Schettkat 2005). In the Anglo-Saxon countries, gender orders change in the direction of the dual earner family, as a result of economic constraints for lower income households and a growing labor supply of highly skilled women (who employ – due to the lack of publicly offered care services – formal and informal care workers, most of them women). These groups are the major sources of growing employment in the expanding private service sector. Men's roles in the division of labor are hardly challenged and if they are, this is the result of economic constraints and not policy initiatives to expand men's choices.

The continental European countries (such as Italy and Germany) and Japan have been successful neither in their macroeconomic performance nor in their gender policy. Walby characterizes the continental European approach as the regulatory led route, which means that major efforts are put into the legal removal of labor market discrimination and regulation of working times. Neither governments nor private firms offer sufficient household related services because reconciling work and care responsibilities, and increasing women's employment are not seen as major policy issues. These countries have followed a policy of supporting the male breadwinner system: in Germany, Japan, and Italy, the neglect of developing care services is reflected both in public spending and tax systems that support private family-based care activities. The development of a care related state welfare system or a formal market for household related services has not been made a political issue. Nevertheless, gender orders – once based on the male breadwinner model – are changing even in these countries. The trend is the development of a model with a male breadwinner and a second earner with formal part-time or even informal employment, partly because men's wages have decreased substantially during the last decade (as a consequence of wage policies), and partly because regulations to create flexible labor market conditions have set incentives for part-time and low paid employment for both firms and women (as part of supply-side policies). This model results in a lower level of female employment, a lower level of employment growth in the private and public care services, and a lower level of overall economic growth.

The macroeconomic policies of the EU and the OECD mention gender differences only in relation to paid employment. Within both strategies, women's integration into the labor market is an essential policy goal. The underlying assumption is that women are a major resource for economic growth (especially given the fact that young women have higher levels of human capital in most OECD countries and it is assumed that their productivity will be relatively high).

The OECD position is quite clear in this respect, as it calls for the reduction of impediments to female labor force participation and stresses full-time employment (OECD 2007). The EU position is less explicit with regard to full-time or part-time, as some of the member states (Germany, the UK, and the Netherlands) follow a part-time strategy to allow women to combine unpaid work and employment.

In a recent publication the OECD makes the following statement concerning women's roles:

> Care of children and household responsibilities fall in large part on women with deleterious effects on their working lives. Women are disadvantaged in the workplace by time poverty (juggling for needs of home and work), intermittency (taking time off to care for children or elderly parents), and lack of mobility (needing a job close to home and family). Countries which have mandated and funded family-friendly policies to address these anomalies are those which are reaping the economic benefits of more working women.
>
> (*OECD 2008a: 14*)

The OECD advocates greater access to affordable and quality childcare (subsidized and monitored by public authorities), family-friendly labor market regulations (e.g. paid parental leaves, flexible work arrangements, remuneration of women's work), non-discriminatory tax systems, and welfare and work incentives for single parents. Moreover, the OECD paper states that "accounting for unpaid female services (household duties and child care) should be included in national wealth calculations to better reflect their workloads and contributions" (OECD 2008a: 14). Accordingly, the OECD states that "mobilizing female and maternal labor supply through explicit targets and programmes is key to sustainable economic growth in the long-term" (OECD 2008a: 15).

Because the objective is narrowly focused on increasing women's paid employment without questioning the underlying gender orders, men's roles are ignored. Men's employment is determined to be the norm, and women's constraints are perceived to be anomalies from the perspective of the pure market model – the underlying concept is that of a free worker with no family responsibilities, no time constraints and no mobility barriers. This model, which is assumed by many mainstream economists, neglects the complicated interrelation between the different working spheres of society. Their major concern is women's integration into the labor market without asking questions such as how labor markets, care work, and public policy are interrelated, how the resources of society and individuals should be allocated, and how macroeconomic policies should be directed to decrease the contradictions and tensions between paid and unpaid work. The strategic concepts do not demand gender equality or a decrease of women's economic and social discrimination. Instead they seek to reap the economic benefits of more women in the labor market using childcare facilities, parental leave regulations, and monetary incentives as instruments to achieve labor market integration. The fact that women's unpaid work creates economic benefits for the society and the individual household – which is not only not counted for in the GDP but is an essential part of well-being – and the reality of tensions and contradictions between market activities, unpaid care work, and individual well-being are not taken into consideration. Similarly, the need for changes in men's economic and social position is also neglected.

Additionally, the impact of the macroeconomic policies on women's economic and social position is not examined. Some elements of the EU and OECD macroeconomic strategy may have a negative impact on women's situation in the labor market – for example restrictions on government spending may occur in the fields of childcare and education, as motorways and ICT infrastructure may have a higher priority in budget processes. Pro-cyclical fiscal behavior and the privatization of services may cut public employment in times of recession and increase prices for household related public services. More flexible working-time arrangements and more flexible wage-bargaining systems may increase the number of women in employment; however, they are accompanied by a lower quality of work and an increase in wage inequality. Cuts in social benefit systems may result in more single mothers and children living in poverty. The example of the well performing countries shows that macroeconomic developments may be connected with different outcomes for women, depending on the interplay between macroeconomic policies and gender orders. What makes the Nordic countries' policy approach so different from the Anglo-Saxon approach are the overall targets. From the perspective of the former, women's labor market integration was not only an economic benefit for the society but also a major element of gender equality policy (integrated into a social model of overall equality, which includes class and ethnicity dimensions). It combines private and public care work, paid employment, social benefits during periods of non-employment due to parental leave or unemployment, and flexibility and security in working conditions in a welfare state model, which has been shown to be more favorable for women. It challenges men's roles by setting positive incentives for changes. It combines successful macroeconomic policies with a high degree of welfare and avoids high levels of poverty. The Anglo-Saxon model distributes the benefits of the successful macroeconomic performance of the last decade quite unequally among different groups, and corresponds to high levels of poverty and a decline in overall working conditions. The impact of women's integration into the labor force on gender roles is not mediated by an overall policy of gender equality but left to market outcomes with limited state intervention.

Notes

1 The Lisbon Strategy, also known as the Lisbon Agenda or Lisbon Process, is an action and development plan. Its aim is to make the EU "the most dynamic and competitive knowledge-based economy in the world capable of sustainable economic growth with more and better jobs and greater social cohesion, and respect for the environment by 2010." It was set out by the European Council in Lisbon in March 2000. In 2004, Wim Kok headed up a review of the program and presented a report on the Lisbon strategy. One of the main conclusions of this report was that the promotion of growth and employment in Europe is the next great European project. In its resolution on the mid-term review of the Lisbon strategy in March 2005, the European Parliament expressed its belief that "sustainable growth and employment are Europe's most pressing goals and underpin social and environmental progress" and "that well-designed social and environmental policies are themselves key elements in strengthening Europe's economic performance."

2 In the actual deep recession all member states have broken the rules of the SGP. It will become important whether the economic policy returns to the SGP targets or allows for

more flexible and sensitive policy after the crisis. Until now there have been no signs of a fundamental change in economic policy concepts on the EU level and no lessons have been learned by the actual recession.

3 This concept is known as "Say's Law": supply and production will create demand. A central element of Say's Law is that recession does not occur because of failure in aggregate demand or lack of money. The more goods (for which there is demand) that are produced, the more those goods (supply) can constitute a demand for other goods. For this reason, prosperity should be increased by stimulating production, not consumption.

Bibliography

Arestis, P. and Sawyer, M. (2007) "Perspectives on Economic Policy in the Economic and Monetary Union," in E. Hein, J. Priewe and A. Truger, (eds) *European Integration in Crisis*, Marburg: Metropolis-Verlag, pp. 331–352.

Beffa, J. L., Boyer, R. Gazier, B., De Grauw, P., Illing, G, van der Ploeg, R. and Solow, R. (2008) *Defining a European Macroeconomic Policy*. Online. Available http://www.sfm.vwl.uni-muenchen.de/makropolitik/index.html (accessed August 20, 2008).

Bertelsmann Stiftung (2007) LiMa-Benchmark – *A Performance Analysis of EU Member States in the Light of the Lisbon and Maastricht Goal Systems*. Online. Available at: http://www.bertelsmann-stiftung.de/bst/en/media/xcms_bst_dms_20480_20481_2.pdf (accessed January 4, 2010).

Blanchard, O. (2006) "European Unemployment: The Evolution of Facts and Ideas," *Economic Policy*, 21(45): 5–59.

Burda, M. and Wyplosz, C. (2005) *Macroeconomics. A European Text Fourth Edition*, Oxford: Oxford University Press.

Carlin, W. and Soskice, D. (2006) *Macroeconomics – Imperfections, Institutions and Policies*, Oxford: Oxford University Press.

Coats, D. (2006) *Who's Afraid of Labour Market Flexibility*? London: Work Foundation.

European Commission (2008a) *Integrated Guidelines for Growth and Jobs 2005–2008*. Online. Available at: http://ec.europa.eu/growthandjobs/guidelines/index_en.htm#gl1 (accessed August 20, 2008).

European Commission (2008b) *Employment in Europe 2008*. Online. Available at: http://ec.europa.eu/social/main.jsp?catId=119&langId=en, (accessed July 20, 2009).

Freeman, R. and Schettkat R. (2005) "Marketization of Household Production and the EU–US Gap in Work," *Economic Policy*, 20(41): 6–51.

Hein, E. and Truger, A. (2008) "Fiscal policy in the macroeconomic policy mix: a critique of the NEW Consensus Model and a comparison of macroeconomic policies in France, Germany, the UK and Sweden from a Post-Keynesian perspective," Working Paper des IMK 3/2008, Düsseldorf.

Heine, M., Herr, H. and Kaiser C. (2006) *Wirtschaftspolitische Regime Westlicher Industrienationen*, Baden-Baden: Nomos Verlagsgesellschaft.

OECD (1994) *The OECD Jobs Study*, Paris: OECD Publications.

OECD (2007) *Going for Growth*, Paris: OECD Publications.

OECD (2008) *OECD Economic Outlook No. 83 Annex Tables*. Online. Available at: http://www.oecd.org/document/61/0,3343,en_2649_34573_2483901_1_1_1_1,00.html (accessed August 20, 2008).

OECD (2008a) *Gender and Sustainable Development: Maximising the Economic, Social and Environmental Role of Women*, Paris: OECD Publication.

OECD (2009) *Growing Unequal? Income Distribution and Poverty in OECD Countries*, Paris: OECD Publications.

Rothschild, K. (2006) "Nairu oder Nauri oder ... ? Eine ideologiekritische Note," *WSI Mitteilungen*, Heft 3, 2006: 162–164.

Saam, M. (2003) "Gender in growth theory," in U. Pasero (ed.), *Gender – From Costs to Benefits*, Wiesbaden: Westdeutscher Verlag, pp. 31–43.

Sozialpolitik aktuell (2009) *Das Informationsportal zur Sozialpolitik*. Online. Available at: http://www.sozialpolitik-aktuell.de/tl_files/sozialpolitik-aktuell/_Politikfelder/Europa-Internationales/Datensammlung/PDF-Dateien/abbII25.pdf (accessed July 20, 2009).

Stotsky, J.G. (2006) "Gender and its relevance to macroeconomic policy: a survey," IMF working paper WP/06/233, Washington: International Monetary Fund.

Walby, S. (2004) "The European Union and Gender Equality: Emergent Varieties of Gender Regimes," *Social Politics*, 11(1): 4–29.

2

CHANGING MACROECONOMIC GOVERNANCE AND GENDER ORDERS

The case of Canada

Isabella Bakker

Introduction

Neoliberal restructuring, fiscal policy, and gender orders

Recent decades have given rise to pronounced economic and political transformation for many, including Canadians. Since the late 1970s, a new economic and political paradigm, neoliberalism, began to impose its market rationality across the global North and South. Characterized by reduced expenditures on state services, the privatization of formerly public services, the expansion and creation of new markets, and the appropriation of assets (such as land, water, or agricultural seeds in the South), neoliberalism signaled a process of restructuring that touches not just states and markets but also the gendered norms and divisions of labor that underpin gender orders.[1]

This chapter explores both the changing and continuing aspects of the Canadian gender order through a consideration of the macroeconomics of fiscal austerity that has marked the last 20 years or so. I will argue that macroeconomic policy rules related to "sound" policies and the resultant social policy regime that has emerged in Canada reflect a strategic silence about the gender order that is inscribed in these regimes. The gender order that appears to be emerging is both continuous and changing. Its change is reflected in the increasing labor force participation of women and the shift to a male wage earner model. Here provisions for care remain privatized, and women continue to perform the bulk of social reproduction work. On the other hand, the prevalence of transnational mothering – care work provided by women from other countries who are hired privately in the home – implies a continuity of the boundaries around productive and reproductive work and the gender divisions of labor that mark this division.

An intersectional analysis reveals the class, race, and spatial differences that are intensifying among women partly as a result of globalization forces. The example of transnational care work is a compelling one that illustrates both the spatial and hierarchical aspects of the privatization of care and social reproduction. As Lourdes Beneria (2008) has noted, the dispersal and fragmentation of families from the global South to the North represents, on the one hand, a gender role reversal, with women migrating and sending back remittances to their families and communities. As such, this can present an "undoing of gender" (Butler 2004) if women experience an increase in financial autonomy and independence. On the other hand, the prevalence of transnational mothering implies a continuity of the boundaries around productive and reproductive work and the gender divisions of labor that mark this division. In a sense, this continuity is hidden, since it conceals not just the complexities of migrant domestic workers' own social reproduction but also that of their employers – middle-class women whose citizenship rights are mediated on the condition they participate as if they were men in the labor markets (Arat-Koc 2006; Bakker and Silvey 2008).

There are, of course, many dimensions to the changing parameters of the Canadian experience, including the current global financial and economic crisis (which other chapters in this volume address more directly). I will focus on two key aspects of economic governance and regulation here: the macroeconomic framing through sound economic policies and the resultant social policy regime with its diverse range of policies and programs (including health care, education, training, housing, income support, unemployment insurance, and care). I argue that both the economic regime and the social policy regime are contributing to a shift in gender arrangements and the disappearance of the gendered subject – both in discourse and practice – from Canadian policy making (Brodie and Bakker 2008). This chapter is only a modest beginning to a more detailed examination of the shift in governance regimes and the links to gender orders.[2]

Macroeconomic policy and social reproduction of gender orders

In Canada, how revenues are raised for public purposes (a shared federal–provincial responsibility) and who is responsible for the necessary programs to meet social progress objectives (mainly the provinces) is shaped by the constitution. The role of government spending at both levels, however, has been reduced over the last two decades and has left markets with a much greater influence (Yalnizyan 2005a). Since the 1980s, Canada has progressively moved toward a neoliberal approach to economic management, which, from the mid-1990s onwards, committed the federal government to fiscal discipline measures and balanced budgets. These measures included rapid deficit reduction, new expenditure and restraint rules, and a push for greater fiscal transparency.

Offloading risk – the changing social policy regime

In Canada, federal spending as a share of the economy shrank from 16 percent of gross domestic product (GDP) in 1993–94 to 11 percent in 2000–01. This was part of a massive neoliberal-inspired plan to eliminate budget deficits through cuts in federal spending, which was first marked by a federal plan in 1995. According to a 2005 *Social Watch* report, these cuts were harshest for the most vulnerable, and, given their place in the distribution of income, women were "doubly jeopardized" (Yalnizyan 2005b). For instance, the dramatic decline in employment insurance coverage has been reflected in a widening gap in coverage between women and men. Only three in ten women who become unemployed are now eligible for benefits due to new rules that ignore gendered differences in employment. As a recent study by Townson and Hayes notes: "while women's patterns of paid employment and participation in the paid workforce are different from those of men, these differences were not recognized when the EI changes were made" (2007: 8). Specifically, the shift from measuring work in weeks to measuring work in hours conceals the significant gender differences in working time and interruptions related to childcare and family responsibilities (Ibid.: 19). In addition, while women have very high labor force participation rates, the nature of their paid employment is quite different from the previous generation of full-time work with a single employer and guaranteed pension. Since the late 1970s, more jobs have become short-term, temporary, contract-based, part-time, and casual, and many workers have become self-employed or hold multiple jobs. These non-standard work arrangements – which constituted 34 percent of all employment in Canada in 2004 – tend to be poorly paid and reflect the job reality of more women than men (40 percent versus 29 percent in 2004). Given the shift in work measurements, and the gendered nature of these non-standard work arrangements, women often do not meet the work hour requirements that would qualify them for EI benefits. Townson and Hayes conclude that:

> the gender gap in coverage has serious implications for women workers. While they must contribute to the program from the first dollar of their earnings, their likelihood of being able to receive benefits if they become unemployed is much less than that of men. In effect, the EI contributions of women workers are being used to subsidize the benefits of the male workers who find it easier to qualify under the new rules (2007: 9).

The new rules not only reinforce a male breadwinner bias but also have different applications among women. For example, maternity leave benefits tend to be given to more affluent, better-educated women, who are more likely to be employed in large firms. This leads Townson and Hayes to conclude that "the switch to an hours-based system for maternity and parental benefits tended to exclude the most disadvantaged women – those who were less well educated, had lower earnings and worked for small firms – from access to maternity and parental benefits" (2007: 16). In sum, changes in EI reflect the broader shift in social policy that is driven by an adult-worker model and its emphasis on human capital and entitlements linked to labor force attachment (MacDonald 2009: 81).

Another important aspect of women's "double jeopardy" resulting from rapid deficit reduction and spending cuts relates to their place in the distribution of income and levels of poverty. The vast majority of Canadian households living on less than $20,000 a year are female-headed (Yalnizyan 2005b: 5).

In a detailed report for Status of Women Canada on Canada's social policy regime and its changes over the last decade, Brodie and Bakker conclude that the continued fragmentation and erosion of the social assistance regime, along with tax-delivered social policies that do not benefit low income women (since they generally do not have enough taxable income),[3] has left Canada's poorest – who are disproportionately women, children, aboriginal peoples, and visible minorities – poorer and more insecure than they were before the reforms were enacted (2008).

For example, according to Statistics Canada's Low Income Cut-Off (LICO), a measure usually employed as an approximate measure of the incidence and depth of poverty in Canada after tax, about 2.7 million Canadians, 54 percent of them women, lived in poverty in 2003 (Brodie and Bakker 2008). According to the Canadian Council on Social Development, female-headed lone-parent families had much higher poverty rates than male-led lone-parent families – 35.6 percent compared to 14.2 percent in 2004. Between 2000 and 2004, lone-parent families faced virtually unchanged poverty rates, having made significant gains in the mid- to late-1990s when their poverty rate dropped from 45 percent to 32.3 percent.[4] Single-parent mothers continue to account for the majority of all lone-parent families in Canada and accounted for 90 percent of all poor lone-parent families in 2001 (Brodie and Bakker 2008). In the case of identifiable groups of women, Townson notes that 36 percent of Aboriginal women lived in poverty (compared to 17 percent of non-Aboriginal women), as did 29 percent of visible minority women, 35 percent of recent women immigrants (arriving between 1991 and 2000), and 26 percent of women with disabilities (Townson 2005: 2–3).

The feminization of poverty is a persistent phenomenon despite women's increasing labor force participation rates. The employment rate for women increased from 42 percent in 1972 to 81 percent in 2005, yet in both full- and part-time work, and across all age groups, women earn less than men. In 2003, the average income of women aged 15 and over from all sources (including employment, government transfer payments, investments and other income) amounted to 62 percent of what men earned (Statistics Canada 2005). The wage gap between male and female workers in Canada remains significant, as full-time female workers earn about 71 percent of what males earn (Statistics Canada 2005: 14). Despite this disparity, in recent years, certain jurisdictions in Canada have eliminated pay equity laws (Cohen and Cohen 2006). While women have increased their representation in several professional fields (making up over half of those employed in certain medical fields and business and financial positions), the majority of women continue to be employed in traditionally female occupations in the characteristically low-paid service and retail sectors. Women are also more likely to be "precariously" employed in part-time, limited-term, contractual, and non-standard work, often in order to accommodate ongoing family responsibilities.

Compounding the lack of government support for women facing economic pressures, is the decision of federal policy makers to redirect resources to tax-based incentives and expenditures through what has been termed the "fiscalization of social policy" (Yalnizyan 2005a). Fiscalization means that social policy goals are pursued indirectly through the tax system (for example, through tax credits) and the individual spending priorities of families, while taxable income determines both who is eligible for support and the level of support attained. Some argue that fiscalization is a preferable way to provide income support for the poor, because it is a private mechanism that avoids stigmatizing the poor. Yet fiscalization is, at best, an indirect social policy instrument that is both precarious and lacking transparency.

More importantly, in terms of our analysis of the strategic silences within macroeconomic instruments, tax expenditures are not gender neutral. Lisa Philipps (2006) has argued that these tax-delivered social policies have two systemic disadvantages for many women. First, tax-based measures generally do not benefit low-income women (and men) because these earners do not have enough taxable income or tax liability to claim deductions, exemptions, or credits. Second, underlying tax expenditures is the assumption that the primary breadwinner will share these gains with the household. This ignores a good deal of evidence about intra-household financial inequalities, assumes caregivers are in a spousal/partner relationship, and leaves out those cases in which neither partner earns sufficient taxable income to benefit from the credit (Philipps 2006). The male breadwinner bias of tax-delivered social policies structures any claims on the state for social benefits around the norm of full-time, lifelong participation in the labor force, and assumes that a wage paid to the male breadwinner provides for the cash needs of dependants, leaving women with little or no autonomy of decision making and control (Elson and Cagatay 2000: 1355).

Sound macroeconomics, budgets, and paid/unpaid work

So-called sound macroeconomic policies, which promote low inflation and high mobility of capital, have been common to neoliberal perspectives of governments in Canada since the 1980s. Their adoption often creates policy incoherence between overall macroeconomic stewardship and social justice commitments (Elson 2006; Floro and Hoppe 2008). For example, the social investment commitments to poverty alleviation and gender equality require public spending to counterbalance deflationary policies (Elson and Cagatay 2000), not fiscal contraction. Aside from a contradiction between the stated objectives of governments and the actual budgetary resources dedicated to meet commitments, there is also the issue of the type of gender order that is being configured through macroeconomic decision making and planning. This is the point of departure for the following section.

Budgets and gender-based analysis (GBA)

The Canadian Parliamentary Standing Committee on the Status of Women (FEWO) has recently completed a year-long set of hearings on the challenges of implementing gender-responsive budgeting at the federal level with the objective of enhancing the GBA of fiscal policies. It is clear that one key aspect of attaining more gender-responsive budgeting involves scrutinizing the approach to economic policy in the prevailing economic and budgetary consensus. For instance, recent studies conclude that focusing too narrowly on macroeconomic stability can have adverse effects on economic and human development. Sound policy to defeat inflation, for instance, has led to very high interest rates in a number of countries. Higher interest rates, in turn, have led to increased unemployment, thereby perpetuating poverty (Rodrick 2004; Stiglitz 2005; Berik *et al.* 2009). Economic growth does require measures such as employment creation. Yet viewed from a gender equality perspective, notions of "full employment" also need to be scrutinized for ignoring the unpaid work in which most women are engaged. For instance, lower income women in developing countries often suffer from "overfull employment" based on the excessive demands on their time and energy to fetch fuel and water, produce meals, and so forth. Lower income women in the more developed countries continue to face many care responsibilities that compromise their ability to seek full employment in the formal labor market, a fact that is reflected in their higher concentration in part-time jobs in most countries (Elson 2006: 119–120).

These points underscore what appears to be a conceptual separation in Finance Canada – Canada's Treasury Department – between "structural" policies and "macroeconomic" policies. In her testimony to FEWO, the newly appointed Gender Based Analysis Champion at Finance, who is responsible for mainstreaming a gender analysis into the budget, notes that:

> Macro-economic policies deal with aggregate economic variables such as fiscal surpluses and fiscal deficit targets and the level of public debt. These policies provide the economic and fiscal framework within which structural policies are developed. Since macro-economic policies are by definition not targeted to any sector or any group of individuals in particular, gender-based analysis is not applicable. Structural policies, on the other hand, can impact specific sectors and segments of the population. Since these policies could potentially have different measurable impacts on women and men, it is on those policies that gender-based analysis is carried out. Examples of structural policy for which the Department of Finance is responsible include tax, tariff policy, managing federal borrowing, administering transfers to the provinces, and developing an effective system of regulation for the financial sector.[5]

Feminist and heterodox economists have documented how broader macroeconomic strategies and discourses about the role of government, in particular public investment, shape the direction of economic growth, the nature and level of job creation, poverty reduction efforts, and time spent in social reproduction activities. These issues are significantly related to the appropriate level of budget deficit and surplus, which neoliberal economists argue should be in a situation of balance. A contrasting approach is offered by heterodox economists who argue for the medium-term need for budget deficits to facilitate the process of private sector deleveraging[6] and to help restore growth. In their view, deficit-financed investment can make a positive contribution to growth; public capital spending on infrastructure has a multiplier effect that raises the productivity of private capital and contributes to improved quality of life. Also, government can use its special financial power to issue money and bonds to offset fluctuations in private sector demand and it can increase budget deficits in downswings while reducing them in upswings (Palley 2009).[7] Feminist macroeconomists generally tend to support a more heterodox economics approach that allows for greater government discretion in the management of public finances and in terms of how the deficit/surplus is managed (see Elson 2006 for a detailed discussion). Yet they caution that this approach too may suffer from an implicit or explicit "breadwinner bias" through which priority is given to men's employment and women are treated as dependents with a contingent relationship to public services and social protection (Bakker 2003; Elson 2004).

The capacity to undertake GBA of macroeconomic policies within the federal government (and within the Department of Finance in particular) has also been significantly undermined by the spending cuts discussed earlier. As Brodie and Bakker (2008) note, despite a long history of gender-based policy units within the Canadian federal government, from the mid-90s onward, broader social and political forces have served to erode the resources assigned to these units. This retrogression was starkly apparent in 2006 when, after years of successive cutbacks to the status of women machinery (e.g. Status of Women Canada) under the Liberals, the new Conservative government under Stephen Harper cut even deeper, some $2 billion worth, at the expense of Canada's equality-seeking groups. Brodie (2007, 2008) argues that this dismantling of GBA within government is part of a broader process of delegitimizing the women's movement and women's claim-making vis-à-vis public policy making and underscores the disappearance of women as an analytical category of policy analysis in favor of, for example, the child.

These developments suggest that at the very time when more effective analysis of expenditures and revenues is needed (and indeed, government has commitments to results-based management of public funds) we have fewer resources (financial and human) to undertake such analyses. For example, in response to the recent financial and economic crisis, the Federal Budget 2009 announced $64 billion in new deficit-financed spending and tax cuts, yet very little GBA accompanied these plans. Infrastructure spending, which was announced at $8 billion over the next two fiscal years, had no gender equity requirements nor is it targeted at child care facilities, which are needed to enable women on the economic margins to enter paid work (Lahey 2009). Such an approach echoes the earlier fiscal austerity measures undertaken by federal governments of different political stripes, and the choices they ultimately made not to reallocate the resulting budget surpluses from 1998–2004 into depleted social programs (Yalnizyan 2005a).

Feminist economists have highlighted how achieving macroeconomic balance through cuts to public provisioning offloads care work to women's unpaid labor (Elson 1995). While some women can afford to hire other women to undertake this work, in doing so they are relying on a private solution to the paid work/unpaid care dilemma that fails to facilitate women's full-time employment in good jobs through public services or to influence the traditional gender-based division of labor in a more progressive way. In effect, this signals a shift from providing care services to placing the responsibility on individuals to meet these needs through an adult dual-earner model or through cash allowances, tax credits, or tax incentives to pay domestic workers (Williams 2009: 13). The tensions around this private form of meeting caring needs will only increase with the aging of the population. It is estimated that by 2026, one Canadian in five will have reached the age of 65 (Health Canada 2002). In addition, an inadequate strategy toward meeting the needs of care and social reproduction agitates against the government's own social investment strategy of having all "able bodied" adults engage in paid work.

In the policy domain and across a variety of countries, at least three potential alternative approaches have emerged with regard to the politics of care and the shaping of more equitable gender orders. The first gives *indirect policy recognition* to the relationship between paid and unpaid labor through, for example, pension schemes and employment equity policies, which encourage a more equitable choice and distribution of unpaid work (unemployment related provisions). The second *recognizes the importance of unpaid work* through policies such as tax breaks for those staying at home to raise young children (i.e. financial or in-kind social security and tax benefits in the Netherlands). These policies may also provide a separate paid paternity leave to fathers on a "use it or lose it basis" such as in the Nordic countries. The third recognizes women as both mothers and workers through *public sector provision of services* and removes some of the individual burden of unpaid labor (such as child care), by shifting this to the public sphere (i.e. France) (see Daly 2001; Williams 2009 for a detailed discussion). There are obviously many hybrids of these three approaches (see Jenson (2003)) and policy makers are rarely explicit about how assumptions about who should do care work and under what conditions guide their decision making. Yet social policy development in Canada is informed by these implicit (and often paradoxical) models of the macroeconomy (Bakker 1997), the family, and models of social policy. The implementation of a social investment approach that seeks to promote human capital also encourages women to increasingly engage in paid work without sufficient public policy attention to the necessities of unpaid work, including child care and, increasingly, care for the elderly.

A new gender order?

This analysis suggests that a new gender order may be emerging in Canada: one that is shaped by a shift in political rationality away from post-war social liberalism to twenty-first-century neoliberalism and the accompanying erosion of the foundations of the post-war welfare state along with the male breadwinner model of social provisioning and its gender identities and relations (Brodie 2008: 147). Brodie identifies three sets of forces – what she calls the 3Ds – that have contributed to this shift: the *delegitimization* of feminist voices (and those of virtually all equity-seeking groups) as claims-makers in the policy process; the *dismantling* of the gender-based policy capacity in the federal and provincial governments; and the *disappearance* of the gendered subject in policy discourses and practices (2008: 171). Overall, there has been a move toward policy discourses and practices committed to a gender-neutral market citizen and worker who is not impeded by systemic discrimination and unequal structures of representation (Brodie and Bakker 2008).[8]

This move to a genderless market citizen can, to some extent, be substantiated through *labor market* data. Based on the 2005 Canada General Social Survey, women's labor force participation rate is one of the highest in the world, at 81 percent in 2005 (up from 70 percent in 1986) compared to men's, which has edged down to 91 percent in 2005 (compared to 94 percent in 1986). This convergence of participation patterns reflects longer workdays for both men and women since 1986. Most of the increase for men, however, came from unpaid work in the house – about 2.5 hours per day. Men's time in paid labor also rose from 6.1 to 6.3 hours. By comparison, women's increased workday came from paid work: in 2005, an average of 4.4 hours compared to 3.3 in 1986, with a half-hour decline in unpaid work from 4.8 hours to 4.3 hours. In the end, daily participation rates for housework remain significantly higher for women than for men in all family types. Notably, it is only within higher personal income brackets that either sex is spending more time at a job and less on housework. Statistics Canada found that when wives have an income of $100,000 or more, the division of paid labor and housework is more likely to be split equally by couples (Statistics Canada July 2006).

These findings are interesting when compared with Broomhill and Sharp's (2004) for Australia. Covering a similar period of time, these authors conclude that the extent to which the breadwinner model is changed depends on place, class, and socioeconomic differences in structuring experiences around paid and unpaid work. They note that in working-class areas, women provide an increasingly important component of household income but this is because male employment levels and income have dropped. By contrast, in more affluent areas, the increased earnings of women have contributed substantially to the household and this may reflect "a shift towards a more symmetrical breadwinner model among some more affluent Australian households" (Broomhill and Sharp 2004: 1). These conclusions appear to echo the recent Canadian developments in paid and unpaid work discussed above.

What can we conclude from this brief consideration of labor patterns in Canada? At the most general level, there appears to be a convergence toward a model that relies on both members of households to earn a living.[9] The General Social Survey notes that, on average, the proportion of men and women aged 25–54 who did some housework daily rose from 72 percent in 1986 to 79 percent in 2005. At the lower end of the income scale, this has meant some adjustment in the amount of unpaid labor both men and women are doing; the former have increased their share, while the latter have reduced the time spent on housework. At the high end of income, there has been a convergence between men and women toward a "genderless" breadwinner model. Given, however, that the work of social reproduction is secured through the market and done by women who are paid to undertake these tasks, we can question the extent to which this model is in fact "genderless." For instance, the Survey of Household Spending (2004) found that while only 7 percent of households with less than $40,000 paid for domestic help (spending an average of $813), 43 percent of households with $160,000 or more did so (spending an average of $2,150).[10] In that sense, the "genderless" breadwinner model continues to rely on women's labor – in this case, the labor of migrant women and working-class women – but the collectivization of responsibility and risk for that work has been individualized and removed from the purview of states and capital.

The gender order, macroeconomic governance, and social reproduction: some preliminary conclusions

The foregoing discussion points to some tentative conclusions that must be developed further through what Elson and Warnecke refer to as the "macro–meso–micro approach," which relies on stylized facts about the economy and the gender order derived from case studies and time series analysis (see Chapter 6).

1. Neoliberal restructuring of fiscal policy has prioritized debt reduction and the individualization of risk through reduced social spending and an increased reliance on the delivery of social programs through the tax system, developments that have punished those at the lower end of the income scale who can be said to have borne the burdens of adjustment. Risk is greater for women, especially the most marginalized, as both poverty rates and the nature of labor market attachment (non-standard) suggest.
2. At the very time when GBA and gender-responsive budgeting are needed, less capacity to conduct these exists within federal and provincial governments due to cuts in women's machineries. This is not merely a reflection of spending cuts; rather, it signals a shift in the legitimacy of claims making around social markers such as gender. This is reinforced by the budget process, which – both in terms of representation and content – does not consider gender a significant factor in the construction of macroeconomic policies and concepts. The conventional macroeconomic framework that guides fiscal, monetary, and exchange rate policy only addresses women's needs and experiences to the extent that they conform to male norms. But a substantial part of women's time and resources is dedicated to unpaid work – the work of producing and caring for human beings – that underpins the paid economy. This omission of the activities from macroeconomic inquiry and, by extension, policy, is not simply an omission based on complexities of measurement; rather, it reflects assumptions built into this model that exclude women's time in unpaid work as a used economic resource. It also increasingly masks the exploitative extraction of care resources that results from decisions taken by individuals in the North and South in response to the economic conditions and imperatives they are facing (Beneria 2008).
3. A gender order that is both constant and changing appears to be emerging in Canada as elsewhere (Elson 2006). At the formal policy level, many policy assumptions and implementations (such as EI and tax expenditures) are

reinforcing a male breadwinner notion. At the material level of everyday life, workers – be they women or men – are working longer hours to meet their social reproduction needs. At the lower end of income, new data suggest that men are doing slightly more unpaid work, while women are doing less. At the high end, there appears to be convergence toward a seemingly gender-neutral (yet ultimately male) breadwinner model, with a private, marketized solution to meeting the needs of care and social reproduction. Within this model, it is still women who are performing unpaid work but they are often from another place and compelled by the social reproduction needs of their own families, communities, and sending governments. As feminist migration studies have revealed, the state is not neutral in either the sending or receiving countries (Kofman and Raghuram 2009). Capital is also offloading social reproduction costs with shifts in taxation away from business to individuals and this further contributes to the fiscal squeeze of governments at the national and sub-national levels (UNDESA 2005).

Notes

1 Many definitions of "gender order" exist. The concept derives from R.W. Connell, who uses the term to describe the social organization of gender relations at different levels of social life. For Connell, modern gender orders are constituted and reconstituted through intersecting processes of industrialization, urbanization and globalization (1995). The term as it is used here reflects this understanding and incorporates the broader institutionalized relations of power and privilege, and divisions of labor that are organized around gender difference.

2 For a recent detailed examination, see Alexandra Dobrowolsky (ed.) (2009) *Women and Public Policy in Canada: Neo-liberalism and After?* Don Mills: Oxford University Press. This volume offers discussions of shifts in childcare, employment insurance, and many other social policies within a consideration of both the neoliberal and social investment perspectives. See also Brodie and Bakker (2008) *Where are the Women? Gender Equity, Budgets and Canadian Public Policy*, Ottawa: Canadian Centre for Policy Alternatives for the argument that neoliberal rationality of the social has contributed to the erosion of women as the subject of public policy.

3 See Phillipps (2006).

4 http://www.ccsd.ca/factsheets/economic_security/poverty/index.htm.

5 http://cmte.parl.gc.ca/Content/HOC/committee/392/fewo/reports/rp3551119/feworp11/08-chap5-e.htm, note 158.

6 The following is the explanation of deleveraging from *The Economist* in the context of the current financial crisis: "Financial institutions, desperate to repair the damage inflicted on their balance sheets by mortgage-related securities, sell assets. In doing so, they exacerbate the problem. Forced sales push down the prices of assets, worsening the balance sheets of other investors, forcing more asset sales, and so on. In the end, the government is the only entity left in the game with a balance sheet strong enough to keep buying." http://www.economist.com/businessfinance/displaystory.cfm?story_id=12306060, Sept. 25, 2008.

7 Palley (2009) also considers and rejects arguments that deficits pose an inflationary threat and crowd out the private sector.

8 In Brodie and Bakker, there is an interesting discursive analysis of speeches from the Throne that traces the shift from women as objects of public policy to genderless workers and consumers with an ascendant focus on the child as the main focus of social policy (pp. 77–78).

9 The total paid and unpaid work day for people aged 25–54 has increased from 8.2 hours in 1986 to 8.8 hours on average in 2005, or the equivalent of about nine extra days. See Statistics Canada, *The Daily*, "General Social Survey: Paid and Unpaid Work", July 19, 2006.

10 See http://www.statcan.ca/Daily/English/060719/d060719b.htm.

Bibliography

Arat-Koc, S. (2006) "Whose Social Reproduction? Transnational Motherhood and Challenges to Feminist Political Economy," in K. Bezanson and M. Luxton (eds) *Social Reproduction: Feminist Challenges to Neo-liberalism*, Montreal and Kingston: McGill-Queen's University Press.

Bakker, I. (1997) *Unpaid Work and Macroeconomics: New Discussions, New Tools for Action*, Ottawa: Status of Women Canada. Online. Available at: http://dsp-psd.pwgsc.gc.ca/Collection/SW21-33-1998E.pdf

Bakker, I. (2003) "Neoliberal Governance and the Reprivatization of Social Reproduction: Social Provisioning and Shifting Gender Orders," in I. Bakker and S. Gill (eds) *Power, Production and Social Reproduction: Human In/Security in the Global Political Economy*, Houndsmills Basingstoke/New York: Palgrave Macmillan.

Bakker, I. and Silvey, R. (eds) (2008) *Beyond States and Markets: The Challenges of Social Reproduction*, London: Routledge/RIPE Series.

Beneria, L. (2008) "The Crisis of Care, International Migration, and Public Policy," *Feminist Economics*, 14(3): 1–22.

Berik, G., van der Meulen Rodgers, Y. and Seguino, S. (2009) "Feminist Economics of Inequality, Development, and Growth," *Feminist Economics*, 15(3): 1–33.

Brodie, J. (2003) "Globalization, In/Security, and the Paradoxes of the Social," in I. Bakker and S. Gill (eds) *Power, Production, and Social Reproduction*, London: Palgrave.

——— (2007) "Canada's 3D's: Gender and Social Policy in Canada," in M. Cohen and J. Brodie (eds) *Remapping Gender in the New Global Order*, London: Routledge.

——— (2008) "We Are All Equal Now: Contemporary Gender Politics in Canada," *Feminist Theory*, 9(2): 145–164.

Brodie, J. and Bakker, I. (2008) *Where are the Women? Gender Equity, Budgets and Canadian Public Policy*, Ottawa: Canadian Centre for Policy Alternatives. Online. Available at: http://www.policyalternatives.ca/reports/2008/09/reportsstudies1962/.

Broomhill, R. and Sharp, R. (2004) "The Changing Male Breadwinner Model in Australia: A New Gender Order?" *Labour and Industry*, 15(2): 1–23.

Butler, J. (2004) *Undoing Gender*, New York and London: Routledge.

Cohen, M. G. and Cohen, M. (2006) "Privatization: A Strategy for Eliminating Pay Equity in Health Care," in K. Bezanson and M. Luxton (eds) *Social Reproduction: Feminist Political Economy Challenges Neo-liberalism*, Montreal: McGill-Queen's University Press.

Connell, R. W. (1995) *Masculinities*, Cambridge: Polity Press.

Daly, M. (2001) *Care Work: The Quest for Security*, Geneva: ILO.

Dobrowolsky, A. (2009) *Women and Public Policy in Canada: Neo-liberalism and After?* Don Mills: Oxford University Press.

Elson, D. (1995) *Male Bias in the Development Process*, Manchester: University of Manchester.

——— (2006) "The Changing Economic and Political Participation of Women: Hybridization, Reversals and Contradictions in the Context of Globalisation," GEM-IWG Working Paper 06-8. Online. Available at: www.genderandmacro.org (accessed August 5, 2009).

Elson, D. and Cagatay, N. (2000) "The Social Content of Macroeconomic Policies," *World Development*, 28(7): 1347–1364.

Floro, M. and Hoppe, H. (2008) "Towards Globalisation with a Human Face: Engendering Policy Coherence for Development," in I. Bakker and R. Silvey (eds) *Beyond States and Markets: The Challenges of Social Reproduction*, London: Routledge/RIPE Series.

Health Canada (2002) *Canada's Aging Population*, Ottawa: Minister of Public Works and Government Services Canada.

Jenson, J. (2003) *Redesigning the Welfare Mix for Families: Policy Challenges*, Ottawa: Canadian Policy Research Networks Discussion Paper.

Kofman, E. and Raghuram, P. (2009) "The Implications of Migration for Gender and Care Regimes in the south," Social Policy and Development Programme paper No. 41, Geneva: UNRISD.

Lahey, K. (2009) *Gender Analysis of Budget 2009*. Online. Available at: http://www.progressive-economics.ca/2009/01/31/gender-analysis-of-budget-2009 (accessed May 12, 2009).

MacDonald, M. (2009) "Women and EI in Canada: the First Decade," in A. Dobrowolsky (ed.) *Women and Public Policy in Canada: Neo-liberalism and After*? Don Mills: Oxford University Press.

Palley, T. (2009) "The Fiscal Austerity Trap," *New American Foundation*, 15 September. Online Journal. Available at: http://www.newamerica.net/publications/policy/fiscal_austerity_trap (accessed September 9, 2009).

Philipps, L. (1996) "The Rise of Balanced Budget Laws in Canada: Fiscal (Ir)Responsibility," *Osgoode Hall Law Journal*, 34(4): 681–740.

——— (2006) "Gender Responsive Tax Policy Making: What Would it Look Like in Canada?" Paper prepared for the Levy Institute, Bard College, April 26, 2006.

Rodrik, D. (2004) *Rethinking Growth Policies in the Developing World*, October 2004, *Harvard University and How to Save Globalization from its Cheerleaders*, July 2007. Online. Available at: http://www.ksghome.harvard.edu/-rordik/papers.html, (accessed August 21, 2007).

Statistics Canada (2005) "Statistics Canada. 2005," *Women in Canada: A Gender-Based Statistical Report*, 5th edn, Ottawa: Statistics Canada. Catalogue Number 89-503-XIE.

——— (2006) "General Social Survey: Paid and Unpaid Work," *The Daily*, July 19. Online. Available at: http://www.statcan.gc.ca/daily-quotidien/060719/dq060719b-eng.htm (accessed August 12, 2009).

——— (2008) *Perspectives on Labour and Income*, 9(8), Ottawa: Statistics Canada. Catalogue Number 75-001-X.

Stiglitz, J. (2005) "Finance for Development," in M. Ayoen and D. Ross (eds) *Development Dilemmas: The Methods and Political Ethics of Growth Policy*, London and New York: Routledge.

Townson, M. (2005) *Poverty Issues for Canadian Women*, Prepared for Gender Equality Consultations, Ottawa: Status of Women Canada.

Townson, M. and Hayes, K. (2007) *Women and the Employment Insurance Program*, Ottawa: Canadian Centre for Policy alternatives. Online. Available at: http://www.policyalternatives.ca/reports/2007/11/reportsstudies1763/?pa=BB736455 (accessed August 13, 2009).

UNDESA (2005) *The World Economic and Social Survey 2005*, New York: UNDESA.

Williams, M. (2009) "Women's Economic Empowerment in a Time of Recession," United Nations Division for the Advancement of Women Expert Group Meeting on World Survey on the Role of Women in Development. Copenhagen, February 17–19, 2009.

Yalnizyan, A. (2005a) *Canada's Commitment to Equality: A Gender Analysis of the Last Ten Federal Budgets (1995–2005)*, Ottawa: Canadian Feminist Alliance for International Action.

——— (2005b) *Divided and Distracted: Regionalism as Obstacle to Reducing Poverty and Inequality*, Ottawa: Canadian Centre for Policy Alternatives, September.

3

EU MACROECONOMIC GOVERNANCE AND GENDER ORDERS

The case of Austria[1]

Elisabeth Klatzer and Christa Schlager

Introduction

> The low importance of emancipatory and redistributory goals in budget policy, linked to the suppression of the role of the state, is not primarily the result of globalization, rather a conscious neo-liberal policy at the national and international level constantly creating factual constraints that are then sold to the population as the fiscal non-viability of the social state, with the enthusiastic support of the masculine economic mainstream.
>
> (*Schuberth 2006: 49*)

In the context of gender budgeting, analysis is often carried out without sufficient attention to macroeconomic conditions. Over the course of the past decade, macroeconomic policies and policy rules have been changed decisively in the European Union (EU). Essential budget policy processes have been transferred away from nation states to the EU level in preparation for the construction of the Eurozone in the 1990s. With the Treaty of Maastricht, fiscal policies have become rule-based and strict limitations have been placed on deficits and debt levels (known as the Maastricht criteria). A second source of additional regulations (which are even more restrictive in nature) is the Stability and Growth Pact (SGP) established by the European Union's Economic and Financial Affairs Council (Ecofin). Many national budget policies have been reshaped in accordance with the SGP, which also contains the possibility of imposing sanctions in cases of non-compliance. In addition to these fiscal policy rules a third set of regulations emerge from the "Quality of Public Finance" discourse.

The effects of macroeconomic policies are, however, by no means gender-neutral. Whether macroeconomic measures are primarily aimed at actively stabilizing the economy and stimulating growth or simply achieving price stability, these measures have significant impacts on the living conditions of women. For this reason, it is important to address macroeconomic framework conditions – particularly those at the European level – in analyses of gender budgeting.

This paper explores the gendered influence of EU macroeconomic policies and governance on national budgetary policies, drawing on the example of Austrian budgetary policies. In the second section, we describe the relevant framework conditions at the EU level (as indicated in the Maastricht Treaty provisions, the SGP, and the Quality of Public Finance discourse). In the third section we analyze how these EU policies increasingly limit the room for maneuver at the national level by drawing on the example of Austria. In the fourth section we discuss the impact of these rule-based budgetary policies on women and gender orders.

Analysis will show that the shifts in framework conditions at the European level have reduced the room for economic policy maneuver on the part of EU member states. As monetary policy has shifted to the European level and the scope for fiscal policy has been severely reduced, basically wage setting remains the adjustment mechanism. As is illustrated by severe macroeconomic imbalances which have been built up due to very restrictive wage policies in Germany (and some other member states) – an important, though often forgotten element in the "Greek crisis" – even in wage setting policies the degree of dependence within the members of the Eurozone has increased dramatically.

By bringing into focus the relationship between changes in EU governance and regulatory levels and the management of revenues and expenditures at the national level, we pave the way for a gender-sensitive analysis of EU policies. In particular, our analysis shows that the ability to pursue counter-cyclical policy making has been heavily constrained. Furthermore, the prioritizing of rule-based monetary policy and restrictive fiscal policies over concerns with employment, sustainable growth, and stabilization of overall demand in the economy has not only led to contractionary economies at the level of wages and income but also to gender-specific effects, such as increased gender pay gap and increased risk of poverty, especially for women.

In order to promote gender equality, changes in EU macroeconomic policies and framework conditions are necessary. This requires a focus on both the contents and processes of macroeconomic policy making at the EU level.

EU macroeconomic governance and the gender equality deficit: framework conditions for national fiscal policy at EU level

EU economic governance is comprised of a complex set of formal and informal rules, institutions, and agreed-upon objectives (Collignon 2004: 909). The institutional framework introduced by the 1992 Maastricht Treaty consists of the independent European Central Bank (ECB) (Article 105), the Excessive Deficit Procedure (Article 104), and multilateral surveillance through the Broad Economic Policy Guidelines (Article 99). In previous years a broad range of complementary processes, methods, and strategies have been introduced. Among these are the SGP, the European Employment Strategy, the Cardiff Process (for product and capital market reform at the microeconomic level) and the Macroeconomic Dialogue (Cologne Process). The 2000 Lisbon Strategy brought these separate processes together and introduced the open method of coordination (OMC) as a main policy tool.[2] In the context of the Lisbon strategy, and its successor, the so-called Europe 2020 strategy adopted in 2010, the Integrated Guidelines for Growth and Jobs is a core strategic economic policy document that combines the Broad Economic Policy Guidelines (both macroeconomic and microeconomic) with the Employment Guidelines. With the exception of a marginal inclusion in the Employment Strategy, all relevant economic policy strategies, processes and governance mechanisms neglect gender.

This chapter will focus on the macroeconomic policies and governance mechanisms that have a direct impact on public finance.

The system of decision making in economic governance spans a broad range of degree of commitment, from legal rules and sanctions to various forms of new policy instruments, such as benchmarking, best practices, and the OMC. Whereas legal rules such as the Excessive Deficit Procedure and the SGP are justiciable and subject to infringement procedures before the European Court of Justice, the new modes of governance, which are at the core of the Lisbon process, are based on procedures that are "voluntary, open, consensual, deliberative, and informative" (Caporaso and Wittenbrinck 2006: 472). They "insist on the non-coercive processes based on the will of the participants to agree, by way of collective deliberation, on procedural norms, modes of regulation and common political objectives" (Bruno *et al.* 2006: 520).

The Treaty of Maastricht represents the legal basis of the European Economic and Monetary Union (EMU). It introduced a set of convergence criteria that initiated strict fiscal rules for the transition of member states to the EMU. For example, it stipulates that at the end of the preceding fiscal year, the ratio of annual government deficit to gross domestic product (GDP) must not exceed 3 percent and the ratio of gross government debt to GDP cannot exceed 60 percent. Subsequently adopted in 1997 by EU secondary legislation (Regulation 1466/97 and 1467/97), the SGP established that these convergence criteria should continue to be respected following the introduction of the Euro. As a result, the provisions of the SGP tied national budget policies in the member states even more closely to stringent rules. The multilateral surveillance procedure specified in the SGP (Reg. 1467/97) aims at preventing "excessive" deficits (defined as surpassing 3 percent of GDP) and sets a medium-term budgetary objective close to balance or in surplus.

Because these budget regulation criteria proved to be unviable for several member states, the SGP was reformed in 2005. Although fiscal flexibility was increased to a certain extent, it did not widen the scope for states to pursue anti-cyclical fiscal policies. Furthermore, fiscal sustainability continues to be prioritized over other economic targets, such as growth, employment, and distributive justice.

In addition to the SGP, an agenda for restructuring public finance is being pushed by the Ecofin Council in the context of the Quality of Public Finance process at the EU level (cp. Ecofin 2006, 2007a–d). In this framework, "future-oriented" spending (e.g. research and infrastructure) is prioritized over "past-oriented" spending (e.g. social expenditure and pensions). The "quality" of public finances is assessed in light of a reform program – dictated by the major players in the monetary industry – that aims at expenditure cuts and transporting one-sided political goals: The supposed theoretical foundation for this program is nothing more than the ideological and politically driven prioritizing of the market as well as transformation and reduction of the state sector, i.e. the promotion of *a slim "Wettbewerbsstaat"* (Hirsch 1998), a state which promotes radical liberalization, dilution of the social welfare state and serves the interests of the international capital. The state and democratic processes are primarily perceived as disruptive factors.

Goals such as distributive justice or gender equality have no place in this approach; they are explicitly suppressed in favor of abstract concepts and rules that favor fiscal discipline and budgetary cuts. This rule-based approach – in line with an international trend for which Gill (1998) coined the term "the new constitutionalism of disciplinary neo-liberalism" – makes it more difficult to enact new socio-political initiatives to influence budget issues.

The key players in this rather concealed process come from the executive branch, mainly from ministries of finance and central banks, which remain male-dominated and feature strongly masculine characteristics in terms of values and norms but also male dominated decision-making processes and traditionally male policy preferences. As these actors and institutions become more important in the process of (limiting) public spending, one can perceive a re-masculinization of budgetary processes. This reverts modest developments of the last 2–3 decades to bring questions of economic policy and budgetary decisions to a broader public scrutiny and include voices of women (e.g. by more women entering national parliaments).

The consequences of introducing these budget rules were predominantly visible in their pro-cyclical effect; the rules were not capable of counteracting the economic downturn observed in the EMU and the measures necessary to trigger a recovery were not created.

Furthermore, the pursuit of price stability as the primary and often sole economic goal has led to a macroeconomic policy mix that negates the interdependence of different economic domains and seeks to achieve specific goals with the exclusive use of an economic policy recipe with a high degree of rigidity and little flexibility. Surprisingly enough, even after the big financial and economic crisis the same economic policy strategy continues to be on top of the agenda (compare the "exit strategy" and the new "Europe 2020" medium-term economic policy strategy of the EU). This has particularly negative consequences for growth, employment, and distribution, as we will show by drawing on the case of Austria. This apparently gender-blind framework has consequences for social justice and gender equality goals and commitments. It is within this context that we ask whether the restrictive fiscal rules are implemented to women's disadvantage and what is the impact of these rules on unpaid work and gender relations.

Transformation of EU and Austrian budgetary policies 1995–2006

Economic growth and the asymmetrical effects of the Stability and Growth Pact

Given the important countersteering function of fiscal policy in the face of business cycle fluctuations, it is important to look at the cyclical development in order to estimate the effects of budgetary policies. In the present context we analyze the period from Austria's accession to the EU in 1995 up to 2006. The majority of Eurozone countries[3] had relatively low real growth rates (below 3 percent) in the period 1995–2006 and thus faced economic problems. Austria was among these. Fundamental weaknesses in growth emerged especially in the large European economies, such as Germany, France, and Italy. Due to the economic size of these countries, this had negative impacts on the overall European business cycle (Hein and Truger 2006: 27).[4]

The slump of the world economy in the year 2001 was the trigger for an economic downturn in Europe, which lasted until 2005. During this long period of stagnation, the EMU was put to a reality test. It turned out that the available instruments are not adequate: the SGP only allows for very limited anti-cyclical countersteering. The effects of the SGP are not symmetrical in different phases of the business cycle. The SGP was established for one central economic problem: If the economy is producing at full employment and to full capacity, then an increase of deficit-financed public expenditure leads to higher inflation and higher interest rates in the whole monetary union. Due to the potential negative external effects of individual countries' expansive fiscal policies in such special circumstances, coordination in the form of common rules is necessary in order to prevent this kind of expansionary strategy (Angelo and Schweighofer 2003: 14f).

In case of an economic downturn with under-utilization of capacities and below capacity employment, however, the fiscal policy problem is very different. Through stabilization policies, the state intends to set economic policy impulses for the economy that will increase demand in order to reach a better utilization of capacities. The SGP has been shown to be too rigid to apply to this situation. The focus of the SGP is on consolidation of public finance, even in times of economic downturn. As we will see, the effects of the SGP were pro-cyclical; it aggravated the economic downturn in the Eurozone. Given the difficult economic situation in many member states, these asymmetries of the SGP mechanism led to political and economic discussions and an eventual reform of the SGP in 2005. This reform has somewhat increased the room for economic policy maneuver regarding national fiscal policies in comparison to the original version of the SGP. With the reform it has become easier to countersteer with public investments in times of economic downturn. Still, this reform is not a fundamental change of the system; the SGP still prioritizes fiscal sustainability (Rossmann 2006a: 140f). Also the big financial and economic crisis of 2008/2009 has again highlighted the still existing severe deficiencies of the SGP as almost all member states are subject to an Excessive Deficit

Procedure – in times when continued fiscal expansion would be necessary to bring the European economy back on a growth trajectory.

Development of fiscal balances in the EU 1995–2006

In the period 1995–2006, the big EU member states such as Germany, France, and Italy surpassed the 3 percent criteria of overall new indebtedness.[5] Furthermore, the southern EU member states such as Portugal and Greece showed higher deficits. According to the Treaty measures have been taken against these states: A deficit procedure was initiated based on article 104 of the EC-Treaty (known as the "pink slip" to a larger public). All states concerned were obliged to take measures to reduce the deficit within the agreed-upon time limits.[6]

Despite the differences in real economic developments, a continuous improvement of budget balances has been observed since 2000. In this context we find only few exceptions, such as Luxembourg. Still, the new debt of Luxembourg was always below the 3 percent limit. Since 2000, only three EU member states have surpassed the deficit criteria significantly: Greece, Italy, and Portugal. Thus, this shows that an increasingly rule-based fiscal policy has impacted the budget balance of EU-15. Consolidation was prioritized over fiscal policy measures in order to stimulate growth.

Since 1997, the Austrian Maastricht-deficit has remained far below the 3 percent threshold. The Scandinavian countries and Ireland have shown the "best" budget balances. Among new member states, Estonia and Bulgaria have shown constant budget surpluses, whereas Hungary and Poland have had problems with budget consolidation.

Consolidation of public expenditure in EU member states

The public expenditure ratio has been decreasing in most member states since 1995 (see Table 3.1).

Finland has reduced its public expenditure ratio most strongly (21 percent), Germany, Ireland, Sweden, and the Netherlands experienced a decrease by 17 percent and Denmark by 14 percent. With a 12 percent reduction, Austria is not leading this development, but demonstrates a clear trend to reduce public expenditure nevertheless. Interestingly, the UK has maintained its public expenditure ratio almost constant at 44 percent.[7] Still, compared to other large European economies, the UK has a level of expenditure below average. The public expenditure ratio of France has also remained relatively constant (2006 = 53.5 percent). This resulted in France moving upward in the ranking, surpassing Denmark and Finland. In 2006, only Sweden (2006 = 55.5 percent) has had a higher public expenditure ratio than France. In spite of clear reductions, Austria (2006 = 49.2 percent) remains above the Eurozone (2006 = 47.4 percent) and EU-27 averages (2006 = 46.8 percent).

Regarding public expenditure, one can talk about a trend reversal since the mid-1990s: After 1945 we observed a steadily increasing trend. Since the mid-1990s,

TABLE 3.1 Public expenditure after Maastricht (1995–2006)

	% of GNP		*Changes 2000–2006*		*Changes 1995–2006*	
	1995	*2006*	*in %-Pts.*	*in %*	*in %-Pts.*	*in %*
Belgium	51.9	49.1	0.06	0.1%	−2.80	−5.4%
Germany	54.8	45.7	0.60	1.3%	−9.06	−16.5%
Ireland	41.0	34.1	2.47	7.8%	−6.96	−17.0%
Greece	51.0	46.1	−5.08	−9.9%	−4.95	−9.7%
Spain	44.4	38.5	−0.55	−1.4%	−5.99	−13.5%
France	54.5	53.5	1.89	3.7%	−0.92	−1.7%
Italy	52.5	50.1	3.92	8.5%	−2.41	−4.6%
Luxemburg	39.7	40.4	2.83	7.5%	0.74	1.9%
Netherlands	56.4	46.7	2.50	5.7%	−9.77	−17.3%
Austria	**56.0**	**49.2**	**−2.21**	**−4.3%**	**−6.84**	**−12.2%**
Portugal	42.8	46.1	3.01	7.0%	3.39	7.9%
Slovenia	:	46.3	−1.88	−3.9%	:	:
Finland	61.6	48.6	0.24	0.5%	−12.99	−21.1%
EU−13	**:**	**47.4**	**1.08**	**2.3%**	**·:**	**:**
Denmark	59.6	51.4	−2.83	−5.2%	−8.25	−13.8%
Sweden	67.1	55.5	−1.60	−2.8%	−11.64	−17.4%
UK	44.3	44.1	5.03	12.9%	−0.19	−0.4%
Estonia	43.6	33.2	−3.26	−8.9%	−10.40	−23.9%
Poland	47.7	43.3	2.25	5.5%	−4.40	−9.2%
EU-27	**:**	**46.8**	**:**	**:**	**:**	**:**

Source: Eurostat; March 2007 Notification; Calculations by Schlager.

increased public expenditure cuts have been realized leading to a decreasing public expenditure ratio. Only Luxembourg and Portugal do not share this trend. In some states this development has been slowed down since 2000. Great Britain has increased its public expenditure to a certain degree, while the ratios of Ireland and Italy have increased but remain below the level of 1995. One has to be aware though, that decreasing public expenditure ratios cannot be equated with expenditure cuts (see discussion of the Austrian budgetary consolidation below).

Changes in the budget policy strategy in Austria 1995–2006

Since Austria's decision in 1995 to accede to the EMU, the country has been obliged to ensure that the ratio of the annual government deficit to GDP does not exceed 3 percent. With the introduction of the SGP, the members of the EMU committed themselves to providing stability programs and updating these on a yearly basis – a requirement that Austria has fulfilled since 1998. The rule-based financial policy has had a deep impact on the development of the budgetary balance. Austria has fulfilled the Maastricht deficit criteria since 1997 and has not approached the 3 percent deficit range since then (leaving aside the most recent developments due to the financial crisis management). This was due to a change in the budgetary strategy in 1995, which prioritized budget consolidation over other economic objectives. In this section we show that the new priority setting and the establishment of a new logic in public finance, leading to a revaluation of the hitherto existing economic policy objectives, has had problematic impacts on economic growth and led to stagnating income and high unemployment in Austria.

The endeavor to comply with the fiscal Maastricht-criteria has led to restructuring processes in public finance. In its first Stability Program, presented in 1998, Austria committed itself to reducing the deficit so much that in case of normal cyclical fluctuations, the public deficit would remain within the reference value of 3 percent of GDP, even without countersteering measures. Furthermore, the debt ratio was projected to reach the reference value of 60 percent of GDP in the year 2002. The concrete budgetary goal was to keep public finance debt at an overall level of 1.5 percent of GDP in normal cyclical situations. This was supposed to be sufficient to keep the debt ratio permanently below 60 percent of GDP (BMF 1998: 3). These objectives were temporarily accepted by the European Commission. However, the tightened interpretation of the SGP by the European Commission led to a warning in 2000 that the Stability Program was not ambitious enough (Rossmann 2006a: 143). This had consequences for the economic policy agenda in Austria. The new conservative government used the warning as an occasional and welcome support for a fundamental change of budget policy. In the face of a projected growth rate of 1.3 percent, a balanced budget was announced for the years 2002 and 2003 along with a budget surplus for the years to come (BMF 2001: 9). This budget policy strategy, known as "Zero-Deficit," was not realized due to a business cycle downturn. Actually, a balanced budget was only accomplished once – in the year 2001 – by increasing the tax and contribution ratio by 0.9 percent of GDP compared to 2000 and undertaking numerous hive-offs from the public budgets (Stübler 2005b: 1149f). In order to relieve the budget and to ensure the "sustainability of public finance," pension reforms were implemented in 2000 and 2003, which led to considerable pension cuts for large parts of the population, along with a harmonization of pension schemes in 2004. These reforms were lauded by the EU Commission, which attested the Austrian reform a long-term relief of public finance (European Commission 2006: 144). The high human and social implications and costs of the pension reform were not taken into account in the evaluation by the European Commission.

Since 2004/2005 the "zero-deficit" strategy has been abandoned and a "balanced budget over the business cycle" has been aimed at instead (BMF 2003: 9).[8] Additionally, the reduction of the tax and contribution ratio to below 40 percent of GDP (until the year 2010) was declared to be the new budget policy objective (cp. ibid.). The subsequent tax reduction in 2004/2005 involved the reduction of corporate income tax to 25 percent and the creation of both an internationally attractive group taxation model for enterprise as well as a tax break for monthly gross wage income below 1,100 euros and an increase in tax deductibles for children. It was also announced that expenditure in future-oriented areas, such as research, education, and infrastructure, would be increased in order to strengthen competitiveness (BMF 2004: 27).

Overall, business benefitted much more from the tax reforms in the years 2000–2006 than wage earners (Rossmann 2006a: 148). Budget policies supported the interests of capital owners much more than the interests of employees. This is important to note when considering the development of the relation between wage ratio and profit ratio (see below). Note that an average employee has received lower net real wage in 2008 than in 1992.[9]

With a different coalition (social democrats and conservative people's party) entering government in 2006, the aim of reaching a balanced budget over the business cycle remained in place, as well as the emphasis on future-oriented public expenditures. Still, it was stated that the overall social balance should not be lost sight of (BMF 2007a: 4). As economic forecasts for 2007 and 2008 were good and revised upwards several times, the stability program for 2007 and 2008 was classified as anti-cyclical (BAK 2007: 12f).[10] Public expenditure and revenue were projected to decrease slightly. The Austrian fiscal balance was significantly better than the Eurozone and EU averages (BMF 2007b: 80). The European Commission has used the positive economic developments to demand a "strengthening of the preventive component" of member states' budgets. This means that the member states have been asked to intensify consolidation efforts in order to reach sustainable solid public finances (European Commission 2007a: 10f). Thus, the main objectives of the Austrian and European budget policies remained an increase in competitiveness (through improving the quality of public finance) and an improved budget balance.

The focus on the Maastricht-deficit criteria has been criticized as "balance-fetishism" (Rossmann 2005: 501), which has had far-reaching consequences for economic and social developments. The emphasis on fiscal sustainability has led to a hierarchy of economic policy objectives, rather than a balanced set of economic policy objectives, such as sustainable growth, full employment, price stability, distribution, and gender equality. The aim of fiscal sustainability has displaced other objectives of public finance, such as stabilization over the business cycle, promotion of growth, sufficient provisioning of public infrastructure, distributional justice, and reduction of unemployment. Furthermore, the term "sustainability" has been used very narrowly to refer only to the fiscal and economic sphere, leaving out environmental and social objectives.

Political projects and budget balances contain very limited information about economic effects of budgetary measures (Nowotny 1999). For the analysis of the relation between economic development and budget balances, we used the following hypothesis: Rule-based budget policy has led to a pro-cyclical behavior in countries with low economic growth; the policies to reach balanced budgets primarily have favored expenditure cuts to consolidate budgets. Such behavior has reinforced the cyclical downturn. Research about the Eurozone, for the period 1999–2003, confirms this hypothesis. The effects of automatic stabilizers have been counteracted by discretionary policies (e.g. budget cuts); thus, pro-cyclical behavior can be observed for the Euro-11 overall (Van den Noord in Rossmann

2005: 521ff).[11] Deficits have been reduced in nearly all countries, irrespective of economic developments.

To summarize the case of Austria, a bad overall economic development has coincided with a consolidation of public finance. This has had a double-negative impact on the population. Stagnating income and high unemployment emerged as a result of restrictive budget policies and numerous budget cuts. The uncertainty in the population led to precautious saving, with a decrease in private consumption. Especially low-income receivers experienced real wage cuts in combination with reduced benefits. This led to deteriorating living conditions for the majority of the population.

Budgetary consolidation in Austria since 1995 and its economic and social impacts

This section of the paper looks at both public expenditure and public revenue in more detail in order to analyze how the consolidation policies have been implemented and with what effects.

Consolidation on the public expenditure side

By exploring the example of Austria in more detail, we will illustrate how the public expenditure ratio has been reduced since 1995 through a combination of three effects: (1) retrenchments; (2) reclassification, hive-offs, and privatization; and (3) the operating of automatic stabilizers. Automatic stabilizers refer to effects within public budgets which lead to counter-cyclical effects without the necessity of discretionary measures, e.g. income taxes and transfer payments such as unemployment insurance.

The budget policy targets in Austria, since 1995, were primarily oriented at an expenditure-side consolidation, and several *Sparpakete* (expenditure cut programs) have been carried out. The impact of these measures has not been analyzed to date. As a matter of fact, expenditure cuts were more pronounced before 2000 than afterwards. Some of the reform measures are difficult to quantify. Reforms of public administration, for example, went hand-in-hand with hive-offs at all levels. In Austria, a complicated system of revenue sharing between national, provincial and local levels adds complexity. All this makes it even more difficult to trace developments (Rossmann 2005: 513).

In any case, we see lower public expenditure ratios for the state sector. According to economic criteria, the investment ratio decreased by 69 percent, the ratios for intermediary consumption and salaries and wages decreased by 26 percent, and the interest ratio decreased by 27 percent (1995–2006). The social transfer ratio stagnated, whereas the subsidy ratio increased by 12 percent and the capital transfer ratio increased by 18 percent. These major changes are affected by hive-offs, restructuring, and privatization in the public sector, all of which have been accelerated by the pressure for retrenchments or budgetary cuts and specific accounting rules at the European level. In order to make budgets comparable, public deficits are represented within the EU using macroeconomic accounting standards (European System of National and Regional Accounts, called ESA 95). This representation by economic criteria has motivated a variety of measures in order to reduce the state sector by introducing reforms which reduce expenditure items accounted for by the state sector. These reclassifications putting certain categories of public expenditures outside the public budget have become widely known as "budgetary tricks" in the public sphere. The new "units outside general government" – a list of about 300 institutions in Austria – accounted for expenditures of about 7.4 billion euros and revenue of about 6.4 billion euros in 2003 (Stübler 2005a: 660). Thus, a "sector close to the state" emerged. In 2002, the fiscal deficit of this sector close to the state was even bigger (1.1 billion euros) than the fiscal deficit of the state sector (0.9 billion euros) (Stübler 2005a: 663).

As a result of hive-offs, personnel cost and investments of the public sector decreased considerably. In particular, the financing of infrastructures (e.g. roads, railways, and real estate[12]) has been reallocated outside the public budget. The strategies of these hive-offs are increasingly less able to be influenced by the state (e.g. price setting of public transport) as these public companies are managed according to market criteria and the management is acting increasingly independently from public authorities. This tendency leads to fundamental concerns about what constitutes the public, issues of control, accountability, and quality of service delivery. For example, the plan to privatize mountains has led to citizen involvement and protests (e.g. *Rettet Salzburgs Berge* – the Save the Salzburg Mountains campaign). This issue publicly raised the question of limits to "privatization" of the state.[13] Institutions in the sector close to the state are increasingly less visible in public budgets. It becomes very complicated to retrace financial transactions and to capture the whole picture, as every company produces its own reports. The few existing evaluations of the trends to locate outside the public budget give a very mixed picture about the alleged improvement of service delivery (Rechnungshof o. J.; Leitsmüller and Rossmann 2001: 147ff).

The responsiveness of the public budget in Austria by means of automatic stabilizers – indicated by the changes in fiscal balance in relation to changes in output gaps – is below the EU average (Breuss 2002: 594). In Austria the relation tends to change less than in other EU member states with the effect that the reduced burden on the state budget due to automatic stabilizers (e.g. increases in tax revenue or decrease in public benefits) in a business cycle upturn is much lower than in other EU states.

To summarize public expenditure developments, it is remarkable that even though expenditure cuts have been announced as a priority, the decreasing expenditure ratio is more heavily influenced by hive-offs and privatizations as well as "budgetary tricks" at all levels of government. This leads overall to large changes in the public budget and in budgeting, but mainly to a rapidly increasing sector close to the state, which is very intransparent and partly out of the reach of public control.

Consolidation on the public revenue side

> In line with the EU trend,[14] the public revenue ratio has decreased since 1995 by 5 percent. Various changes in the level of revenues are the result of the following four factors: (1) changes in tax, contribution, and fee revenues due to reforms; (2) changes of revenues due to one-time effects; (3) changes in other revenues (e.g. revenue from production and dividends) due to a changing role of the public sector; and (4) changes due to the effects of automatic stabilizers (see above).

The revenue of the Austrian state is comprised – on long-term average – of 84 to 87 percent from taxes and social security contributions, about 4 percent from production revenue, and 3 percent from income (from assets, e.g. interests and dividends) (Stübler 2005b: 1144). So, taxes and social security contributions are clearly the main source of state revenue. Since 1995, there have been several tax reforms, most of which have lowered or abolished property, capital, and corporate taxes. In contrast, the tax rate on wages has steadily increased. It is important to mention the 1994 tax reform, which was intended to prepare Austria economically to join the EMU. The property tax and the business tax have been abolished. To compensate public revenue losses, social lump sum taxes as well as the corporate tax were raised. Moreover, a final taxation of capital gains has been introduced (Pasterniak 2006: 148). Already in 1993, Austria had introduced the possibility of establishing private foundations with very favorable taxation, which led to Austria being perceived and criticized as a tax haven for big companies and rich persons (Beigewum 2000: 37ff).[15] In 2004 and 2005, further preferential treatments for corporations were introduced: the corporate tax rate in Austria was reduced from 34 to 25 percent. A favorable taxation of undrawn profit for private companies and group taxation for business were also introduced (Pasterniak 2006: 148). The tax rate in Austria is still above the EU-15[16] average. But property taxes account for only 2.2 percent of the tax revenue and 0.5 percent of the gross national product (GNP) (in 2005), which is extremely low in comparison to other OECD countries.

At federal level, most of the public enterprises have already been sold. ÖIAG, a public holding in charge of the privatizations, gained 10.3 billion euros from selling national companies in the period 1995–2006. Moreover, new financing instruments such as Cross Border Leasing (Rügemer 2004), and Sale and Lease Back (Stübler 2005a)[17] were implemented to improve the budgets. The public did not perceive the privatization of public firms positively. Many post offices in the countryside were closed and many privatized firms raised charges and fees for previously public services. People felt that services of common interest were becoming increasingly threatened by privatization and feared that privatized firms were more focused on profit than social and economic objectives (ÖGPP 2007; Raza 2004).

To summarize, the decrease of the public revenue ratio by 5 percent between 1995 and 2006 is due to several factors. Tax cuts, especially on property and on companies are important elements, accompanied by irregular revenue from privatizations.

Privatizations and an increase of transfers to the sector close to the state (hive-offs) led furthermore to a decrease in revenue from production. The state has become increasingly financed by taxes and contributions, and the reduction of the tax and contribution ratio aggravates the fiscal squeeze of the public sector. In order to maintain and eventually increase flexibility for political decision making in the long run, the financing of the welfare state must be secured by additional sources (e.g. imposing taxes on the increasing wealth – of individuals, corporations and foundations – and the increasing profits of firms).

Structural changes of the national budget 1995–2008

One could assume that the decrease of the revenue and expenditure ratio as well as the numerous hive-offs outside the general government budget have led to structural changes. Furthermore, budgetary priorities have changed. Looking at the national level budget, the decrease of the expenditure ratio is influenced by hive-offs, which lead to decreasing personnel cost, investments, and interests. Regarding the structure of specific expenditure priorities since 2004, the expenditure for science and research has increased disproportionately, while expenditures for families remained at a high level. Even though most areas experienced expenditure cuts, far-reaching structural changes have not taken place on a large scale.[18] Regarding the revenue side, larger structural changes can be observed: wage earners have been increasingly burdened, which contributed to a decreasing net wage ratio (see Figure 3.1), and thus a decrease in the disposable income and the purchasing power of large segments of the population.

In the face of weak consumer demand, policies leading to decreased disposable income were the wrong economic policy measures. Furthermore, an increased

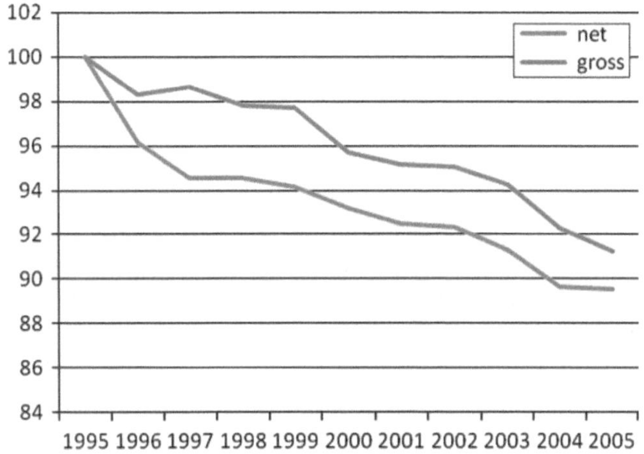

FIGURE 3.1 Development of wage ratios (gross and net) 1995–2005

Source: Data AK-Wien, calculations by Schlager.

burdening of immobile factors (e.g. excise taxes and fees) has contributed to a further burdening of lower income earners in particular. This increased burden on wage earners in general and lower income earners in particular, has increased the social cleavage and the social tilt over the last few years and taken away purchasing power from lower income earners (Rossmann 2006b: 145).

In spite of rapidly increasing profit ratios, taxation on companies and wealth has been reduced dramatically. This is a problem from the perspective of both financing and distributive justice, as there has been no increase in "sustainability" (both defined narrowly in terms of public finance or more broadly in terms of social equality). This paper challenges the tendency to define sustainability in terms of expenditure cuts, which is common in the EU discourse of public finance quality.

Impact of rule-based budgetary policies on women and gender relations

The analysis of the main changes of budgetary policies in Austria shows that the macroeconomic framework conditions specified at the EU level substantially influence the budget policy strategies of member states. Fundamental changes in the function and level of public budgets have been observed as follows:

- A rule-based financial policy has been established at all levels of government by means of the inner-Austrian Stability Pact. This has led to a reduction in room for maneuver on budget policy issues.
- The goal was to achieve budget surpluses in line with the Treaty of Maastricht and the SGP, which resulted in all the member states – at both national and subnational levels – attempting to portray their fiscal balances in as positive a light as possible.
- In financial policy issues, binding rules are preferred to discretionary interventions at individual state level. The primary objective is to achieve fiscal stability, with even economic stability policy being subordinated.
- The goal of redistribution, which can be achieved effectively primarily through the expenditure side, is forced to take a back seat.

All of these changes have had a significant impact on women's living conditions, gender relations, and the possibility of gender budgeting initiatives to exert influence on budget processes.

Influence on women's living conditions

The Maastricht criteria and the SGP have led to a restrictive budgetary policy in Austria. Because this restrictive budgetary policy has had pro-cyclical effects, it has reinforced negative economic development on a number of fronts, with differential impacts on women and men.

Due to the weakening economic development, women were faced with several negative consequences. First, there was a considerable increase in unemployment with women bearing the larger share. Second, when comparing inflation and increases of nominal wages and salaries, it can be shown that women with low income (2nd decile of income statistics) suffered real wage losses over the decade 1995–2005. In other words, they could afford less than they could ten years ago, although the GNP rose in the same period. The wages of female employees with an average income stagnated in the period 2000–2005 (Schlager 2007: 78ff).

The third negative effect is an increase in women's dependence on welfare aid (*Sozialhilfe*). In 2006, the proportion of female welfare aid recipients in private households was 53 percent (sole, main, and additionally supported) or 55 percent (durable assistance) (Statistik Austria 2008a). Since the mid-1990s to 2006, there has been a massive increase in welfare aid. Since 1996, the number of welfare recipients has increased by approximately 77 percent. This increase is primarily due to the development of welfare aid for private households: +67,300 or +105 percent (Statistik Austria 2008a) but not for elderly people, who are living in retirement homes. (The increase of welfare aid recipients is especially concentrated in Vienna, with a 2.5 fold increase from 32,600 persons in 1996 to 83,500 persons in 2006.) In the capital, those who have an income below the social support threshold (*Sozialhilferichtsatz*) are supported by complementary payments. According to the Viennese welfare administration, the increase of atypical and precarious employment relationships (e.g. part time, marginal employment, and temporary employment), along with respectively low earnings potential in relation to unemployment and low social benefits (unemployment benefits, social support, etc.) constitute the main reasons for the sharp increase in social support (ibid.).

The fourth negative effect is women's increasingly precarious employment. This increase is best understood as an indirect effect of changes in budgetary policies. Supply-side economic policy favors independence of the ECB and thus of monetary policy and rule-based budget policies. Accordingly, in order to counterbalance economic imbalances, more flexible labor markets are necessary. In Austria, the flexibilization of the labor market has primarily taken place in female employment. Women's part-time employment is over 41 percent, while men's part-time employment is 7.2 percent (Statistik Austria 2008b). Among the marginally employed in 2007, (*geringfügig Beschäftigte*) 69.4 percent were women (AMS Österreich 2008: 38ff). Moreover, the volume of women's paid work has not increased. In terms of full-time equivalents, employment of women has stagnated in the last decade.

Precarization of employment has negative impacts on one's eligibility for social benefits. Two-thirds of women receiving unemployment insurance benefits in 2006 received a daily amount below the Austrian poverty risk rate. This contributed to increasing dependency in partnerships. The poverty risk rate in single-parent households was among the highest (27 percent in 2005 – which is double the average). In addition, 90 percent of single parents at risk of poverty are single mothers (Statistik Austria 2007b: 40).

In the area of social transfers, pension reforms led to significant reductions in payments. These reforms privilege the male breadwinner model and assume a full-time and uninterrupted work trajectory for all individuals. The duration of employment used as the basis for pension calculations has been extended to 45 years. In spite of slight improvements in the recognition of childcare, the pension reforms continue to disadvantage women. This consolidates the "additional income earners" role of women in the male breadwinner model and works against women's autonomy and independence.

Impact on women regarding the provision of public goods and employment in the public sector

Beigewum states that "only rich men can afford a slim state" (Beigewum 2002: 173). The development of public expenditure is characterized by a reduction of expenditures on the one side and hive-offs (*Ausgliederungen*) on the other. The public sector has been diminished and access to public employment and public services has been reduced. Outsourced enterprise and enterprise outside the public budget are managed according to market economy criteria; this means that services are being sold and bought primarily at market prices. In this context, limited access to services and lack of sufficient incomes become central issues. As women have, on average, much lower market incomes, they disproportionately profit from a public supply of resources, goods, and services (Beigewum 2002). Women have a higher interest in maintaining public property and public services, along with the welfare states that provide basic protection. Thus, the fight for public goods and services has become a primary social issue (Hirsch 2007; Klein 2001; Marterbauer 2007; Pelizzari and Zeller 2007). It is therefore necessary that these issues be incorporated into gender budgeting. An analysis and design of the provision of public goods and services is necessary from a gender perspective that takes into account the interconnections between the different sectors of economy, state, non-profit, for-profit, households, and the illegal sector (Gubitzer *et al.* 2008).

An increased provisioning of public tasks by the private sector is supposedly aimed at providing the services at reduced costs. What this means for women, however, are considerably lower wages in the private sector compared to the public sector as lower wages are the main cost reducing factor. So far, no analysis has highlighted the gender aspect of reform and hive-off projects that exist in Austria.

As argued above, women are significantly impacted by this shift from public to private provisioning of goods and services: women are now employed as low-wage workers in the private service sector and they also become low income consumers of good and services that were previously available for free.

Gender aspects of revenue and redistributive effects of tax policies

On the revenue side, steps have been taken with far-reaching consequences which are questionable from a gender perspective. Even though profit ratios have increased, corporations and the wealthy have benefitted disproportionately from tax reforms. Lower income individuals have been burdened disproportionally with indirect taxes. This development must be challenged from a gender perspective. Women continue to earn much less than men in all employment groups. In 2006 women's average gross income (including apprentices) was 60 percent of men's (STA 2007a: 386ff). But not only when comparing average income, especially at the margins of the income distribution, a very unequal distribution can be observed: In 2006, 393,857 employees – a rise of 11 percent compared to 2005 – had annual gross wages/salaries of 50,000 euros and above, among these 80 percent were men. The share of male wage earners increases continuously with increasing gross wages/salaries. Among earners of 200,000 euros annually (and above) 93.7 percent were men. At the opposite end of the distribution we observe a very different picture, as women are represented disproportionately in low-income brackets: 31 percent of women earn less than 10,000 euros annually; 44.8 percent had an income of less than 15,000 euros; and nearly three-fifths (59 percent) earned less than 20,000 euros in 2006 (ibid.: S.37f).

The distribution of wealth is even more unequal than that of income, thus taxation of wealth is necessary from a gender perspective. To date, there is no analysis for Austria, but a preliminary analysis of the gender wealth gap in Germany shows that only 15 percent of married couples have an equal distribution of the stock of wealth. Women own more assets in 26 percent of households, and men hold higher assets in about 50 percent of households. For Germany, the average gender wealth gap is around 30,000 euros in households consisting of couples. With increasing wealth, the gender wealth gap increases further (Sierminska *et al.* 2008: 14).

Securing public revenue is an important prerequisite in order to maintain the social welfare state, as distributive policies in Austria take place mainly by means of public expenditure. Thus, policies that endanger the financial sustainability of public finance have distributional consequences, especially on gender relations in the distribution of income, wealth and social well-being in Austria.

We can conclude that the new rules-based budget policy, which brings with it neo-liberal economic policy making, has had many direct and indirect negative effects on the living conditions of women in Austria. The interests and needs of women are, once again, "blind spots" in budget policies (Bakker 1994: 4).

Conclusion: impacts on the gender order

Despite changes in Austria, the male breadwinner model still prevails. While men are allocated to full-time, uninterrupted work life, women constitute the "flexible mass" of part-time, flexible, precarious, and low-wage employment. The distribution of work in the unpaid economy, especially regarding care work in and outside families, assigns the responsibility of child and elderly care, as well as household chores to women. The Austrian social welfare state can be labelled as conservative in the European context (Schlager 2009). Social insurance is strongly income-related and differentiated according to professional groups (Talós 1981). The social system is oriented toward maintaining the standard of living. Social services are increasingly performed less by the public sector and more by women in families and welfare organizations in the non-profit and private sectors. In such a conservative welfare state model, the gendered perception of men and women in social policy hold the former to be gainful worker/earner and husband and the latter to be wife and mother, a dependent in traditional family structures (Mairhuber 2000: 24).

Thus, social policy has a gender bias. Indeed, we see both a double structural exclusion as well as a double specific inclusion (Mairhuber 2001: 138ff). By premising social policies on the male breadwinner model, social protection for women is inadequate (both in terms of the requirement of entitlement as well as the amount of entitlement). This is especially true for unemployment and pension insurance. Structural exclusions are set in place for most women who have career interruptions due to family responsibilities and who are segregated in low pay, part-time work.

In contrast, marriage provides a specific type of inclusion: women (and men) get entitlements to widow's pensions, which increase their financial protection. In 2005, 431,522 women (38 percent of female pension recipients) received a widow's pension of 568 euros per month (on average). For 62 percent of recipients this was the only pension payment. Thus, there is social protection of sorts for women, but it is does not secure subsistence (Schlager 2009: 118).

Individual-based entitlements, such as a basic provision for the elderly, has not been developed in Austria. About 13 percent of women above 60 years of age are without independent or deduced pension entitlements (Schlager 2009: 119). Furthermore, the alimony perspective is translated into a system that excludes women, as the income of one's partner is taken into account when calculating entitlement to social benefits (e.g. unemployment benefit for long-term unemployed persons) (Mairhuber 2001: 142f).

Women can acquire entitlements through motherhood or other care services (e.g. child care payments, co-insurance that is free of cost in health insurance schemes, and substitute qualifying periods for child care in pension schemes). These payments are not intended to secure existence. Furthermore, exit from the labor market is better facilitated than re-entrance (AK-Wien 2006: 53).

The structural exclusions within the social system have a poverty-enhancing effect. The inclusions are reducing poverty, but they are not designed to provide a decent existence. As the social insurance system is oriented toward full-time standard employment, it has created a higher risk of poverty for women.

Reforms and expenditure cuts in the period under examination have reinforced these aspects of structural exclusion and the insufficient inclusion of women as caretakers and dependents in budgetary policy considerations. These are reinforcing the prevalent gender order in Austria, which is still characterized by the male breadwinner role and the female additional earner, flexible reserve army, and primary caregiver role. The pension reform is one of the central measures that maintain and reinforce the existing gender order. Increases of family benefits and tax policy measures that set perverse incentives by increasingly rewarding sole wage earners (e.g. tax deductions for sole wage earners which have a tendency to discourage women from entering the labor market by putting a cost on women's labor market participation in the form of higher taxes for their spouse) equally reinforce the prevalent gender order. While discussions about the increased recognition of care activities exist, these are undermined by insufficient incentives for an affordable market-based provision of care.

This analysis demonstrates that gender budgeting needs to take into account the macroeconomic policy frame in order to capture important effects of budgetary policy on women and men, as well as on gender orders. The prevalent fiscal policy rules at EU level have not only considerably limited the room for fiscal maneuver by member states but also contributed to sizeable reforms of the public sector.

The subsequent consolidation of public expenditure and revenue has also significantly reduced possibilities of democratic influence by restructuring the public sector. Additionally, masculine institutions – such as finance ministries and central banks – have gained influence and significance in all policy areas.

Notes

1 This paper draws on the findings of the research project "Innovation in European Democracy through Engendering Budgets" (see Gubitzer *et al.* 2008) carried out by an interdisciplinary research group, financed by the Austrian Federal Ministry of Science and Research. Participants in this project were Luise Gubitzer, Elisabeth Klatzer, Katharina Mader, Monika Mayrhofer, Katharina Muhr, Anna Obermair, Birgit Sauer, and Christa Schlager. International researchers – Diane Elson, Regina Frey, Mascha Madörin and Susanne Schunter-Kleemann – have participated at different stages of the project.

2 The OMC has been designed to help member states to progressively develop their own policies according to common objectives in policy fields, which remain in the competence of member states. It involves fixing guidelines and objectives for the Union combined with specific timetables for achieving the goals, establishing quantitative and qualitative indicators and benchmarks as a means of comparing best practices. Periodic monitoring, evaluation and peer review organized as mutual learning processes are essential parts of the OMC in order to induce desired policy changes at the national and regional levels.

3 Eurozone countries in 2006 (Euro12): Austria, Belgium, Finland, France, Germany, Greece, Ireland, Italy, Luxemburg, the Netherlands, Portugal, and Spain.

4 Hein/Truger 2008 show that the New Consensus Models (NCM) argument that real stabilization should effectively be brought by monetary policies and that fiscal policy essentially cannot be accepted when analyzing the economic performance of the major EU countries.

5 See: http://europa.eu/scadplus/glossary/excessive_deficit_procedure_de.htm.

6 See: http://europa.eu/scadplus/glossary/excessive_deficit_procedure_de.htm.

7 The UK is not a member of the Economic and Monetary Union.

8 This referred to a cyclically adjusted budget balance of zero in the year 2008 (cp. ibid.).

9 Our own calculation based on national income accounting.

10 The spring economic forecast of the OeNB (Austrian National Bank) predicted for 2007, 3.2 percent and for 2008, 2.7 percent real growth, http://www.oenb.at/isaweb/report.do?lang=DE&report=7.2.1.

11 Automatic stabilizers are public expenditure/public revenue, which have counter-cyclical effects. On the expenditure side, unemployment benefits are the most effective as they serve as a substitute for wage income, and thus reduce the fall in private consumption. On the revenue side, a progressive tax system is the most effective against an overheating of the economy.

12 Managed by outsourced public companies, such as ASFINAG, ÖBB, BIG.

13 http://www.rettet-salzburgs-berge.at/pdf/pedition.pdf.
14 Interestingly, again, Great Britain and Portugal go against this trend with increases in public revenue ratios in 2006 by 7 percent and 12 percent respectively. Also, Greece (+6 percent), Spain (+6 percent) and France (+4 percent) have increasing revenue ratios.
15 In May 2007, the Austrian Federal Chancellor got media attention by promoting the abolition of inheritance tax in Austria in the neighboring Germany with the slogan: "Steuern runter, macht Österreich munter" (Reducing taxes animates Austria).
16 EU-15 = member states without Central and Eastern European Countries (CEEs)
17 Lecture at the WIFO, on January 27, 2006.
18 This does not mean that smaller expenditure rearrangements might not also have large implications for the population affected.

Bibliography

AK Wien (2006) *AK Frauenbericht 1995–2005. Arbeit – Chancen – Geld*, Vienna: Kammer für Arbeiter und Angestellte für Wien.

AMS Österreich (2008) *Arbeitsmarktlage 2007*, Vienna: Arbeitsmarktservice Wien.

Angelo, S. and Mesch, M. (eds) (2003) *Wirtschaftspolitische Koordination in der Europäischen Währungsunion*. Series "Wirtschaftswissenschaftliche Tagungen der Arbeiterkammer Wien," 7, Vienna: LexisNexis.

Angelo, S. and Schweighofer, J. (2003) "Wirtschaftspolitische Koordination in der Europäischen Währungsunion. Ausgangsüberlegungen für eine notwendige Debatte," in S. Angelo and M. Mesch (eds) *Wirtschaftspolitische Koordination in der Europäischen Währungsunion*, Series: Wirtschaftswissenschaftliche Tagungen der Arbeiterkammer Wien, 7, Vienna: LexisNexis: 5–18.

Bakker, I. (1994) *The Strategic Silence, Gender and Economic Policy*, London: Zed Books.

Beigewum (2000) *Mythos Nulldefizit, Alternativen zum Sparkurs*, Vienna: Mandelbaum.

——— (2002) *Frauen macht Budgets, Staatsfinanzen aus Geschlechterperspektive*, Vienna: Mandelbaum.

Breuss, F. (2002) "Die wirtschaftspolitische Architektur der WWU," *WIFO-Monatsberichte*, 9/2002: 581–607.

Bruno, I., Jacquot, S. and Mandin, L. (2006) "Europeanization Through its Instrumentation: Benchmarking, Mainstreaming and the Open Method of Coordination ... Toolbox Or Pandora's Box," *Journal of European Public Policy*, 13(4): 519–536.

Bundesarbeitskammer Österreich (BAK) (2007) *Bundesvoranschlag 2007/2008, Analyse der Bundesarbeitskammer Österreich*, Stand 13.4.2007, Vienna.

Bundesministerium für Finanzen (BMF) (1998) *Österreichisches Stabilitätsprogramm für die Jahre 1998 bis 2002*, Vienna.

——— (2001) *Österreichisches Stabilitätsprogramm – Fortschreibung für die Jahre 2001–2005*, Vienna.

——— (2003) *Österreichisches Stabilitätsprogramm – Fortschreibung für die Jahre 2003–2007*, Vienna.

——— (2004) *Österreichisches Stabilitätsprogramm – Fortschreibung für die Jahre 2004–2008*, Vienna.

——— (2007a) *Österreichisches Stabilitätsprogramm für die Jahre 2006 bis 2010*, Vienna.

——— (2007b) *Budgetbericht 2007/2008, Bericht der Bundesregierung*, Vienna.

Caporaso, J. A. and Wittenbrinck, J. (2006) "The New Modes of Governance and Political Authority in Europe," *Journal of European Public Policy*, 13(4): 471–480.

Collignon, S. (2004) "Is Europe Going Far Enough? Reflections on the EU's Economic Governance," *Journal of European Public Policy*, October 2004: 909–925.

Ecofin (2006) *Conclusions: The Quality of Public Finances*, European Union, Council Dok. 5462/06, January 24, 2006, Brussels.

——— (2007a) *Report on Quality of Public Finances Issues. Work Accomplished and Way Forward*, European Union, Council Doc. 9916/07, Brussels.

——— (2007b) *Initiatives to Improve the Efficiency and Effectiveness of Public Spending: "Modernising Public Administration,"* Issue note from the European Commission, October 1, 2007, Doc. 13317/07, Brussels.

——— (2007c) *Conclusions on the Quality of Public Finance*, European Union, Council Dok. 9936/07, June 5, 2007, Brussels.

——— (2007d) *Conclusions "Quality of Public Finances: Modernising Public Administration,"* European Union, Council Dok. 13316/07, October 9, 2007, Brussels.

Elson, D. (2002a) "Macroeconomics and Macroeconomic Policy from a Gender Perspective," Public Hearing of Study Commission 'Globalisation of the World Economy – Challenges and Responses', *Deutscher Bundestag*, February 18, 2002. Online. Available at: http://www.eclac.org/mujer/curso/elson3.pdf (accessed December 8, 2008).

European Commission (2007a) *Mitteilung der Kommission an den Rat und das Europäische Parlament: Die öffentlichen Finanzen in der Wirtschafts- und Währungsunion (WWU) – 2007, Die Wirksamkeit der präventiven Komponente des SWP*, KOM(2007) 316, Brussels.

——— (2007b) Public Finances in EMU – 2007. Online. Available at: http://ec.europa.eu/economy_finance/publications/publication338_en.pdf (accessed December 8, 2008).

Feld, L. P. and Schneider, F. (2002) "Zum Wandel des föderalistischen Aufgaben- Ausgaben- und Finanzierungsspektrums: Österreich und die Schweiz im Vergleich," in E. Theurl, R. Sausgruber, H. Winner (eds) (2002) *Kompendium der österreichischen Finanzpolitik*, Heidelberg: Springer: 675–703.

Europäische Kommission (EU 2006) "The long-term sustainability of public finances in the EU," *Communication from the Commission*, Brussels, 12.10.2006, COM (2006) 574. Online. Available at: http://eur-lex.europa.eu/smartapi/cgi/sga_doc?smartapi!celexplus!prod!DocNumber&lg=en&type_doc=COMfinal&an_doc=2006&nu_doc=574 (accessed December 8, 2008).

Eurostat (2008) "Armut und soziale Ausgrenzung." Online. Available at: http://epp.eurostat.ec.europa.eu/portal/page/portal/living_conditions_and_social_protection/publications/income_social_inclusion_living_conditions_sub (accessed December 8, 2008).

Gill, S. (1998) "New Constitutionalism, Democratisation and Global Political Economy," *Pacifica Review*, 10(1): 23–38.

Gubitzer, L., Klatzer, E., Mader, K., Mayrhofer, M., Muhr, K., Obermair, A., Sauer, B. and Schlager, C. (2008) Gender Budgeting als Beitrag zur Demokratisierung europäischer Wirtschaftspolitik? Unpublished research report.

Hein, E. and Truger, A. (2006) "Fiscal Policy and Macroeconomic Performance in the Euro area – Lessons for the Future," *Working Paper 7/2006*, Düsseldorf: Macroeconomic Policy Institute, Hans Böckler Stiftung.

Hein, E. and Truger, A. (2008) "Fiscal policy in the macroeconomic policy mix: A critique of the New Consensus Model and a comparison of macroeconomic policies in France, Germany, the UK and Sweden from a Post-Keynesian perspective," *Working Paper, 3/2008*, Düsseldorf: Macroeconomic Policy Institute, Hans Böckler Stiftung.

Hirsch, J. (1998) *Vom Sicherheitsstaat zum nationalen Wettbewerbsstaat*, Berlin: Id-Verlag.

——— (2007) "Der Kampf um öffentliche Güter – oder weshalb der Ausbau einer sozialen Infrastruktur nötig ist," in R. Klautke, B. Oehrlein (eds) *Prekarität – Neoliberalismus – Deregulierung*, Hamburg: VSA-Verlag: 137–146.

Klein, N. (2001) "Reclaiming the Commons," *New Left Review*, 9. Online. Available at: http://www.newleftreview.org/A2323 (accessed January 8, 2010).

Leitsmüller, H. and Rossmann, B. (2001) "Ausgliederungen aus dem Bundeshaushalt – eine Evaluierung aus volks- und betriebswirtschaftlicher Sicht" in K. Kropf (ed.) *Ausgliederungen aus dem öffentlichen Bereich*, Vienna: Verlag des ÖGB: 147–318.

Lichtenecker, R. and Salmhofer, G. (ed.) (2006) "Gender Budgeting. Theorie und Praxis im internationalen Vergleich," *Studien zur Frauen- und Geschlechterforschung*, 4/2006, Innsbruck: Studienverlag.

Marterbauer, M. (2007) *Wem gehört der Wohlstand? Perspektiven für eine neue österreichische Wirtschaftspolitik*, Vienna: Zsolnay.

Mairhuber, I. (2000) *Die Regulierung des Geschlechterverhältnisses im Sozialstaat Österreich*, Frankfurt: Peter Lang Verlag.

——— (2001) "Frauenarmut – Ein sozialpolitisches Problem?!" in K. Heitzmann and A. Schmidt (eds) *Frauenarmut: Hintergründe, Facetten, Perspektiven*, Frankfurt: Peter Lang Verlag: 137–162.

Nowotny, E. (1999) *Der öffentliche Sektor, Einführung in die Finanzwirtschaft*, 4. Aufl., Berlin/Heidelberg: Springer.

Österreichische Gesellschaft für Politikberatung und Politikentwicklung (ÖGPP) (2007) "Privatisierung und Liberalisierung öffentlicher Dienstleistungen in der EU: Entwicklung in ausgewählten kommunalen Dienstleistungsbereichen." Online. Available at: http://www.politikberatung.or.at/wwwa/documents/zusammenfassung.pdf (accessed December 8, 2008).

Pasterniak, A. (2006) *Budgetregeln und die Qualität der öffentlichen Finanzen. Europäische Perspektiven und österreichische Praxis*, Wiesbaden: Deutscher Universitäts-Verlag.

Pelizzari, A. and Zeller, C. (2007) "Perspektiven jenseits Privatisierung öffentlicher Daseinsvorsorge", in R. Klautke and B. Oehrlein (eds) *Prekarität – Neoliberalismus – Deregulierung*, Hamburg: VSA-Verlag: 147–183.

Raza, W. (2004) "Editorial," *Privatisierung öffentlicher Dienstleistungen, Kurswechsel* 3/2004, Vienna: 3–6.

Rechnungshof (2006) Bericht des Rechnungshofes gemäß Art. 1 § 8 Bezügebegrenzungsgesetz, BGBl. I Nr. 64/1997. Online. Available at: http://www.rechnungshof.gv.at (accessed December 8, 2008).

Rechnungshof (o.J.) Kernaussagen von Ausgliederungen. Online. Available at: http://www.rechnungshof.gv.at/berichte/kernaussagen/ausgliederungen.html (accessed December 8, 2008).

Rossmann, B. (2005) "Die Budgetpolitik Österreichs seit dem EU-Beitritt," *Wirtschaft und Gesellschaft*, 4/2005: 493–534.

——— (2006a) "Der Stabilitäts- und Wachstumspakt und seine Folgen für die österreichische Fiskalpolitik," *WISO*, 3/2006: 135–152.

——— (2006b) "Die Budgetpolitik nach der politischen Wende 2000 – Versuch einer Bilanz," in E. Tálos (ed.) *Schwarz-Blau, Eine Bilanz des "Neu-Regierens,"* Vienna: LIT-Verlag: 137–153.

Rügemer, W. (2004) "Cross Border Leasing. Wie fiktive Kapitalbildung zur realen Auszehrung des öffentlichen Sektors führt," *Privatisierung öffentlicher Dienstleistungen, Kurswechsel*, 3/2004: 54–61.

Schlager, C. (2007) "Zunehmende Einkommensunterschiede 1990–2005," *Wirtschaft und Gesellschaft*, 1/2007: 73–92.

——— (2009) "Soziale Ungleichheit und Armut aus Geschlechterperspektive," in N. Dimmel, K. Heitzmann and M. Schenk (eds) *Handbuch Armut in Österreich*, Innsbruck: Studienverlag: 116–128.

Schuberth, H. (2006) "Fiskalische Strategien auf EU Ebene – Implikationen für Gender Budgeting," in R. Lichtenecker and G. Salmhofer (eds) *Gender Budgeting. Theorie und*

Praxis im internationalen Vergleich, Studien zur Frauen- und Geschlechterforschung, 4/2006, Innsbruck: Studienverlag.

Sierminska, E., Frick, J. and Grabka, M. (2008) *Examining the Gender Wealth Gap in Germany*, IZA DP No. 3573, Bonn.

Staatsschuldenausschuss (2006) *Die Budgetpolitik der Bundesländer im Lichte der Maastrichtvorgaben 2001 bis 2004*. Online. Available at: http://www.staatsschuldenausschuss.at/de/img/studie_laenderbudgets_2001bis2004-endversion_tcm163-43335.pdf (accessed December 8, 2008).

Statistik Austria (STA 2007a) Statistik der Lohnsteuer 2006, Vienna.

——— (STA 2007b) Einkommen, Armut und Lebensbedingungen, Ergebnisse aus EU-Silc 2005, Vienna.

——— (STA) (2008a) Sozialleistungen auf Landesebene. Online. Available at: http://www.statistik.at/web_de/statistiken/soziales/sozialleistungen_auf_landesebene/sozialhilfe/index.html (accessed December 8, 2008).

——— (STA 2008b) Teilzeitarbeit. Online. Available at: http://www.statistik.at/web_de/statistiken/arbeitsmarkt/arbeitszeit/teilzeitarbeit_teilzeitquote/index.html (accessed December 8, 2008).

Stübler, W. (2005a) "Budgetentlastung durch Ausgliederungen – Entwicklungen seit dem EU-Beitritt Österreichs," *Statistische Nachrichten*, 7/2005: 658–665.

——— (2005b) "Staatsquoten 2000 bis 2004, " *Statistische Nachrichten*, 12/2005: 1142–1150.

Talós, E. (1981) *Staatliche Sozialpolitik in Österreich. Rekonstruktion und Analyse*, Vienna: Verlag für Gesellschaftskritik.

Watchgroup Gender und Öffentliche Finanzen (2006) "Elemente einer Genderanalyse des Steuersystems," *Kurswechsel: Steuern! Alternativenzur neoliberalen Steuerpolitik*, 1/2006: 25–36.

Young, B. (2001) "Genderdemokratische Governance der Finanzpolitik in der Europäischen Währungsunion," *Zeitschrift für Frauenforschung & Geschlechterstudien*, 19/2001: 79–91.

——— (2004) "Das Korsett der Europäischen Zentralbank und eine geschlechtergerechte Budgetpolitik," in L. Gubitzer and B. Trukeschitz (eds) *Frauen und Budget*, Frankfurt am Main: Peter Lang, 137–153.

4

TAXATION, EMPLOYMENT, AND GENDER

The case of state taxes in the USA

Elissa Braunstein and Caren Grown

Introduction

This chapter contributes new empirical research to gender-aware analyses of public finance by examining the effect of state taxes on female and male employment in the USA from 1978–2004. While there is a large literature dealing with the relationship between taxation and economic or business development, fewer studies focus on employment creation, and none (to our knowledge) disaggregate employment effects by sex. Further, no study attempts to assess whether the public services that are provided through taxes have gender-differentiated impacts, measured in terms of employment or other variables.

Why should gender matter for the impact of state taxation on employment? First, there are well-known gender differences in employment and economic activity. Males tend to have higher labor force participation rates than females, although the gap is closing (Jacobson 2007). Within paid employment, industrial and occupational segregation by sex is extensive and has not changed much in the past 30 years (Blau *et al.* 2006). If female-dominated industries or jobs are linked to either the level or structure of state taxes in different ways than male-dominated industries or jobs, we should expect to see sex-specific employment effects of state tax policy.

Second, there is a large literature showing that personal income taxes have gender-differentiated impacts on labor supply (see LaLumia 2008 and Smith *et al.* 2003 for recent contributions). For instance, in the USA, married women who are secondary family income earners face strong disincentives to work for pay, as the system of joint personal income taxation means their income is taxed at a higher marginal rate than income earned by unmarried women. The effects of other types of taxes (such as corporate taxes) on female employment have not been investigated.

Third, there are also gender-differentiated needs for public expenditure because of gender differences in responsibilities for care (Himmelweit and Perrons 2006).

For instance, public expenditure on child and dependent care may be more important for women's labor force participation than for men's. Thus, state taxes may affect female employment indirectly via the level and composition of public expenditures.

These potential differences are important from a political economy perspective because the public discourse around the relationship between taxes and economic activity is highly contested in the USA. Long suspicious of the economic efficiency and administrative capability of the government sector, firms and some state policy makers use the term "business-friendly environment" to refer to states with low taxes and limited government involvement in economic activity. Knowledge of whether the empirical relationship between employment and state taxation is both positive and gender specific would enable citizens and state policy makers to better address the political processes that structure state tax policy.

In light of these issues, this chapter explores the following: First, we ask whether overall tax levels create or detract from employment in sex-specific ways. We then consider whether financing a greater proportion of tax revenues from corporate income taxes has gender-differentiated employment effects. And lastly, we investigate the potential effects of interstate tax competition on the relationship between taxation and employment, again differentiated by sex. Our results indicate that there is indeed a positive and robust relationship between state tax levels and employment for both women and men, that women's employment is much more (positively) sensitive to corporate income taxes than men's, and that both women and men suffer employment losses as the result of interstate tax competition – though women's employment declines more than men's when that competition takes the form of corporate income tax competition.

The impact of taxation on employment

Literature on the impact of fiscal policy variables (i.e. taxation and expenditure) on economic activity is large and inconclusive, partly because of the wide variety of questions asked, time periods used, and variables and models chosen (Wasylenko 1997; Wheeler 2006). Hence, for the most part, we restrict this discussion to the literature that focuses on the relationship between state taxation and employment as opposed to business start-ups or investment. At the outset it is important to note that nearly all studies include both government taxation and expenditure as independent variables in their specifications. The resulting taxation coefficients are interpreted as the marginal effect on employment holding public expenditure constant. Thus, we would expect a negative correlation between taxes and employment, though even here the results are quantitatively small and vary in terms of statistical significance.

Bartik's (1991) review of 70 studies conducted from 1950–1990 determined that studies using data from the 1950s, 1960s, and 1970s generally established no statistically significant or negative effects of taxes on state and local employment growth, even when controlling for expenditure. By contrast, the five studies that measured the effects of state and local business taxes on employment using data from the 1980s found some evidence of extremely small negative effects.[1] A later review by Michael Wasylenko (1997) found that in analyses using data from the 1990s, the effect of state and local taxes on employment and business location was negative but smaller than the magnitude suggested by the studies of the 1980s.[2] Still, Wasylenko noted that intra-regional tax elasticities were, on average, four times those of the more commonly studied inter-regional estimates. Thus it is important for these types of analyses to account for interstate tax competition, particularly within regions.

Another important finding of these studies is that different types of taxes will affect employment in distinctive ways. Carroll and Wasylenko (1994) develop an empirical model of the level of non-agricultural employment that includes separate variables for state and local tax revenue from property, income, corporate, sales, and other tax revenue, as well as the structure of public expenditures. Their study focused on structural changes between 1967–1976 and 1978–1988, and finds evidence of a decline in tax elasticity in the latter period relative to the former, as well as differences in elasticity by type of tax.

Harden and Hoyt (2003) also find that different types of taxes have different effects on non-agricultural employment growth. Using state level data from 1980–1994, they examine the effects of corporate, income, and sales taxes and find that corporate income tax revenue has negative and significant impacts on employment growth (while controlling for expenditures) in a sample of 43 states with contiguous borders, but statistically insignificant negative impacts on the rate of growth in employment when all 48 states are included in the analysis. They also find a negative impact on employment from increases in individual income and sales taxes, but the results are not statistically significant. Importantly, the authors are the only ones in this literature to include a gender variable in their specification, the fraction of women aged 18–65 in the labor force, which is added as a proxy for productivity. It is not clear from their analysis why this variable would function as a proxy for productivity, and there is no discussion of the econometric results.[3]

From this brief review, it is clear that the literature is inconclusive about the effects of the level and composition of state taxes on employment generally, even when investigators control for the level of expenditures. When compelled to generalize, most would acknowledge that the effects are probably small and slightly negative, with the type of tax and some measure of intra-regional tax competition an important part of any specification. In order to put the discussion in context, we provide a brief overview of recent empirical trends in state tax revenues and then turn to our own empirical approach.

Trends in state taxes

The trend rate of growth of state tax revenue as a proportion of personal income is generally positive over the period 1970–2004, but with brief declines, predictably, during periods of economic recessions (Figure 4.1). State tax revenue was 5.7 percent of personal income in 1970, but rose to just over 6.1 percent in 2004. This graph

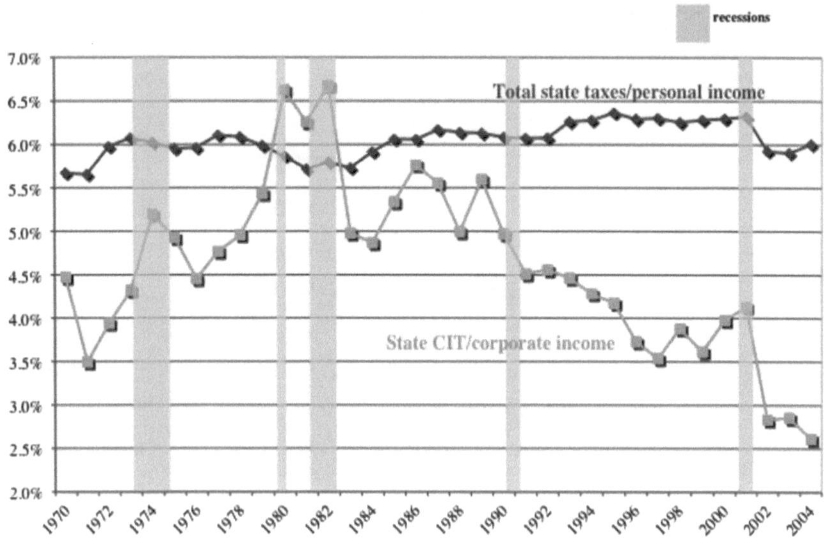

FIGURE 4.1 State tax revenue base, US totals 1970–2004

Source: Authors' calculations based on data from US Census, the Bureau of Economic Analysis, and the National Bureau of Economic Research.

also shows the yield in the state corporate income tax, measured as the sum of state corporate income tax (CIT) revenue for all 50 states as a proportion of corporate income (as recorded in the national income and product accounts). After increasing over the 1970s, the state CIT yield declined precipitously, a pattern that cannot be explained by decreases in statutory rates, as state CIT rates have been roughly constant, on average, since 1980 (Wilson 2006). It is more likely that firms (and their accountants) have become better at avoiding state taxation, which suggests that it is important to determine whether state governments that prioritize corporate income tax collection incur some sort of employment cost as a result.

The decline in the yield of state CIT can also be inferred from Figure 4.2, which illustrates changes in the composition of state tax revenue over the same period. Personal income taxes grew to become a much larger share of total state taxes, from about 20 percent in 1970 to 34 percent in 2004, while the share of corporate income taxes declined from 8 percent in 1970 to 5.3 percent in 2004. Sales and other taxes as a share of total state taxes declined somewhat over the period, further underscoring the much larger role played by personal income taxes in recent years.

The empirical approach

Hypotheses

There are several likely channels through which the level and composition of state taxation influence employment. On the negative side, taxation increases production

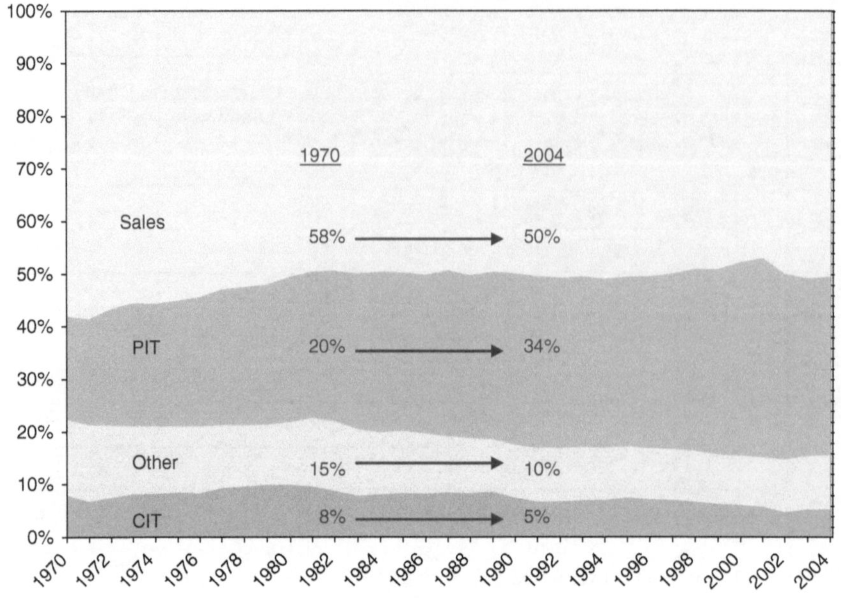

FIGURE 4.2 State tax revenue distribution, US totals 1970–2004

Source: Authors' calculations based on data from US Census.

costs, discouraging new investment and employment creation. Though taxes directly lower private sector disposable income, they also raise resources for public expenditure, which may be more or less efficient than private expenditure in creating economic growth. On the positive side, taxation finances public expenditure, which creates public sector employment with associated multiplier effects. It also promotes private sector employment through public infrastructure and services that facilitate investment and labor market participation (akin to a "crowding-in" effect).

In order to sort out some of these issues, we test three distinct effects measured alternatively by tax levels, tax composition, and tax competition. The level effect tests whether higher overall state taxes relative to personal income are associated with lower employment growth for both men and women. If the widespread presumption of state-level policy makers that the negative effects of state taxes on employment outweigh the positive ones is accurate (Wasylenko 1997), we expect the level effect to be negative.

The composition effect measures whether a higher proportion of corporate income taxes in state revenue results in lower growth of female and male employment. If states with a higher proportion of corporate income taxes in state revenue sacrifice employment as a result, there should be a negative correlation between the composition variable and employment.

The last measure captures competition effects – the potential loss of employment to neighboring states with lower tax rates, if both firms and individuals try to minimize their tax bills. This is a significant policy issue. One of the main reasons that scholars give for negative correlations between state taxes and economic activity is precisely that higher-tax states are less attractive places to locate and hence often lose out to lower-tax neighbors. If this reasoning is correct, the competition effect should be negative for both male and female employment.

The above three hypotheses are deliberately stated in gender-neutral terms. The tax literature does not provide any theoretical guidance for predicting a priori whether male employment and female employment respond differently to taxation, or whether the effects should be stronger or weaker for males or females. Nor has any empirical study tested for gender-differentiated effects. Our work is thus a first test of whether there are statistically significant differences between the coefficients on male and female employment, which would demonstrate that gender indeed matters. Although it is beyond the scope of this paper to empirically test the reasons why state taxes may affect female and male employment differently, we suggest some preliminary explanations that should be pursued in further research.

Data and specification

We use a reduced-form model of employment demand to assess the role of state taxation in women's and men's employment. The basic model is summarized by equation (1). The dependent variable, employment by sex in state at time *i*, at time *t*, (y_{it}) depends on a vector of measures of state taxation (TAX_{it}), a vector of control variables that also determine employment (Z_{it}), and a state fixed effect (v_i).

$$y_{it} = \alpha + TAX_{it}\beta + Z_{it}\delta + v_i + \varepsilon_{it} \qquad i = 1,\ldots, N; t = 1,\ldots T$$

The employment variables use three-year moving averages based on the March Current Population Survey (CPS) series, limited to workers between the ages of 16 and 65.[4] Since we use a moving average, one-time shocks are smoothed out and thus we do not include any year controls in the specification.

Let's turn now to the independent variables. The *TAX* variables include the three measures of taxation discussed above – level, composition, and competition. Tax level is measured as total state tax revenue as a proportion of state personal income (*Taxes/PI*), sometimes referred to as the "effective tax rate."[5] As Harden and Hoyt (2003) point out, there are two reasons for constructing tax rates in this way. First, no single marginal tax rate applies to every household or corporation with progressive income taxes. Second, if employment responds to taxes because of interstate mobility of firms and workers, then it is the average tax rate, not the marginal tax rate, that would influence decisions to move. The composition variable is measured as the ratio of state corporate income tax revenue to total state tax revenue (*CIT/Taxes*).

To measure competition effects, we grouped each state into eight regions based on the groupings used by the Bureau of Economic Analysis (BEA) (a list of each region and its constituent states are included in Appendix 4A). We then created population-weighted level (*Taxes/PI*) and composition (*CIT/Taxes*) variables for each region. While the difference between a state's effective tax rate and its region's effective tax rate measures the tax level competition effect (*Taxes/PIdif*), the difference between the proportion of corporate taxes in a particular state's tax revenue and its region's measures the tax composition competition effect (*CIT/Taxesdif*). Take Massachusetts as an example. When *Taxes/PIdif* > 0, Massachusetts has a higher effective tax rate than that of its region, New England. Similarly, when *CIT/Taxesdif* > 0, Massachusetts has a higher proportion of corporate income taxes in state revenue than that of New England as a whole. To the extent that tax competition plays a role in attracting and maintaining economic activity, we would expect these coefficients to be negative.

All of the tax variables are based on figures published by the US Census, inflated to 2004 US$, using the national CPI-U from the Bureau of Labor Statistics. It is important to note that tax revenue is published by state fiscal year, hence an observation at time *t* is typically six months preceding the calendar year observation at time *t*. As a result, the regressions include tax-related observations at time *t*, which should be treated as a six-month lag. Harden and Hoyt (2003) point out that lagging these variables is important for two reasons. First, it provides a means for controlling for the endogeneity of current tax rates given that they are constructed from tax revenues themselves. Second, firms and workers are likely to base current employment decisions on past rather than current taxes because of the time required to relocate.

We do not include any controls for government spending. As a result, the tax coefficients capture the *net* effect of taxation on employment – not only the potential negative impact on employment as taxes are a cost to firms and individuals, but also the potential positive impact on employment from public expenditure financed by the taxes.[6]

The remaining independent variables make up the non-tax controls on employment. These include lagged growth of gross state product (GSP) and GSP per capita, both based on GSP data published by the BEA. In addition, we include a measure of human capital based on the CPS data discussed above – the proportion of the state's working age population with a college education or above, lagged one year. This variable is sex specific in that the equations for women include only the data on female education, and the male equations include only data on male education.

Table 4.1 shows the means and standard deviations of all the variables in the pooled sample. The panel is made up of a time series that runs from 1978–2004 with the 48 contiguous US states.

Econometric modeling

Since we use time series data, the first issue we address is whether the variables are stationary. Comparing results of the Levin-Lin-Chu test (a pooled augmented Dicky-Fuller test that restricts all states to a common unit root), with those of the Im, Pesaran and Shin panel unit root test (where unit roots are allowed to vary across states), we could not reject the null of non-stationarity for the following series: female and male employment and education, total taxes as a proportion of personal income, and corporate income taxes as a proportion of total taxes. To correct for this, we first differenced these series and retested them for stationarity;

TABLE 4.1 Summary statistics

	Mean	*Standard deviation*
GSP growth	2.4%	0.036
GSP per capita	$31,437	$6,440
Taxes/PI	6.4%	0.012
CIT/Taxes	6.4%	0.039
Women		
Employment	1,061,726	1,099,283
College and above	17.8%	0.055
Men		
Employment	1,262,756	1,339,515
College and above	21.1%	0.046
Observations (for each sex)	1296	
States (groups)	48	

we were able to reject the null of non-stationarity in all cases after first differencing. In the regressions that follow, we also differenced the remaining level variable, GSP per capita.

Next, we tested whether and how to pool the data. After rejecting the null hypothesis that states have a common intercept, we performed a Hausman test on the random effects estimator and found it to be biased. Hence we start with a fixed effects estimator in the regressions discussed below.[7]

In terms of the regression model, we compare results of two different specifications. The first estimates equation (1) using panel-corrected standard error estimates (PCSE), where parameters are estimated using the Prais-Winsten estimator. PCSE is an alternative to feasible generalized least squares (FGLS), and allows for state-level heteroskedastisity, contemporaneous correlation of errors across states, and autocorrelation within states. The difference between PCSE and FGLS is in their estimation procedures, with evidence that FGLS underestimates variability (Beck and Katz 1995).

The second specification is the same as the first, except for the addition of a one-year lag of the dependent variable (female or male employment) as another independent variable. Adding lagged employment controls for a wide variety of potential problems, in particular any variables that have been omitted due to data limitations or misspecification. This desirable feature leads us to treat this model as the standard in our discussion below, though we compare its results to the PCSE estimates throughout (as a robustness check). Still, using lagged employment does introduce a new problem into the system because there is autocorrelation of the disturbances, and lagged employment will thus be contemporaneously correlated with the autocorrelated disturbances. The Arellano-Bond estimator identifies how many lags of the dependent variable can be combined with first differences of the exogenous variables to create an instrument matrix for the lagged dependent variable. Using this matrix, the estimator is a one-step generalized method-of-moments (GMM) estimator (StataCorp 2005: 25). We use robust standard errors to account for heteroskedasticity and first differencing to address autocorrelation.

Results

Table 4.2 presents the regression results for both specifications. The dependent variable is the first difference in the natural logs of female and male employment levels respectively, so it can be interpreted as employment growth. Given the focus of this study, we discuss only the results for the tax variables.

Examining the results in light of our first hypothesis, that higher effective tax rates are associated with lower growth of female and male employment, we see that neither of the level coefficients in the PCSE model is significant. In the GMM model, however, the correlation between effective tax rates and employment changes for both women and men is positive and highly significant. In terms of economic significance, increasing the effective tax rate by one standard deviation (1.2 percent) in the GMM model would add about 13,300 more jobs for women and 13,800 more jobs for men to average employment – a substantial addition – and the numbers are statistically similar for women and men. These results do *not* support policy makers' belief that higher effective tax rates lead to lower levels of employment, though they do suggest that the effects are similar for women and men.

Turning to the second hypothesis, that a higher contribution of corporate income tax relative to state tax revenues results in lower rates of growth in female and male employment, we find a significant positive correlation between *CIT/Taxes* and employment levels for both females and males regardless of model specification. Again, this does not support the conventional wisdom. The correlation for women's employment is stronger than that for men's in the GMM model, and the difference between the male and female coefficients is statistically significant. Evaluated at mean employment, an increase of one standard deviation in corporate income taxes as a proportion of total taxes (3.9 percent) yields about 20,000 more jobs for women and about 15,400 more jobs for men.

The positive correlation between *CIT/Taxes* and employment could be the result of several factors. States that have a high share of corporate income tax revenues could have a broad tax base with firms generating high profits and employment, though the strength of the results in the GMM specification casts doubt on this possibility as lagged employment would presumably control for this effect (as would GSP growth and levels). Alternatively, states with a high share of corporate income tax could also have a political culture of effective corporate taxation coupled with allocation of those revenues in ways that generate employment. The answer requires a detailed analysis of state expenditures and a consideration of other types of economic structures or policies that might be simultaneously correlated with corporate tax structures and gendered employment conditions. These are both goals for future research.

Even though the level and composition effects are, for the most part, strongly positive, the competition effects are not. Effective tax rates in states that are higher than the population-weighted regional average of effective tax rates (as measured by

TABLE 4.2 Regression results

	PCSE		*GMM*	
	Female	*Male*	*Female*	*Male*
D.ln $\text{employment}_{(t-1)}$			0.868 (0.024)***	0.902 (0.020)***
GSP $\text{growth}_{(t-1)}$	0.442 (0.155)***	0.475 (0.138)***		
D.GSP $\text{growth}_{(t-1)}$			0.112 (0.028)***	0.166 (0.028)***
D.ln GSP per capita_t	0.369 (0.159)**	0.311 (0.145)**	0.002 (0.019)	−0.013 (0.019)
$\text{D.ed45}_{(t-1)}$	0.100 (0.084)	−0.015 (0.067)	−0.186 (0.069)***	−0.151 (0.068)**
D.Taxes/PI_t	0.100 (0.208)	−0.131 (0.193)	1.052 (0.366)***	0.920 (0.199)***
D.CIT/Taxes_t	0.149 (0.065)**	0.143 (0.056)**	0.482 (0.129)***	0.312 (0.098)***
Taxes/PIdif_t	−0.300 (0.188)	−0.328 (0.150)**		
D.Taxes/PIdif_t			−1.324 (0.419)***	−1.139 (0.273)***
CIT/Taxesdif_t	−0.144 (0.064)**	−0.053 (0.048)		
D.CIT/Taxesdif_t			−0.303 (0.145)**	−0.119 (0.091)
Observations	1200	1200	1200	1200
Number of states	48	48	48	48
R^2	0.17	0.21		
Wald chi-square	593,179	265,888	2,712	3,644

Notes

Standard errors in parentheses; * significant at 10%; ** significant at 5%; *** significant at 1%

Dependent variable is D.ln employment; D – the difference operator; ln – natural log. All regressions include state dummy variables, though for the GMM estimation state effects are differenced out.

Taxes/PIdif$_t$) are negatively correlated with employment for both women and men. Increasing this difference by one standard deviation (1.3 percent) costs about 18,500 jobs for both women and men in the GMM model. These results support the third hypothesis that states with higher levels of taxes than their neighbors experience employment losses as a result (after controlling for the employment promoting impact of expenditure financed by these taxes). It also confirms the finding above that male and female employment respond in similar ways to effective tax levels.

When a state's share of corporate taxes in total tax revenue is higher than the population-weighted regional average (as measured by *CIT/Taxesdif*$_t$), there are statistically significant negative consequences for female but not for male employment (and the differences between the sex-specific coefficients are statistically significant.) In the GMM model, this translates into a loss of about 11,400 jobs for women and 5,300 jobs for men when the competition variable difference is raised by one standard deviation (3.5 percent). Similar to the case of tax level competition, states face competition from their lower corporate tax neighbors, but the employment costs of lower taxes are primarily borne by women. I will discuss this further below.

These gender differences strengthen the findings on the composition variables in that they reflect similar elasticities. Corporate tax policy is more strongly correlated with women's employment, both positively in the sense that states with a higher share of corporate income tax also have higher female employment growth, and negatively in the sense that states with a higher share of corporate taxation relative to their neighbors have lower female employment growth. Thus, the situation most supportive of female employment would be in a region where all states have a high share of corporate tax in total tax revenue.

Why should there be gendered employment differences with respect to corporate tax competition? It could be that states with a lower share of corporate taxation in total state taxes may also have a socially conservative culture that discourages female employment. It could also be that these states have higher marginal rates on secondary income, which discourages the labor force participation of married women (Ridao-Cano and McNown 2005). But the competition effect – that female employment is more negatively correlated with corporate tax competition than male employment – is also consistent with a third explanation having to do with the industrial mix of male and female employment. If women are predominantly employed by firms that are smaller, more vulnerable, or more mobile than those that predominantly employ men, intra-regional differences in corporate tax policy will exact a higher cost on women's employment prospects.

With tax levels and composition both positively and negatively correlated with employment, what is the net effect? Is more employment lost to intra-regional tax competition than is gained through higher taxes or through higher corporate taxes in particular? To answer this question we ran Wald tests on two linear combinations for each model; the results are displayed in Table 4.3. The column headings correspond to the models in Table 4.2. The row headings specify the variable difference tested. The null hypothesis is that this difference equals zero and the coefficient gives the magnitude and direction of the effect.

Taking the results for female employment in the PCSE model, *D. Taxes/PI* plus *Taxes/PIdif* tests the net effect of taxes as a proportion of income on the first difference of the natural log of female employment. The coefficient is negative (–0.2), indicating that higher taxes cost more in female employment due to competition losses than higher taxes add due to positive level effects. However, we cannot reject the null hypothesis that the net result is zero in the PCSE model. The positive level effect is counterbalanced by the negative competition effect, an unsurprising result in light of the lack of statistical significance for both coefficients in the original model. The GMM model results are similar for female employment.

TABLE 4.3 Crowding in versus losing out

	PCSE		*GMM*	
	Female	*Male*	*Female*	*Male*
D.Taxes/PI + Taxes/PIdif	−0.200 (0.1913)	−0.4591 (0.1908)**		
D.Taxes/PI + D.Taxes/PIdif			0.2721 (0.2208)	−0.2188 (0.2357)
D.CIT/Taxes + CIT/Taxesdif	0.005 (0.600)	0.095 (0.0523)*		
D.CIT/Taxes + D.CIT/Taxesdif			0.1787 (0.0783)**	0.1931 (0.0781)***

Notes

Standard errors in parentheses; * significant at 10%; ** significant at 5%; *** significant at 1%; D – difference operator; the null hypothesis is whether the expression in the left-hand column is different from zero.

Looking at the results for *D.Taxes/PI* and *Taxes/PIdif* for men, the coefficient on male employment is negative and statistically significant in the PCSE model, and negative but not statistically significant in the GMM model. This suggests that for male employment, there are greater employment losses from competition based on overall tax levels than there are gains from higher taxes.

Analyzing tax composition (e.g. corporate tax revenue as a proportion of total tax revenue) reveals a different picture. The coefficients are positive for all four cases, though for female employment in the PCSE model this result is not statistically different from zero. In contrast, male employment shows a positive and statistically significant net effect in both models, though the difference between men and women in the GMM model is not significant.

Examining these results together with the coefficients reported in Table 4.2 shows that women's employment is more sensitive to changes in corporate tax structures. Women's employment is higher in states with higher corporate tax collections (ceteris paribus), but lower if corporate taxes are not commensurate in surrounding states (ceteris paribus). Thus, women seem to benefit from high corporate taxation but lose out to corporate tax competition.

Why should this be the case? As noted above, one explanation is that women's employment is more sensitive to cyclical changes. However, our specification controls for cyclical changes in both female employment and corporate taxation, so this cannot be the explanation. A more compelling explanation may be that the industries characterized by high female employment are those that are also more intra-regionally footloose, meaning that firms are likely to create employment in high tax (and perhaps also high female productivity) environments, but are also likely to relocate when a nearby low-tax alternative is available. That many typically female-dominated occupations and industries are less skill- and capital-intensive further supports the mobility hypothesis. On the other hand, women are also concentrated in the service sector, which tends to be location specific and therefore less mobile, so firm mobility may not be the whole explanation for these results. Clearly, more research is required to better understand these findings.

Concluding remarks

This study contributes to the literature that explores the effects of public finance on gender equality by examining the gender-specific employment effects of tax levels, composition, and competition in the USA. Our results suggest that a gender-blind approach to tax policy and employment analysis is not appropriate. Taxation, like other economic policies, does not have gender-neutral effects. As feminist economists have long argued, all economic policies must be evaluated for their effects on males and females.

Our econometric results counter two of the three hypotheses we tested: that higher tax levels are associated with lower employment growth, and that a higher contribution of corporate taxes to state tax revenues is associated with lower employment growth. The econometric analysis confirmed the hypothesis that taxes that are higher in states relative to those in states in the same region have a negative impact on employment, but these effects tend to be outweighed by the positive employment impact of overall tax levels and the share of corporate income in total state taxes.

For total taxes as a proportion of income, the effects for women's and men's employment are statistically similar: positive direct effects but counterbalancing losses due to intra-regional tax competition. The picture is gender specific, however, for corporate tax policies. Women's employment is more elastic than male employment with respect to corporate taxes as a proportion of state tax revenues, though the net effects of higher corporate taxes (the positive direct effect plus the losses due to tax competition) range between zero and strongly positive for both male and female employment.

A number of key empirical and policy questions emerge from this analysis. It is important to understand the precise mechanisms behind the responsiveness of women's employment to corporate taxation policy. Alternative explanations could include:

1. Progressive public spending, which is correlated with higher corporate taxation, more strongly supports female employment than male employment.
2. Progressive public attitudes might result in higher rates of female employment and corporate taxation.
3. Sectoral differences between male and female employment might concentrate women in industries that yield higher corporate tax collections and that are more mobile.

Regardless of the particular mechanisms involved, our results make a strong case for adopting public policies that alleviate the negative competition effects of higher taxes. This is especially important from a gender perspective because our results provide strong evidence that women take on a disproportionate share of the burden of interstate corporate tax competition.

Acknowledgement

Thanks are due to Diane Elson, Robert Lynch, Tom Masterson, and Stephanie Seguino, seminar participants at Colorado State University and American University, and discussants on panels at the 2008 ASSA-IAFFE and 2007 EEA conferences. The usual disclaimers apply.

Appendix A

Regions and Population Weights for 2004*

	Population Distribution (%)		*Population Distribution (%)*
New England		Southeast	
Connecticut	24.6	Alabama	6.2
Massachusetts	45.1	Arkansas	3.8
Maine	9.2	Florida	23.8
New Hampshire	9.1	Georgia	12.2
Rhode Island	7.6	Kentucky	5.7
Vermont	4.4	Louisiana	6.2
		Mississippi	4.0
Mideast		North Carolina	11.7
Delaware	1.7	South Carolina	5.7
Maryland	11.7	Tennessee	8.1
New Jersey	18.3	Virginia	10.2
New York	40.8	West Virginia	2.5
Pennsylvania	26.3		
Washington, D.C.	1.2	Southwest	
		Arizona	17.1
Great Lakes		New Mexico	5.7
Illinois	27.6	Oklahoma	10.5
Indiana	13.5	Texas	66.8
Michigan	22.0		
Ohio	24.9	Rocky Mountain	
Wisconsin	12.0	Colorado	46.7
		Idaho	14.2
Plains		Montana	9.4
Iowa	15.0	Utah	24.6
Kansas	13.9	Wyoming	5.1
Minnesota	25.9		
Missouri	29.2	Far West	
Nebraska	8.9	California	74.7
North Dakota	3.2	Oregon	4.9
South Dakota	3.9	Washington	7.5
		Nevada	12.9

*Mideast population weights are for 2003. Population data from the Census

Notes

1 Specifically, they had a negative tax elasticity of only 0.08.
2 Lynch (2004) and McGuire (2003) also provide useful – if somewhat contrasting – summaries of the literature.
3 The coefficient on this variable is negative and statistically significant in both samples.
4 This variable includes full-time and part-time workers. Personal income taxes may have different effects on part-time and full-time workers because of threshold effects. Furthermore, part-time work is often a way of accommodating a lack of public services financed through taxation.
5 Some state and local taxes are deductible, which tends to reduce differences among states in effective tax burdens, however, the data do not permit us to account for deductibility in this analysis.
6 It is likely that different types of government spending will have different types of employment effects. Some types of spending, such as spending on social services, may be more important for generating employment opportunities for women than other types of spending. Preliminary tests by the authors that incorporate government spending variables in the specification, however, do not affect the tax variables and are not reported here.
7 It is likely this sort of cross-section data contains heteroskedasticity (i.e. the variance of each of the states will differ), even just by virtue of the varying sizes of different states. Generating a modified Wald statistic for the specifications, we rejected the null of homoskedasticity across panels. We also conducted tests for autocorrelation, finding evidence of first-order serial correlation using a test written by Drukker (2003), as well as evidence of correlation of the residuals across panels as evidenced by the Breusch-Pagan statistic. Thus, the econometric models used apply the appropriate statistical fixes for state-level heteroskedasticity, serial and cross-sectional correlation of the residuals.

Bibliography

Bartik, T. (1991) *Who Benefits from State and Local Economic Development Policies?* Kalamazoo: W.E. Upjohn Institute.

——— (1994) "Jobs, productivity, and local economic development: what implications does economic research have for the role of government," *National Tax Journal*, 87(4): 847–862.

Beck, N. and Katz, J. N. (1995) "What to do (and not to do) with time-series cross-section data," *American Political Science Review*, 89(3): 634–647.

Blau F., Ferber, M. and Winkler, A. (2006) *The Economics of Women, Men, and Work*, 5th edn, New Jersey: Prentice-Hall.

Carroll, R. and Wasylenko, M. (1994) "Do state business climates still matter? Evidence of a structural change," *National Tax Journal*, 157(1): 19–37.

Drukker, D.M. (2003) "Testing for serial correlation in linear panel-data models," *State Journal*, 3: 168–177.

Harden, J. and Hoyt, W. (2003) "Do states choose their mix of taxes to minimize employment losses?" *National Tax Journal*, 56(1): 7–26.

Helms, L. (1985) "The effect of state and local taxes on economic growth: a time series-cross section approach," *The Review of Economics and Statistics*, 67(4): 574–82.

Himmelweit, S. and Perrons D. (2006) "Gender and Fiscal Rules: How Can We Afford the Rising Cost of Care," Paper prepared for the Levy Institute Symposium "Gender Equality, Tax Policies & Tax Reforms in Comparative Perspective," Annandale on Hudson: Bard College.

Jacobsen, J. (2007) *The Economics of Gender*, 3rd edn, Malden, MA: Blackwell Publishing.

LaLumia, S. (2008) "The effects of joint taxation of married couples on labor supply and non-wage income," *Journal of Public Economics*, 92(70): 1698–1719.

Lynch, R. (2004) *Rethinking Growth Strategies: How State and Local Taxes and Services Affect Economic Development*, Washington, DC: Economic Policy Institute.

Mark, S., McGuire, T. and L. Papke, L. (2000) "The influence of taxes on employment and population growth: evidence from the Washington, D.C. metropolitan area," *National Tax Journal*, 53(1): 105–123.

McGuire, T. (2003) "Do taxes matter? Yes, no, maybe so," *State Tax Notes Magazine*, 28(10): 885.

Ridao-Cano, C. and McNown, R. (2005) "The effect of tax-benefit policies on fertility and female labor force participation in the US," *Journal of Policy Modeling*, 27(9): 1083–1096.

StataCorp (2005) *Longitudinal/Panel Data Release, 9*, College Station, TX: Stata Press.

Smith, N., Dex, S., Vlasblom, J. and Callan, T. (2003) "The effects of taxation on married women's labour supply across four countries," *Oxford Economic Papers*, 55: 417–439.

Wasylenko, M. (1997) "Taxation and economic development: the state of economic literature," *New England Economic Review*, March/April: 37–52.

Wheeler, L. (2006) "The potential effect of eliminating the state corporate income tax on economic activity," *State Tax Notes*, 39(9): 705–717.

Wilson, D. (2006) "The Mystery of Falling State Corporate Income Taxes," Federal Reserve Bank of San Francisco Economic Letter 2006–35: 1–4.

5

CENTRAL BANKS, EMPLOYMENT, AND GENDER IN DEVELOPING COUNTRIES

Elissa Braunstein and James Heintz

Introduction

The dominant policy position of central banks in most developing countries is to maintain very low rates of inflation without much consideration for how these restrictive policies impact the real economy – outcomes such as employment, investment and economic growth (Epstein 2003). There is scant evidence that maintaining very low rates of inflation raises economic growth. Nevertheless, these policies remain a key feature of neoliberal approaches to monetary development policy (Epstein 2000). Gerald Epstein and Juliet Schor argue that anti-inflation policy and neoliberal approaches to central banking reflect the "contested terrain" of central banks – the class and intra-class conflicts over the distribution of income and power in the macroeconomy (Epstein 2000; Epstein and Schor 1990). Their work underscores the importance of understanding monetary policy from a political perspective, as the distribution of the gains and costs of economic policy lends insight into both a policy's genesis and its longer-term consequences. Class is one dimension of this contested terrain; gender is another.

We build on this analysis by considering the employment costs of inflation reduction in developing countries from a gender perspective. We explore two broad empirical questions: (1) What is the impact of inflation reduction on employment and is the impact different for women and men? (2) How are monetary policy indicators (e.g. real interest rates) connected to deflationary episodes and gender-specific employment effects? We find a common pattern among countries undergoing what we term *contractionary inflation reduction*, which refers to periods of declining inflation that are accompanied by loss of employment (as captured by the available time-series data). After controlling for long-term employment trends, we find that the ratio of women's to men's employment tends to decline during these periods in the majority of countries examined. During the fewer periods of expansionary inflation reduction, however, there are no clear patterns to the relative changes in women's and men's employment. In terms of monetary policy, we find that countries that respond to inflation by raising real interest rates or tightening the real money supply (both relative to their long-run trends) are more likely to experience employment contractions, with concomitantly higher costs for women's employment. Conversely, those that maintain competitive real exchange rates are likely to reverse the negative impact of contractionary inflation reduction on women's relative employment.

That the costs of inflation reduction are, at least in terms of employment, inequitably distributed by gender means that the contested terrain of monetary policy is also affected by the gender order, with the result that the costs of implementing these sorts of policies are actually quite different – and potentially higher – than is generally presumed. After discussing the literature on the differences in women's and men's unemployment in developing countries and presenting our empirical results, we will develop this last point in more detail.

Gender differences in employment and unemployment in semi-industrialized countries

In thinking about the differences between women's and men's unemployment, it is helpful to think in terms of supply-side factors and demand-side factors (Seguino 2003). On the supply side, differences in human capital are probably the most commonly considered. However, gender-based differences in education, skill, and experience are themselves rooted in workers' productive roles outside the factory door and the institutional, social, and material contexts in which they live. These structures create gendered differences in choice and opportunity. A useful way of considering these differences is through what Folbre (1994) terms "structures of constraint" – the preferences, norms, assets, and rules that shape individual choice.

Beginning with preferences, women make decisions about whether or not to look for wage work, a process sometimes referred to as "exercising agency" or, in the language of utilitarian economics, "desire fulfillment." But self-perception, what individuals value, and what choices they perceive to be possible are constituted by the social world (Sen 1990), thus the putative preferences that underlie an individual's objectives must be understood in this light. The objectives that drive women into the labor market can be different from those governing men, the implications of which bear upon the price of labor and unemployment. Women who expect to leave the labor force for full-time motherhood may prefer the structure of easy-access, high-turnover jobs that give them a chance to live away from home and exercise freedoms they would not otherwise be able to enjoy.

Norms refer here to the traditional structures of gender and kinship that constitute the meaning and social expectations of women and men. Perhaps the most salient factor here is the sexual division of labor. While women are primarily responsible for the care and reproduction of the family, and, as a result, much of their work time is spent outside of the market, men's work is typically viewed as more directly productive and more fully incorporated into the market sphere. These divisions have implications not only for whether women look for market work at all, but also what types of jobs are considered feasible (in terms of combining market and non-market work) or even suitable (in terms of conforming to gender norms).

Norms about divorce and remarriage also shape women's labor. They partly determine the possibility and terms of exit from a conjugal union and affect daughters' attitudes about market work. In East Asia, where divorce rates are extremely low, wage work for married women is less important as insurance against the economic stress of divorce. Conversely, in parts of Southeast Asia, divorce and remarriage rates are high (Lim 1990: 106), and high labor force participation rates in this region provide a way for women to insure against the costs of divorce (Papanek and Schwede 1988: 79).

Assets, or wealth, engender labor supply as well. Systematic differences by gender in ownership or control over assets are common and partly determine how much wage employment women seek as well as the extent to which women are influenced by other (typically male) household members. Asset ownership also influences the returns to labor from various forms of informal self-employment, including own-account employment. In many countries, women are disproportionately concentrated in forms of non-agricultural own-account employment, often characterized by low and unstable earnings (Chen *et al.* 2005).

Legal constraints on women's movements, such as officially sanctioned purdah or rules against night work, limit labor supply in gendered ways. Property rights and family law also influence labor market decisions. Patriarchal property rights, by which eldest men have the right to claim and apportion the fruits of all household members' labor, can create incentives for high fertility and lower female labor force participation (Braunstein and Folbre 2001). Conversely, not having a legal claim on a spouse's income in the event of separation means that a paying job can be an insurance policy against loss of that support (Folbre 1997).

On the demand side, both overt and subtler forms of gender discrimination can result in gender differences in unemployment. In terms of direct discrimination, the male breadwinner ideal – the presumption that men should and do bear the primary financial responsibility for providing for their families – has been linked with higher unemployment for women relative to men in OECD countries (Algan and Cahuc 2004). Women are laid off first because employers presume that it is more important for men to be able to fulfill their traditional breadwinning responsibilities. The same link has been made between gender gaps in unemployment and gender-biased attitudes in general among OECD countries (Azmat *et al.* 2006).

Discrimination in hiring practices also contributes to gender segregation in industries and occupations. A clear example is the nearly universal increase in women's share of the non-agricultural labor force among high-growth developing countries in the past few decades (UN 1999), a result of tremendous growth in manufacturing, trade, and export processing from these countries (Standing 1989, 1999). This increased demand is not just a matter of expanding the available labor force when male labor is in short supply. With labor costs such a crucial part of international competitiveness, labor intensive exporters prefer to hire women both because women's wages are typically lower than men's and because employers perceive women as more productive in these types of jobs (Elson and Pearson 1981). Reasons that employers cite for the latter include: women's putative "nimble fingers," being obedient and less prone to worker unrest, their suitability for tedious work; and their reliability and trainability relative to men (Anker and Hein 1985; Elson 1996; Elson and Pearson 1981; Fernández-Kelly 1983).[1] By extension, women may lose their comparative advantage in these job markets as industries upgrade, leading to a defeminization of manufacturing employment (as has happened in Mexico, India, Ireland, and Singapore) (Elson 1996; Fussell 2000; Ghosh 2001; Joekes 1999). Subcontracting may also have a role to play, as women doing own-account work for subcontractors linked with international trade may underlie defeminization in formal manufacturing sectors. Women working in the informal sector are undercounted in official employment statistics (Carr *et al.* 2000).

Increases in women's employment that are associated with lower unit labor costs have important implications for inflation. For the non-tradable and import-competing sectors in which some degree of competition exists, the lower unit labor costs associated with increases in demand for female labor reduce inflationary pressures in the countries where the women work. The concentration of women in certain export sectors worldwide also has implications for inflation dynamics in importing countries. The expansion of low-wage manufactured exports from developing countries can lower prices to consumers in relatively more affluent markets, including those with significant market power in the retail sector (Heintz 2006).

That women are segregated into certain sectors and jobs underlies the notion of crowding, where an increased supply of female labor in certain classes of jobs or industries raises unemployment and lowers wages in those industries (Bergmann 1974). In a study of gender differentials in unemployment in the Caribbean, Seguino (2003) finds a positive correlation between female share of the labor force and female unemployment (with no such correlation for men), suggesting that job segregation by sex has contributed to higher rates of unemployment for women.

As a result of these gender differences in labor demand and supply, changes in macroeconomic structure and policy have differential effects on men's and women's work (Seguino 2003). From a macroeconomic perspective, some of the most important insights we have on the link between macroeconomic policy and women's employment in developing countries come from the feminist literature critiquing structural adjustment policies (SAPs) imposed largely in Latin American and African countries in the 1980s. Feminists argued that the interaction between gender relations and SAPs have implications both for the distribution of costs and benefits between different groups of women and men, and for the achievement of the economic objectives of the SAPs themselves (Bakker 1994; Benería and Feldman 1992; Benería and Roldan 1987; Cagatay *et al.* 1995; Elson 1991, 1995).

Turning more specifically to issues of gender differences in employment and unemployment in the context of SAPs, Cagatay and Ozler (1995) use cross-country data from 1985 and 1990 to show that SAPs have led to increased feminization of the labor force due to factors such as worsening income distribution and the impact of economic liberalization. These findings touch on gender differences in both labor supply and demand.

Economic downturns may affect labor supply in one of two ways: by either discouraging workers and pushing them out of the labor market completely, or by inducing households to add more workers to the labor market as protection against lower or more volatile household incomes. It is widely argued that the added worker effect is a dominant factor in crisis-related increases in labor force participation in Latin America (with women accounting for much of this increase) (Cerrutti 2000). Increasing labor force participation by women was also accompanied by an increase in the number of hours they devoted to paid work (Arriagada 1994). These supply effects underlie Cagatay and Ozler's finding that the worsening income distribution associated with SAPs lead to an increase in women's share of the labor force. Such dynamics are not limited to SAPs. For example, research into the determinants of women's labor supply in post-apartheid South Africa shows that female labor force participation rises in response to growing unemployment, thereby further increasing the country's average unemployment rate (Casale 2003).

On the demand side, Cagatay and Ozler's finding that SAPs, together with economic liberalization, are positively correlated with women's labor force participation reflects the shift away from import substitution and toward export-orientation, as export sectors provide an increasing number of job opportunities to women. But women's traditional industries have also been subject to contractionary effects. SAPs linked with deflationary stabilization that lowers domestic consumption can have adverse effects on women who produce traditional consumption goods (Standing 1999). In semi-industrialized countries, female-intensive export-oriented industries are more cyclically volatile than men's industries, resulting in higher overall rates of unemployment (Howes and Singh 1995). Emphasis on export-oriented industrialization has also been associated with increases in informalization as firms continue to minimize wage and non-wage costs (Standing 1999). So, as female labor force participation and unemployment rose in the context of crisis and structural adjustment, informal work became a key feature of new labor markets for women (Arriagada 1994; Benería 2001; Patnaik 2003).

Similar work has been done on the gendered employment effects of the Asian financial crisis (1997–1998). Women were typically the first to be laid off both because they worked in more cyclically volatile firms, such as small export-oriented enterprises and because of efforts to protect the jobs of "male breadwinners" (UN 1999). In Korea, women lost jobs at twice the rate of men despite the fact that their unemployment was half that of men's before the crisis (UN 1999). According to a 2000 World Bank report, women constituted 75 percent of discouraged workers and 85 percent of retrenched workers in the banking and financial service sectors (Aslanbeigui and Summerfield 2000). Immediately after the crisis in Indonesia, 46 percent of the unemployed were women, although they made up only one-third of the workforce. And as more men became unemployed, the percentage of women engaged in paid and unpaid work increased (ibid.). Similarly, women in Thailand constituted between 50 and 60 percent of the unemployed (ibid.). A slightly different pattern was found by Lim (2000) in the Philippines, where the post-crisis decline increased male unemployment more than female unemployment despite a rapid displacement of women from the manufacturing sector (especially in traded goods). The reason for this difference was the relative resilience of the service and trade sectors, which are more female intensive. Women did, however, increase their labor force participation to deal with male unemployment, and their total work hours relative to men increased as well. Similar to the case of structural adjustment reviewed above, the combination of increasing female unemployment and labor force participation is partly absorbed by increases in informalization. Women are increasingly pushed out of the formal sector and into the informal sector, and those who are new labor market entrants trying to preserve their household income are increasingly drawn into the informal sector (UN 1999).

Clearly, there are significant structural distinctions between women's and men's labor markets on both the supply and demand sides that are differently affected by macroeconomic structure and policy. The literature reviewed above on emerging economies suggests that economic contractions have a disproportionately negative effect on women's formal employment, though women tend to increase their labor force participation at the same time to protect household income. In the next section we turn to a more direct test of this employment hypothesis and look at whether the process of inflation reduction in particular can be associated with gender differentials in employment.

Inflation reduction and women's employment

The empirical exercise we present here explores the effects of inflation reduction on women's and men's employment. We compiled data for 51 "inflation reduction episodes" in 17 low- and middle-income countries.[2] To assess the employment effects of inflation reduction periods, we looked at actual employment trends during each inflation reduction episode, disaggregated by gender, and compared these to long-run employment trends.[3] We also examine indicators that suggest how monetary policy responded during inflation reduction episodes using a similar approach. We compare average short-term real interest rates, growth rates of the real money supply, and indicators of the real exchange rate to their long-run trends to see if these variables deviated from trends during inflation reduction episodes. We drew from three different data sources in conducting this exercise: employment data that came from the ILO's LABORSTA on-line database, and macroeconomic data that was compiled from *World Development Indicators* (Washington, DC: World Bank) and *International Financial Statistics* (Washington, DC: IMF).[4]

Our first task was to identify what we call "inflation reduction episodes." An inflation reduction episode is the period from peak inflation to a local trough.[5] Peaks occur when the value in a particular year exceeds the values of immediately adjacent years. Troughs occur when the value in a given year falls below the values of the adjacent years. A deflationary period runs from a peak year to the next trough year. We specifically use the term "inflation reduction episode" to refer to these deflationary periods. The reason for this is that during some of the periods identified, employment actually expands more rapidly than its long-run trend. It seems confusing to refer to these periods as "deflationary." Therefore, we use the terms "expansionary inflation reduction episode" and "contractionary inflation reduction episode" to distinguish between these periods.

We applied the following restrictions in the selection of countries:

- Only low- or middle-income countries were examined.[6]
- Countries must have at least 20 years of gender-disaggregated employment data (it would be hard to estimate a meaningful "long-run trend" with a shorter series).
- Time series with missing values were used. However, time series with two consecutive missing observations were rejected. Missing values were estimated for the purposes of computing a long-run trend by extrapolating between the previous and subsequent values in the series.

Changes in employment across inflation reduction episodes were calculated as the annualized value of the overall rate of change in employment across the entire peak-to-trough period. The employment time series used most likely underestimates the magnitude of informal employment in these countries. The results of this analysis should be interpreted with these considerations in mind.

Table 5.1 summarizes the results for all the inflation reduction episodes studied. The table shows the country name, the dates of each inflation reduction episode, and the deviation from the long-run trend for women's employment, men's employment, and the female to male employment ratio. Negative values indicate that the series grew more slowly than the long-run trend (a negative value could also indicate a more rapid decrease in the actual value compared to the long-run trend). Table 5.1 is divided into contractionary and expansionary inflation reduction episodes. During contractionary inflation reduction episodes, the rate of increase of total employment fell below its long-run trend. During expansionary inflation reduction episodes, the rate of increase of total employment was equal to or greater than its long-run trend.

In 67 percent of contractionary inflation reduction episodes, the rate of change of the female to male employment ratio fell below its long-run trend, indicating that women's employment was disproportionately affected by the slowdown. If India were to be excluded from the sample, this proportion would rise to over 72 percent.[7] However, in expansionary inflation reduction episodes, there was no clear distinction. The female to male employment ratio increased faster than trend in 53 percent of cases and at or below trend in 47 percent of cases – nearly an even split.

The contractionary inflation reduction episodes were associated with a larger decline in inflation from peak to trough relative to the average inflation rate for the

TABLE 5.1 Inflation reduction episodes and deviations from long-run employment trends, disaggregated by gender

	Period	*Deflation as percent of avg. inflation (%)*	*Deviations from long-run employment trends*			
			W (%)	*M (%)*	*Ratio (%)*	
A. CONTRACTIONARY INFLATION REDUCTION EPISODES						
Barbados	1980–86	−143	−1.8	−0.8	−1.0	
	1990–94	−113	−2.5	−2.6	0.1	****
	1996–99	−117	−1.0	0.3	−1.4	
Brazil	1993–99	−305	−0.7	−0.1	−0.6	
Colombia	1980–85	−29	−3.2	−2.5	−0.7	
Costa Rica	1982–85	−123	−1.5	−0.1	−1.4	
India	1973–77	−175	−0.2	−0.4	0.2	****
	1982–86	−37	−0.1	−0.2	0.1	****
	1991–94	−26	0.1	−1.2	0.2	****
	1997–02	−93	−1.0	0.9	−0.2	
Jamaica	1974–76	−45	−0.5	−0.2	−0.3	
	1992–00	−190	−0.5	0.1	−0.6	
Kenya	1975–80	−36	−2.2	−0.1	−2.1	
	1981–87	−66	0.8	−0.3	1.1	****
Malaysia	1981–86	−181	−0.4	−0.8	0.4	****
Mauritius	1980–86	−182	−0.6	−1.6	0.9	****
	1989–93	−46	−1.3	−0.3	−0.9	
	1994–96	−21	−1.8	−0.9	−0.8	
Philippines	1973–76	−69	−1.6	−0.4	−1.2	
	1980–82	−55	0.2	−0.3	0.5	****
	1984–87	−130	−2.4	0.0	−2.3	
Singapore	1974–76	−171	−6.7	−0.7	−5.9	
	1981–86	−267	−1.8	−2.0	0.1	****
South Korea	1980–85	−196	−1.4	−0.9	−0.5	
	1991–94	−45	−0.4	0.0	−0.4	
	1997–00	−82	−1.2	−1.1	−0.1	
Sri Lanka	1981–86	−106	−0.7	0.1	−0.8	
	1997–99	−56	−0.7	−2.6	1.9	****
Taiwan	1974–76	−106	−4.9	0.3	−5.1	
	1980–85	−243	0.6	−0.5	1.1	****
	1991–02	−197	−0.4	−0.2	0.2	****
Thailand	1974–76	−88	−1.3	−0.8	−0.5	
	1980–85	−180	−2.6	−0.7	−1.8	
	1990–93	−31	−0.8	0.1	−0.9	
	1997–00	−136	−0.8	−0.7	−0.1	
Trinidad and Tobago	1980–87	−56	−1.0	−0.6	−0.4	

(Continued)

TABLE 5.1 (*Continued*)

	Period	*Deflation as percent of avg. inflation (%)*	*Deviations from long-run employment trends*			
			W (%)	*M (%)*	*Ratio (%)*	
B. EXPANSIONARY INFLATION REDUCTION EPISODES						
Brazil	1989–92	−39	1.9	−0.8	2.8	★★★★
Chile	1984–88	−39	0.8	2.3	−1.5	
Costa Rica	1991–93	−42	0.2	1.6	−1.4	
Jamaica	1979–82	−101	0.1	0.5	−0.4	
	1985–88	−90	2.9	0.5	2.3	★★★★
Kenya	1993–96	−134	0.9	−0.3	1.3	★★★★
Malaysia	1992–96	−27	0.6	1.4	−0.8	
Mauritius	1974–77	−59	3.9	1.6	2.1	★★★★
Philippines	1990–94	−60	0.2	0.3	−0.1	
Singapore	1990–99	−139	0.1	0.1	0.0	
Sri Lanka	1974–76	−100	1.9	3.1	−1.1	
	1989–94	−50	8.9	3.6	4.9	★★★★
Trinidad and Tobago	1974–77	−48	0.2	1.0	−0.8	
	1989–92	−37	3.8	1.6	2.1	★★★★
	1993–96	−69	0.7	0.6	0.2	★★★★

C. SUMMARY

Contractionary inflation reduction episodes with declining female:male employment ratios relative to the trend: 67
Contractionary inflation reduction episodes with declining female:male employment ratios relative to the trend (excl. India): 72
Expansionary inflation reduction episodes with increasing female:male employment ratios relative to the trend: 53

★★★★ Inflation reduction episodes in which the ratio of women's to men's employment increased more rapidly than the long-run trend.

entire episode. Averaging across all contractionary episodes, the decline in inflation was 115 percent of the average inflation rate during the episode in question. For expansionary episodes, the decline was 69 percent.

The difference in employment experiences (e.g. expansion or contraction of employment) across countries during inflation reduction episodes might be explained, in part, by policy choices. For example, if real interest rates rose above the long-run trend in reaction to an acceleration of inflation, this could trigger a contractionary inflation reduction episode. However, if real interest rates were not raised above the long-run trend (i.e. they were kept in line with the long-run trends of global interest rates), a contraction of employment might be avoided.

TABLE 5.2 Patterns in average real short-term interest rates over inflation reduction episodes in which total employment expanded (only episodes with positive average real interest rates included)

	Period	*Difference in actual and long-run average real interest rates as a percentage of the long-run average (%)*	*Notes*
Chile	1984–88	−31.3	
Costa Rica	1991–93	−9.8	
Kenya	1993–96	−2.1	
Malaysia	1992–96	−9.7	
Philippines	1990–94	−42.8	
Singapore	1990–99	−6.9	
Sri Lanka	1974–76	+24.0	1973–75: avg. neg. interest
	1989–94	−5.6	
Trinidad and Tobago	1989–92	+6.3	1988–91: +5.4%
	1993–96	−3.0	

To examine this possibility, we looked at average real short-term interest rates across the inflation reduction episodes.[8] Table 5.2 shows patterns in short-term interest rates over expansionary inflation reduction episodes. Average actual real interest rates are compared to the average interest rates associated with the long-run trend. The difference in average real interest rates (actual rates minus the rates associated with the long-run trend) is expressed as a percentage of the average long-run trend in real interest rates over the inflation reduction episode. Only inflation reduction episodes with positive actual average real interest rates over the episode in question are included in Table 5.2.

In almost all of the inflation reduction episodes, actual real interest rates were, on average, kept below the long-run trend. This is consistent with the argument that countries that do not raise interest rates in the face of growing inflationary pressures are less likely to experience employment losses or a slow-down in the growth rate of employment during inflation reduction episodes. There were only two exceptions: Sri Lanka (1974–1976) and Trinidad and Tobago (1989–1992). An alternative periodization that accounts for the possibility that policymakers responded to inflation before inflation peaks (by beginning one year before the beginning of an inflation reduction episode and extending half-way into the episode), shows that real interest rates were negative for Sri Lanka during this period.

Table 5.3 shows a similar set of calculations for contractionary inflation reduction episodes. As with Table 5.2, only inflation reduction episodes with positive actual average real interest rates over the episode in question are included.

In most cases, the opposite pattern (observed previously in Table 5.2) is evident. During contractionary inflation reduction episodes, actual interest rates were, on average, kept above the long-run trend. In two cases, Barbados (1996–1999) and

TABLE 5.3 Patterns in average real short-term interest rates over inflation reduction episodes in which total employment contracted (only episodes with positive average real interest rates included)

	Period	*Difference in actual and long-run average real interest rates as a percent of the long-run average (%)*	*Notes*
Barbados	1980–86	+36.7	
	1990–94	+4.4	
	1996–99	−3.3	1995–98: +1.0%
Colombia	1980–85	−1.1	1979–83: +34.6%
India	1982–86	+14.2	
	1991–94	−9.3	1990–93: −19.3%
	1997–02	−18.4	1996–00: −12.8%
Jamaica	1992–00	−8.4	Interest rates are t-bill rates. 1991–96: avg. neg. interest
Malaysia	1981–86	+51.9	
Mauritius	1989–93	−79.2	1988–91: −76.3%
	1994–96	+16.4	
Singapore	1981–86	+17.9	
Sri Lanka	1981–86	+398	
	1997–99	+2.9	
Taiwan	1980–85	+24.3	
	1991–02	−6.5	1990-97: −11.9%
Thailand	1980–85	+6.6	
	1990–93	+5.2	
	1997–00	+14.2	

Colombia (1980–1985), actual real interest rates fell below the long-run trend during the entire inflation reduction episode. However, if we apply the alternative periodization we can see that real interest rates increased before inflation peaked and during the earlier stages of the inflation reduction period. For example, in Colombia, from 1979 to 1983, average actual real interest rates were nearly 35 percent higher than the long-run average over this same period.

These findings suggest that negative real interest rates are important in analyzing the employment trends across inflation reduction episodes. In other papers based on this research, we show that keeping interest rates negative and below the long-run trend will not help to increase employment (Braunstein and Heintz 2008). One reason why negative real interest rates tend to be associated with a contraction in employment relative to its long-run trend is that many of these inflation-reduction episodes are "stagflationary." That is, supply-side shocks produce a situation in which inflation accelerates and economic growth slows down, resulting in negative real interest rates.

Real interest rates are only one set of variables that potentially link monetary policy to inflation reduction and employment dynamics. Two other possibilities are the real exchange rate and the growth rate of the real money supply. Table 5.4 examines trends in these two variables across the various inflation reduction episodes. Specifically, it shows differences between the actual average annual growth rate and the growth rate associated with the long-run trend for the real exchange rate (RER) and the real money supply across various inflation reduction episodes.[9] The inflation reduction episodes are separated into contractionary and expansionary periods.

TABLE 5.4 Differences in the average actual annual growth rate and the average annual growth rate associated with the long-run trend for the real exchange rate (RER) and the real money supply across inflation reduction episodes

Country	*Period*	*RER (%)*	*Money supply (%)*
Total employment contracts on average			
Barbados	1980–86	−0.3	−1.1
	1990–94	+1.1	−1.5
	1996–99	−1.2	+3.0
Brazil	1993–99	+1.1	+0.3
Colombia	1980–85	+2.2	+0.2
Costa Rica	1982–85	−6.7	−9.4
India	1973–77	+1.6	−1.6
	1982–86	+0.8	+0.6
	1991–94	+3.6	−0.4
	1997–2002	+0.4	+1.7
Jamaica	1974–76	−9.0	−0.7
	1992–2000	−0.6	+0.5
Kenya	1975–80	−3.5	+1.9
	1981–87	+1.7	+1.8
Malaysia	1981–86	+4.5	−1.4
Mauritius	1980–86	0.0*	−2.2
	1989–93	+1.8	−1.9
	1994–96	−4.0	−1.4
Philippines	1973–76	−3.9	−1.6
	1980–82	+0.8	−0.4
	1984–87	0.0	−10.2
Singapore	1974–76	+3.9	−0.6
	1981–86	+2.8	−2.4
South Korea	1980–85	+7.0	−1.9
	1991–94	−0.4	−2.7
	1997–2000	+6.7	+6.2
Sri Lanka	1981–86	−0.7	−1.1
	1997–99	+1.7	0.0
Thailand	1974–76	−0.2	−0.3
	1980–85	+3.7	−2.5
	1990–93	−1.9	+2.8
	1997–2000	+7.0	−0.4
Trinidad and Tobago	1980–87	+2.7	−1.0

(*Continued*)

TABLE 5.4 (*Continued*)

Country	*Period*	*RER (%)*	*Money supply (%)*
Total employment expands on average			
Brazil	1989–92	0.0	+4.9
Chile	1984–88	+2.2	+2.7
Costa Rica	1991–93	−4.8	−1.1
Jamaica	1979–82	−2.2	+1.9
	1985–88	−7.8	+4.9
Kenya	1993–96	+5.7	+11.4
Malaysia	1992–96	−4.6	+5.1
Mauritius	1974–77	n.a.	+5.4
Philippines	1990–94	−1.8	−0.5
Singapore	1990–99	+0.4	+1.4
Sri Lanka	1974–76	−1.0	−4.8
	1989–94	−0.3	−0.7
Trinidad and Tobago	1974–77	−1.0	−1.0
	1989–92	−3.8	−2.7
	1993–96	+1.4	+5.4

* Based on 1981–1986 average, due to data limitations.

Source: Authors' calculations based on data from the IMF publication International Financial Statistics. Real US interest rate is T-bill rate less the inflation rate.

There does not appear to be any systematic patterns with respect to changes in the real exchange rate across inflation reduction episodes, regardless of whether the episode was contractionary or expansionary. In 34 percent of inflation reduction episodes, the average annual percent change in the real exchange rate was below that of the long-run exchange rate (i.e. the exchange rate appreciated relative to its long-run trend). In 60 percent of the episodes the difference in average growth rate was positive (i.e. the actual real exchange rate depreciated relative to the long-run trend) and in 6 percent of the episodes there was no difference between the growth rate of the actual and long-run real exchange rates. These ratios were approximately the same for contractionary and expansionary inflation reduction episodes.[10]

Real exchange rates appear, however, to have an impact on the gender bias observed in contractionary inflation-reduction episodes. Recall that in the majority of cases, women's formal employment was disproportionately affected by the slowdown in employment growth. Yet, approximately one-third of the time, the ratio of women's to men's employment actually improved when compared to its long-run trajectory. In each of these cases, the real exchange rate either depreciated or showed no deviation relative to its long-run trend. In other words, maintaining a competitive exchange rate may offset some of the gender bias observed during contractionary inflation-reduction. Why would this be the case? As previously noted, in many countries the growth of women's employment – particularly wage employment – has tended to be concentrated in tradable sectors, either export-oriented or import-competing (Benería 2003; Elson 1996; Elson and Pearson 1981; Kabeer and

Mahmud 2004). A real depreciation of the exchange rate favors tradable sectors and could help protect women's employment in certain cases.

Turning to the real money supply, there is some indication that it grew more slowly during contractionary episodes.[11] In 67 percent of all contractionary episodes for which data is available, actual average annual growth rates in the real money supply fell below the long-run trend. In 60 percent of all expansionary episodes, actual annual growth rates in the real money supply were greater than the average for the long-run trend. Relative to the gendered effects of inflation reduction, tightening the real money supply may be associated with greater sacrifices in women's employment.

Summary

This analysis uncovers a number of important relationships, however, it is important to recognize that a myriad of factors affect the variables examined here – in particular, employment, inflation, interest rates, exchange rates, and the money supply – and any generalizations must be tentative. Although some commonalities do arise, the diversity of country experiences prevents us from drawing definitive conclusions without additional in-depth analysis and country-specific case studies.

Nevertheless, we can make some general observations from the analysis presented:

- If employment contracts during an inflation reduction episode, it is likely that women will experience a larger loss of employment (in percentage terms) than men. In the majority of cases, contractionary inflation reduction has a disproportionately negative impact on women, however, during inflation reduction episodes in which employment expands, the gender-specific impact is ambiguous.
- Countries that respond to inflationary pressures by raising real interest rates above the long-run trend are more likely to experience a slow-down in the growth of employment with concomitantly higher losses for relative female employment relative to those countries that keep interest rates in line with or below the long-run trend. Countries with negative real interest rates, however, do not appear to be able to increase employment growth by lowering real interest rates still further.
- While we did not find a link between changes in the real exchange rate and the impact of inflation reduction on employment in general, we did find that RERs seem to impact the gender bias of contractionary inflation reduction episodes. In all cases where women experienced relative employment gains during employment contractions, exchange rates either depreciated or showed no deviation relative to long-run trends.
- Tightening the real money supply seems to be negatively associated with employment in general and women's employment in particular.

These results suggest that contractionary monetary policy aimed at reducing inflation often has a disproportionately negative impact on women's employment, an effect that may be eased by maintaining a competitive exchange rate. Conversely, non-contractionary inflation reduction is not necessarily favorable to women's employment in all circumstances.

The gendered political economy of central bank policy

In terms of the study's economic implications, the empirical analysis presented here concerns the short-run, gender-specific impacts of policy responses during inflation reduction episodes. The results say little about the long-run impact of different policy responses. Supporters of inflation targeting frequently acknowledge that short-run trade-offs might exist, but that long-run benefits of low inflation for growth and development are more significant. This argument is problematic when transitory policy shocks have long-run consequences for real economic variables (Fontana and Palacio-Vera 2004). Similarly, short-term, gender-specific shocks can have long-run effects for a country's human and economic development.

A number of empirical studies suggest that gender-based inequities in employment and unemployment have implications for long-term development. For example, this body of research shows that a positive relationship exists between gender equality (measured most frequently in terms of educational equity) and economic growth in developing countries (Dollar and Gatti 1999; Hill and King 1995; Klasen 1999). Some studies have shown these effects to be quite large. For example, in a panel data study between 1960 and 1992, Klasen (1999) concludes that had South Asia and sub-Saharan Africa had more gender equity in education, growth would have occurred 0.9 percent faster per year. Investing in girls makes for a more productive workforce, but higher rates of unemployment and cyclical volatility in women's jobs will discourage these types of investments at both the individual and community levels.

In a related sense, lower incomes and higher income volatility for women could lead to lower investments in human capital overall, thereby lowering long-term growth. Theory and empirical research have aptly demonstrated a higher coincidence between a mother's income and the family's basic needs than a father's income (Benería and Roldan 1987; Blumberg 1991; Chant 1991), a finding underlying what has been termed the "good mother hypothesis." Income that is controlled by women is more likely to be spent on children's health and nutrition (Dwyer and Bruce 1988; Hoddinott *et al.* 1998). In many countries, a large proportion of fathers provide little or no economic support for their children (Folbre 1994). But faced with cyclically higher rates of unemployment during disinflation, "good mothers" will have fewer opportunities to invest in their children, compromising future labor force quality.

Moving beyond instrumental arguments, the finding that women as a group shoulder a disproportionate share of the costs of contractionary inflation reduction brings us back to the political economy question posed at the beginning of the chapter: What do the distribution of the costs and benefits of inflation reduction indicate concerning the contested terrain of monetary policy? One might simply respond "not much," and provide an argument such as the following: It is true that the empirical evidence presented in this chapter indicates gender differences in labor supply and demand – the "gender orders" of the labor market – resulting in women's jobs being more cyclically volatile (at least on the economic downturn) than men's jobs. While macroeconomic policies (e.g. trying to reduce inflation by raising interest rates) and structures (e.g. export-oriented industrialization) may have gender-differentiated impacts, these impacts reflect gender dynamics in the labor market, not in the central bank. Monetary policymakers should not be tasked with addressing gender inequality; such issues are, and should properly remain, outside the purview of monetary management. Ultimately, the best thing (indeed perhaps the only thing) a central banker can do for gender equality is to keep inflation low and stable, as these policies provide the sort of macroeconomic stability essential for growth and income generation. Thus, the argument concludes that gender is only a matter of concern for social policy.

The reach of this argument is global in scope. Most central banks in developing countries are constrained by the reactions of international financial markets to their policy choices. This is likely to be the case particularly when capital markets have been liberalized and prudential capital controls have been eliminated. In addition, central banks in many low-income countries – including the heavily indebted poor countries (HIPC) – must craft their policies under the auspices of IMF conditionalities. Monetary policies enshrined in "poverty reduction strategy papers" reflect these biases. Ironically, many of these "post-Washington consensus" development strategies claim to have incorporated a gendered analysis into their poverty reduction program. However, this gender-sensitive analysis does not spill over into the macroeconomic realm.

A different sort of insight comes from thinking about what would happen if gender equity concerns were indeed incorporated into monetary policy. Such a shift would most likely necessitate a move away from inflation targeting as it is currently practiced and could harm the economic interests of those individuals and institutions which benefit from a low inflation, high interest rate environment – largely finance capital. Even a brief survey of central bank leaders and managers around the world reveals that they are largely drawn from the finance and banking sectors, a pool that is also primarily male. From this standpoint – one that acknowledges how gender, class, and nation shape our opinions of the appropriate or feasible reach of macroeconomic policy – resistance to seeing, much less incorporating, the social content of inflation targeting is clearly a political matter. It is not just that central bank policy has gendered effects; it is also that the structures of central banks and global financial markets and institutions, the permissible discourses on monetary policy, and the technical models used to illustrate them are themselves "bearers of gender" (Elson 1998).

Another aspect of the gendered political economy of our empirical findings is the point that if women's labor force participation keeps unit labor costs and inflation lower than it would otherwise be, then a focus on gender equality within the context of sustainable levels of inflation could require other mechanisms for price control that are more consistent with long-run growth and development. Such a move might be resisted by those that benefit (perhaps only in the short run) from women's more precarious employment – for example, women's employers and employed men. Gender-biased central bank policy may help solve the political problems introduced by neoliberal central bank policy in that gender bias concentrates the costs of these policies on a less powerful segment of society – women. Inflation targeting should be considered in terms of its social content (i.e. in terms of the social structures that underlie this policy) as well as its social impact (Elson and Cagatay 2000), as an instance of contested terrain in macroeconomic policymaking.

Acknowledgement

The research for this paper was first conducted as part of a project on "Alternatives to Inflation Targeting," co-sponsored by the Ford Foundation, the UN-DESA, the Rockefeller Brothers Fund, and the Political Economy Research Institute at the University of Massachusetts, and we thank them for their support. We would also like to thank Gerald Epstein, Erinc Yeldan, and Diane Elson for their help and comments, as well as the participants (and our hosts) of the AIT meeting at CEDES in Buenos Aires in June of 2005. All mistakes are our own, of course.

Notes

1 Similar reasoning can be applied to the "pink collar" aspects of the international production of services, a sector where women predominate in the administrative support aspect of the trade.
2 Our choice of countries was limited to those for which reasonably reliable, gender-disaggregated employment data were available.
3 In all cases, long-run trends were estimated by applying a Hodrick-Prescott filter to the data series in question.
4 We conducted the original research featured in this paper in 2005. Our estimates date from this point in time. In addition, the GDP deflator for the US used to construct the real exchange rate measure was taken from the on-line database of the US Bureau of Economic Analysis.
5 Following Ball (1993), we use three-year moving averages to reduce the volatility of inflation in order to better identify inflation reduction episodes.
6 The sample of countries includes Singapore, which could arguably be classified as a high-income country today. However, for much of the period considered in this book, 1970–2003, Singapore can be considered a middle-income country.
7 India is notable in terms of its frequent deviation from the behavior exhibited by other countries, both with respect to the gender dynamics of slower employment growth and the observed trends in real interest rates during inflation reduction episodes.
8 In most cases, short-term rates linked directly to monetary policy choices were used (e.g. a discount rate or bank rate). If these rates were unavailable, yields on short-term (three-month) Treasury bills were calculated instead. Only in the case of Jamaica were the t-bills used to determine actual interest rates and to estimate long-run trends. If actual average real interest rates were negative, these inflation reduction episodes were tabulated separately. Due to its extreme volatility, Brazil was excluded from this analysis.

9 In terms of the real exchange rate, for the purposes of this study, we measured the real exchange rate as the nominal US dollar exchange rate adjusted for changes in the US. GDP deflator relative to the specific country's GDP deflator. A decrease in the value of our real exchange rate measurement, therefore, represents an appreciation in the real exchange rate. Likewise, an increase in value represents a depreciation.

10 In contractionary episodes, 36 percent of the episodes showed an appreciation, 58 percent a depreciation, and 6 percent no difference in the average growth of the real exchange rate relative to its long-run trend. In expansionary episodes, the percentages were 34 percent, 60 percent, and 7 percent, respectively.

11 The definition of the money supply used is money plus quasi-money, corresponding to M2.

Bibliography

Algan, Y. and Cahuc, P. (2004) "Job Protection: The Macho Hypothesis," Society for Economic Dynamics, 2004 Meeting Papers No. 332.

Anker, R. and Hein, C. (1985) "Why Third World Urban Employers Usually Prefer Men," *International Labour Review*, 124(1): 73–90.

Arriagada, I. (1994) "Changes in the Urban Female Labour Market," *CEPAL Review*, 53: 92–110.

Aslanbeigui, N. and Summerfield, G. (2000) "The Asian Crisis, Gender, and the International Financial Architecture," *Feminist Economics*, 6(3): 81–103.

Azmat, G., Güell, M. and Manning, A. (2006) "Gender Gaps in Unemployment Rates in OECD Countries," *Journal of Labor Economics* 24(1): 1–38.

Bakker, I. (ed.) (1994) *The Strategic Silence: Gender and Economic Policy*, London: Zed Books with the North-South Institute.

Ball, L. (1993) "What Determines the Sacrifice Ratio?" NBER Working Paper No. 4306.

Benería, L. (2003) *Gender, Development, and Globalization: Economics as if all People Mattered*, London: Routledge.

Benería, L. (2001) "Shifting the Risk: New Employment Patterns, Informalization, and Women's Work," *International Journal of Politics, Culture and Society*, 15(1): 27–53.

Benería, L. and Feldman, S. (eds) (1992) *Unequal Burden: Economic Crises, Persistent Poverty, and Women's Work*, Boulder, CO: Westview Press.

Benería, L. and Roldán, M. (1987) *The Crossroads of Class & Gender: Industrial Homework, Subcontracting, and Household Dynamics in Mexico City*, Chicago and London: University of Chicago Press.

Bergmann, B. (1974) "Occupational Segregation, Wages and Profits when Employers Discriminate by Race or Sex," *Eastern Economic Journal*, 1(2): 103–110.

Blumberg, R. (1991) "Income under female versus male control," in R. Blumberg (ed.) *Gender, Family and Economy: The Triple Overlap*, Newbury Park, CA: Sage Press.

Braunstein, E. and Folbre, N. (2001) "To Honor and Obey: Efficiency, Inequality and Patriarchal Property Rights," *Feminist Economics*, 7(1): 25–44.

Braunstein, E. and Heintz, J. (2008) "Gender Bias and Central Bank Policy: Employment and Inflation Reduction," *International Review of Applied Economics*, 22(2): 173–86.

Cagatay, N., Elson, D. and Grown, C. (eds) (1995) *Gender, Adjustment and Macroeconomics. A Special Issue of World Development*, 23(11).

Cagatay, N. and Ozler, S. (1995) "Feminization of the Labor Force: The Effects of Long-Term development and Structural Adjustment," *World Development*, 23(11): 1883–1894.

Carr, M., Chen, M. A. and Tate, J. (2000) "Globalization and Home-Based Workers," *World Development*, 6(3): 123–142.

Casale, D. (2003) "The rise in female labour force participation in South Africa: an analysis of household survey data, 1995–2001," Ph.D. dissertation, Division of Economics, University of KwaZulu-Natal.

Cerrutti, M. (2000) "Economic Reform, Structural Adjustment and Female Labor Force Participation in Buenos Aires, Argentina," *World Development*, 28(5): 879–891.

Chant, S. (1991) *Women and Survival in Mexican Cities: Perspectives on Gender, Labour Markets and Low-Income Households*, New York: Manchester University Press.

Chen, M., Vanek, J., Lund, F., Heintz, J., Jhabvala, R. and Bonner, C. (2005) *Progress of the World's Women 2005: Women, Work, and Poverty*, New York: UNIFEM.

Dollar, D. and Gatti, R. (1999) "Gender Inequality, Income and Growth: Are Good Times Good for Women?" World Bank Policy Research Report on Gender and Development Working Paper Series No. 1, Washington, DC: World Bank.

Dwyer, D. and Bruce, J. (1988) *A Home Divided: Women and Income in the Third World*, Stanford, CA: Stanford University Press.

Elson, D. (ed.) (1991) *Male Bias in the Development Process*, Manchester: Manchester University Press.

——— (1995) "Gender Awareness in Modeling Structural Adjustment," *World Development*, 23(11): 1851–1868.

——— (1996) "Appraising recent developments in the world market for nimble fingers," in A. Chhachhi and R. Pittin (eds) *Confronting State, Capital and Patriarchy: Women's Organizing in the Process of Industrialization*, New York: St Martin's Press, Inc.

——— (1998) "Talking to the boys: gender and economic growth models," in C. Jackson and R. Pearson (eds) *Feminist Visions of Development: Gender Analysis and Policy*, New York: Routledge: 155–170.

Elson, D. and Cagatay, N. (2000) "The Social Content of Macroeconomic Policies," *World Development*, 28(7): 1347–1364.

Elson, D. and Pearson, R. (1981) "Nimble Fingers Make Cheap Workers: An Analysis of Women's Employment in Third World Export Manufacturing," *Feminist Review*, 7: 87–107.

Epstein, G. (2000) "Myth, Mendacity and Mischief in the Theory and Practice of Central Banking," Manuscript, University of Massachusetts Amherst.

——— (2003) "Alternative to Inflation Targeting Monetary Policy for Stable and Egalitarian Growth: A Brief Research Summary," PERI Working Paper No. 62.

Epstein, G. and Schor, J. (1990) "Macropolicy in the rise and fall of the Golden Age," in S. Marglin and J. Schor (eds) *The Golden Age of Capitalism: Reinterpreting the Postwar Experience*, Oxford: Clarendon Press.

Fernández-Kelly, M. P. (1983) *For We Are Sold, I And My People: Women and Industrialization in Mexico's Frontier*, Albany: SUNY Press.

Folbre, N. (1994) *Who Pays for the Kids? Gender and the Structures of Constraint*, London and New York: Routledge.

Folbre, N. (1997) "Gender coalitions: extrafamily influences on intrafamily inequality," in L. Haddad, J. Hoddinott and H. Alderman (eds) *Intrahousehold Resource Allocation in Developing Countries. Models, Methods, and Policy*, Baltimore: The Johns Hopkins University Press.

Fontana, G. and Palacio-Vera, A. (2004) "Is long-run price stability and short-run output stabilization all that monetary policy can do?" Mimeo., University of Leeds and Universidad Complutense de Madrid.

Fussell, E. (2000) "Making Labor Flexible: The Recomposition of Tijuana's Maquiladora Female Labor Force," *Feminist Economics*, 6(3): 59–79.

Ghosh, J. (2001) "Globalisation, Export-Oriented Employment for Women and Social Policy: A Case Study of India," Paper prepared for UNRISD project on Globalization, Export-Oriented Employment for Women and Social Policy, July.

Heintz, J. (2006) "Low-Wage Manufacturing and Global Commodity Chains: A Model in the Unequal Exchange Tradition," *Cambridge Journal of Economics*, 30(4): 507–20.

Hill, A. M. and King, E. M. (1995) "Women's Education and Economic Well-Being," *Feminist Economics*, 1(2): 21–46.

Hoddinott, J., Alderman, H. and Haddad, L. (eds) (1998) *Intrahousehold Resource Allocation in Developing Countries: Methods, Models and Policy*, Baltimore: Johns Hopkins University Press.

Howes, C. and Singh, A. (1995) "Long-Term Trends in the World Economy: The Gender Dimension," *World Development* 23(11): 1895–1912.

Joekes, S. (1999) "A gender-analytical perspective on trade and sustainable development," in UNCTAD *Trade, Sustainable Development and Gender*, New York and Geneva: UNCTAD.

Kabeer, N. and Mahmud, S. (2004) "Globalization, Gender, and Poverty: Bangladeshi Women Workers in Export and Local Markets," *Journal of International Development*, 16: 93–109.

Klasen, S. (1999) "Does Gender Inequality Reduce Growth and Development? Evidence from Cross-Country Regressions," World Bank Policy Research Report on Gender and Development, Working Paper Series No. 7, Washington, DC: World Bank.

Lim, L. (1990) "Women's work in export factories: the politics of a cause," in I. Tinker (ed.) *Persistent Inequalities: Women and World Development*, Oxford: Oxford University Press.

Papanek, H. and Schwede, L. (1988) "Women are good with money: earning and managing in an Indonesian city," in D. Dwyer and J. Bruce (eds) *A Home Divided: Women and Income in the Third World*, Stanford, CA: Stanford University Press.

Patnaik, U. (2003) "Global Capitalism, Deflation and Agrarian Crisis in Developing Countries," United Nations Research Institute for Social Development, Social Policy and Development Programme", Paper No. 15, October.

Rives, J. M. and Sosin, K. (2002) "Occupations and the Cyclical Behavior of Gender Unemployment Rates," *Journal of Socio-Economics*, 31(3): 287–299.

Seguino, S. (2003) "Why are Women in the Caribbean so Much More Likely Than Men to be Unemployed?" *Social and Economic Studies*, 52(4): 83–120.

Sen, A. (1990) "Gender and cooperative conflicts," in I. Tinker (ed.) *Persistent Inequalities: Women and World Development*, New York and Oxford: Oxford University Press.

Standing, G. (1989) "Global Feminization through Flexible Labor," *World Development*, 17(7): 1077–1095.

——— (1999) "Global Feminization Through Flexible Labor: A Theme Revisited," *World Development*, 27(3): 583–602.

United Nations (1999) *World Survey on the Role of Women in Development. Globalization, Gender and Work*, New York: United Nations.

6

IMF POLICIES AND GENDER ORDERS

The case of the Poverty Reduction and Growth Facility

Diane Elson and Tonia Warnecke

Introduction

Macroeconomic policy has become circumscribed by rules that limit both the discretion of governments and the scope for democratic accountability (Schuberth 2004). All of these rules have gender implications but are not themselves overtly gendered. In this chapter we examine the case of the rules (or *conditions*) attached to a particular International Monetary Fund (IMF) loan facility, the Poverty Reduction and Growth Facility (PRGF). The PRGF was established in September 1999, ostensibly to "make the objectives of poverty reduction and growth more central to lending operations in its poorest member countries" (IMF 2008). PRGF rules, however, have typically limited public spending in recipient countries. We discuss the extent to which the gender dimensions of these rules have been considered by the IMF, and the extent to which existing critiques of these rules have taken account of gender. We find that both the IMF and its critics have neglected gender issues relating to the PRGF rules.

This chapter considers three ways in which the gender dimension might be introduced:

1) Sex-disaggregated impact analysis.
2) Gender analysis of the extent of fiscal space.
3) Analysis of the way the gender order is invisibly inscribed within the policy rules.

A sex-disaggregated impact analysis considers the potential impact of the PRGF rules on women and girls as compared to men and boys and asks whether the costs and benefits are fairly distributed. In contrast, a gender analysis of the determinants of fiscal space examines how the gendered characteristics of the economy are likely to affect the supply response to increases in public spending. Finally, an analysis of the inscription of the gender order in the policy rules investigates the unspoken assumptions contained in the rules about the gender order. (We understand the gender order to be the system of social power that sustains particular patterns of gender relations.) Here, we consider the extent to which these rules implicitly rely on characteristic features of the gender division of labor and strongly entrenched norms about the responsibilities of women and men.

The IMF and the PRGF

The PRGF[1] provides finance to low income countries at the cost, not only of payments of interest, but also of adhering to certain policy rules (also known as policy conditions or performance criteria). Even though the amounts of finance provided are quite small, a PRGF is valuable to a small, poor country because it opens the door to other forms of finance. The successful negotiation of a PRGF is taken as a sign that the borrowing government has "sound" policies and is thus eligible for access to debt relief and new aid from a variety of multilateral and bilateral donors.

The policy conditions of the PRGF are based on the country's Poverty Reduction Strategy Paper (PRSP), which is prepared by the developing country's government with some limited consultation with various civil society groups. This document sets out a multi-year plan for promoting growth and reducing poverty and identifies financing shortfalls (IMF 2008). Although the PRSP is not prepared by the IMF, it must be approved by the IMF in order for the country to be eligible for funding. This means that the recipient government only has limited policy-making space, and that significant disagreements between a government and the IMF about appropriate policy reforms could lead to the denial of financial assistance. The kind of fiscal and monetary policies that IMF economists espouse are illustrated in Table 6.1.

According to this framework, levels of inflation above 10 percent require reductions in the amount of credit issued to the government through the banking system.

TABLE 6.1 Macroeconomic thresholds and performance criteria

Macroeconomic variable	*Threshold*	*Appropriate performance criteria or benchmark*
Inflation	10%	Credit to the government from the banking system
Domestic Budget Financing (DBF) and Debt	DBF/GDP = 1%	Net domestic financing of the government
Net Present Value of External Public Debt (EPD)	NPV(EPD)/GDP = 40%	Total financing or primary fiscal balance
Revenue (Rev)	Rev/GDP = 15%	Domestic revenue

Source: Fedelino and Zakharova 2006: 5.

If annual flows of government borrowing from domestic sources are above 1 percent of gross domestic product (GDP), domestic borrowing should be reduced. If the present value of external public debt is above 40 percent of GDP, public expenditure should be cut. And if a country has a revenue-to-GDP ratio below 15 percent, methods of increasing revenue, especially through taxation, should be introduced (Fedelino and Zakharova 2006). However, the authors found that this framework was not consistently applied in African PRGF programs in the period up to the end of 2003. For instance, not all governments in countries that had a rate of inflation above 10 percent were required to reduce the amount of credit issued to the government from the banking system, and some governments were required to do this even when inflation was lower.

Research by the Centre for Global Development (CGD), a Washington-based think tank, acknowledges that there is some variation in the size of targeted changes in fiscal deficits and public spending, though it found that most PRGF programs (in the period January 2003–February 2007) have required inflation targets at very low levels. In 12 cases, the inflation target was 3 percent or below; in nine cases, 3–5 percent; and in ten cases, 5–10 percent (CGD 2007: 41). In addition, the IMF has placed conditions on the use of additional foreign aid obtained from other (non-IMF) institutions – requiring countries to use these monies to reduce domestic debt (i.e. reduce the budget deficit) and increase foreign exchange reserves. Only when target levels for the latter have been met, are countries permitted to use additional aid flows to increase public expenditure. A recent study by the Independent Evaluation Office (IEO), which reports on the activities of the IMF and World Bank to the two organizations' executive directors, found that in sub-Saharan Africa, governments were required to hold reserves equivalent to at least two or three months of imports and to have inflation no higher than 5–7 percent before spending any additional aid that they received. As a result, on average, only 27 percent of additional aid was programed to increase public expenditure. In contrast, 37 percent was programed to increase foreign exchange reserves and 37 percent was programed to reduce domestic debt (IEO 2007). In countries that had foreign exchange reserves below the threshold level, 95 percent of additional aid was programed to enlarge foreign exchange reserves. In countries that had higher reserves but also had inflation above the threshold levels, only 15 percent of additional aid was programed to increase public spending. Even in countries with levels of reserves and inflation compliant with IMF requirements, not all aid was programed to increase public expenditure. As much as 21 percent of the additional aid was programed to reduce domestic debt (IEO 2007).

A subsequent IMF working paper argues that the IEO only examined how much aid was programed to increase public expenditure in the year in which the aid was received and that a longer time period should be examined (Berndt *et al.* 2008). Using a larger data set that includes countries outside sub-Saharan Africa, the study finds that on average more than 80 percent was programed to be spent within two years (meaning that on average 20 percent was not to be spent). The paper states that "concerns about fiscal consolidation and reserve adequacy can dampen the programmed spending" (Berndt *et al.* 1998: 16), although it contests the idea that there are specific conditions linked to thresholds. Nevertheless, it reports some weak evidence to support a foreign exchange reserve threshold of approximately 2.9 months and stronger evidence that programed spending drops sharply if inflation rises above 15 percent (Berndt *et al.* 1998: 23).

Besides restraining expenditures of new aid, the IMF has also required an asymmetric treatment of unforeseen increases and decreases in aid. Unexpected decreases in aid trigger cutbacks in public expenditure, while unexpected increases are to be saved (CGD 2007). Moreover, the IMF has imposed ceilings on the public sector wage bill in a large number of countries. In 42 African, Central American, and Caribbean countries with PRGFs (in 2003–2005), 17 were subject to a wage ceiling of some kind (CGD 2007).

Though there has been tension between recipient governments and the IMF regarding such policy constraints (see below), governments usually comply with these rules because of their countries' desperate need for funding and the lack of funding alternatives. According to ActionAid, a growing "despondency on the part of developing country governments, particularly health and education ministries, is regularly reinforced when the IMF demands countries to scale back and tone down their poverty-reducing spending priorities and spending scenarios in their PRSPs" (ActionAid 2005: 42).

Critiques of IMF rules

Critics have particularly focused on the implications of IMF policy rules for education and health, especially in relation to the HIV/AIDS emergency. They point out that the IMF has not made any estimates of the costs of not spending the additional aid (of which preventable mortality and suffering are the most egregious). Among the most active critics have been ActionAid, the CGD, and the UNDP International Poverty Centre (IPC). The key points they have made are briefly discussed below.

Inflation targeting

ActionAid points to the considerable body of academic research finding that moderate levels of inflation have no negative impact on economic growth (ActionAid 2005: 31–32). It recognizes that high rates of inflation may harm poor people by eroding their real incomes, but cites research suggesting that moderate inflation may benefit poor people by reducing the real value of their personal debts. ActionAid cites evidence that policies designed to keep inflation very low adversely affect poor people by constraining employment creation. The IPC has also been very critical of inflation targeting (see for instance, McKinley 2007).

CGD argues that there is no empirical evidence to justify pushing inflation below 5 percent in low-income countries; nevertheless, it concludes that the adoption of higher inflation targets for all borrowing countries would be unlikely to generate higher growth (CGD 2007: 40). It is important to note that there is considerable debate about the threshold at which higher inflation is associated with lower growth; some studies suggest it is between 5 and 10 percent, "while others suggest it is between 20 and 40%" (CGD 2007: 40). Because of this, CGD advocates country-specific inflation targets. In addition, a few researchers from the IMF have concluded that inflation rates of 5–10 percent a year are unikely to harm growth in sub-Saharan Africa (Gupta *et al.* 2006: 18).

Accumulation of reserves

IPC recognizes that it is important for countries to hold an adequate level of foreign exchange reserves in order to offset volatility in foreign exchange receipts. Yet it has also argued that the build-up of reserves has been excessive in many countries: "Developing country reserves as a proportion of imports are now roughly three times those of developed countries" (Lapavitsas 2007). The expected costs and benefits of holding foreign exchange reserves are shown in Table 6.2.

The cost of reserve holding can be measured in terms of "the difference between the market return and the much lower return from holding reserves in (typically) US treasuries" (Cruz and Walters 2008: 666). Using this measure, several studies indicate that the excess of international reserves has a cost of around 1 percent of GDP (Bird and Rajan 2003; Cruz and Walters 2008); this amount is "a multiple of the budgetary cost of even the most aggressive anti-poverty programs implemented in developing countries" (Rodrik 2006: 262).

Given this cost, why is this money being held as international reserves? While the potential for aid volatility plays a role, the main reason is that these reserves are used as a buffer in case of currency speculation or capital flight (Aizenman and Lee 2005). As Cruz and Walters note, however, "a large literature demonstrates that

TABLE 6.2 Costs and benefits of the international reserve accumulation strategy

	Benefits	*Costs*
Development purposes	Foreign exchange stability Export growth (through a competitive real exchange rate)	Forgone resources for development purposes
Policy autonomy	Increased creditworthiness Avoid reliance on the IMF in case a crisis occurs	Moral hazard problems Macroeconomic risks (inflation, high intervention costs, monetary imbalances) No room for industrial and growth policies
Financial stability	Prevents speculative attacks	The economy remains highly exposed to hot money, particularly to capital outflows

Source: Cruz and Walters 2008: 674.

it was not international reserves accumulation *per se* that deterred speculative attacks [...] rather, these aims were attained through the implementation of capital controls" (2008: 666).

IPC concludes that there is a need to regulate capital outflows and for donors to provide more predictable flows of aid (McKinley and Hailu 2006). This point is also made by ActionAid, citing a report of the IEO in 2005 that found the IMF advice on capital account liberalization to be unbalanced and inconsistent, with operational advice failing to take account of the "risks of premature capital account liberalization" (ActionAid 2005: 35–36). As a result of capital account liberalization, government policy is trapped indefinitely in the 'short run,' unable to commit sufficient resources to long run investment because policymakers are afraid of changes in perceptions in international markets of the riskiness of their economies (Nayyar 2003).

Reducing domestic debt

ActionAid is critical of the IMF's demand that governments reduce borrowing from domestic investors, arguing that it fails to differentiate between wasteful use of borrowed money, and investment in productive assets (ActionAid 2005: 13–14). The IMF assumes that government borrowing 'crowds out' private sector investment by leading to rises in domestic interest rates that make it more expensive for domestic investors to borrow. ActionAid argues that the opposite effect prevails: government borrowing funds public expenditure and creates demand that stimulates private investment ("crowding in"), especially in middle-income developing countries that are likely to have underutilized productive capacity. It acknowledges that in low income countries there may be less underutilized productive capacity that can quickly be brought into use, but argues that even in these countries, public expenditure can increase available human and physical capital in the medium term.

UNDP IPC also argues that public expenditure can crowd in private investment, but emphasizes that it is important to distinguish between capital and current expenditure. For example, "public capital expenditures do not [...] have the same impact as current expenditures [...] They create more public capital [...] they help to expand the productive capacity of the whole economy [...] while the government should strive, over time, to keep the current budget in balance, it should have leeway to borrow to finance capital expenditures" (McKinley 2005: 4).

CGD notes that the IMF assumes that paying down domestic debt and reducing the budget deficit will crowd in private investment. However, the evidence on the strength of such an effect is not clear, and much depends on specific country context (CGD 2007: 25).

Wage bill ceilings

CGD points out that wage ceilings have been imposed on the overall public sector wage bill and not on any specific sector, such as health or education. Indeed, some mechanism has usually been included to try to protect priority sectors, though in practice protection has not been enforced or even monitored. In practice, when new hiring took place in non-priority sectors, hiring staff in health and education was constrained. CGD concludes that wage ceilings have been over-utilized and should only be used on rare occasions (CGD 2007: 10, 50–53).

ActionAid (2005) adds that wage ceilings contribute to brain drain in low-income countries and to the problem of providing quality services to their populations. According to the Bangladesh education ministry official, "there are trained and qualified people available to work as professional teachers in Bangladesh, but the wage bill in the public education system is too low to hire them" (ActionAid 2005: 47). This is likely to hamper economic growth in the future, as potential increases in human capital are being forgone.

Investigating the gender dimension of the PRGF rules

None of the critiques discussed above include the gender dimension. This chapter considers three ways in which the gender dimension might be introduced. First, sex-disaggregated impact analysis considers the potential impact of the PRGF rules (and associated policies) on women and girls as compared to men and boys, asking whether the costs and benefits are fairly distributed. Second, a gender analysis of the determinants of fiscal space examines how the gendered characteristics of the economy, such as the gender division of labor, are likely to affect the supply response to increases in public spending. Third, an analysis of the inscription of the gender order in the policy rules examines their unspoken assumptions about the gender order and the system of social power that sustains particular patterns of gender relations.

Sex-disaggregated impact analysis

When the PRGF programs were constructed, it was envisioned that they would be supported by poverty and social impact analyses (PSIA) (IEO 2007: 16). In theory, a PSIA would inform the PRGF by analyzing the potential socioeconomic impacts of various policy options that are geared toward problems defined by the PRGF. The PRGF would then identify appropriate policies, including those countervailing any anticipated adverse outcomes.

In an IMF Working Paper, Caroline Robb (2003) discusses eleven techniques used in PSIA, including both data gathering and analysis. Though five of these eleven techniques are based on household surveys, household surveys have limited value for gender analysis; when data is collected for the household as a whole rather than for individual members, the differences between men and women's activities drop out of focus. Only two approaches are identified that specifically mention gender: participatory poverty assessments (PPA) and benefit incidence analysis.

Unlike household surveys, which sample extensively and use a fixed and predetermined set of questions, PPAs deal with a small sample of communities and use "a variety of flexible participatory methods that combine visual techniques (mapping, matrices, diagrams) and verbal techniques (open-ended interviews, discussion groups)" (Robb 2003: 37). The information that is made available through PPAs is far more detailed and expansive than that of household surveys, as it sheds light on "individuals, intra-household dynamics, social groups [...] and community relationships" (ibid.). Given the flexibility and open-endedness of this technique, it is possible to gain information about the experiences and activities of men and women in various contexts.

Benefit incidence analysis examines how public spending is distributed across different social groups. Most commonly, the data are grouped by household income or expenditure. Robb notes that the analysis can be further disaggregated by region, ethnicity, or gender (Robb 2003: 39). Benefit incidence is a simple technique, but it does not really assess impacts, because outcomes (such as improvements in health and education status) may not correlate strongly with inputs of expenditure. Robb also discusses more complex forms of incidence analysis (including spending incidence analysis, tax incidence analysis, and marginal benefit incidence analysis), but does not mention gender in relation to those.

Given the variety of techniques outlined above, it is clear that there is no set strategy for conducting a PSIA. Possibly because there is no mandatory procedure, many PSIAs have not included sex-disaggregated data or sought to examine the impact on women and girls as compared to men and boys. While there are PSIAs that have explicitly included gender in their focus (i.e. the Ugandan PSIA on a strategic export initiative), this remains the exception rather than the norm (Bird *et al.* 2005). In fact, a study of 23 PSIAs conducted in the agricultural sector led the World Bank (2006) to conclude that there was "considerable variation in the extent to which analysis of social diversity and gender was undertaken" (Gacitua-Mario *et al.* 2008: 9). The study admitted, "in a number of cases, little explicit attention was paid to the impacts on women, children, or landless laborers" (Gacitua-Mario *et al.* 2008: 9). This is associated with the task of identifying stakeholders in the initial stages of the PSIA; it is common for groups with less economic and political power (who are more likely to be invisible to policy makers) to be left off the stakeholder list. Consequently, policy impacts on those groups are not assessed comprehensively, if at all.

Other methods for incorporating gender analysis into PSIAs

An alternative means of incorporating gender into policy impact analysis, which has been explored by the World Bank and others, is to use sex-disaggregated computable general equilibrium models (CGE). Robb (2003) does mention CGE models, though not with reference to gender; she claims that the policy relevance of CGEs may be limited in poverty reduction terms, since CGE models produce information in the aggregate (Robb 2003: 15). While it is true that few gender-aware CGE models have been developed, Fontana (2005) notes that the most common approach so far is to treat female and male labor as imperfect substitutes, and to supplement the typical market sectors with two non-market sectors: household work and leisure. Labor inputs are measured in terms of hours rather than number of workers, and time spent on household work and leisure is valued at the average market wage. These gender-aware CGEs do have several disadvantages, which have been noted by Fontana (2003, 2005). For example, because CGEs are equilibrium models that cannot track processes of adjustment, it is hard to determine what drives the outcomes generated by the model (although their design might be modified to incorporate a dynamic aspect in the future). There are also disadvantages in the way the non-market sector is included: all household work is treated as homogenous, even though different production technologies are used for different tasks, and some tasks provide emotional satisfaction while others do not. Moreover, the leisure sector includes both free time and idle time (the latter imposed on people through lack of employment), which are not of equal benefit.

Another possibility for incorporating gender into PSIAs is to use a macro-meso-micro approach, which can estimate a likely gender impact by considering how fiscal and monetary policies impact women and men in households via public services, markets, and enterprises (Bakker 1994; Elson 1994). For this, one needs to have "stylized facts" about the economy and about the gender order, derived from case studies or cross-country or time-series studies.

For instance, one could consider the differential implications of inflation for poor women and men in terms of different stylized facts about their indebtedness, employment, ability to increase their incomes from earnings or transfers (both from the state and intra-household) in line with increasing prices, responsibility for purchases of household goods, patterns of inflation (i.e. does it occur across all goods and services or are price increases relatively higher for those goods that women or men are specifically responsible for purchasing?), and ability to produce substitutes for market-based goods. Very high inflation is likely to have different implications for poor women than for poor men if women have little or no earnings of their own, are responsible for purchasing essential items whose prices are rising fast, and are unable to easily negotiate an increase in income transfer from their husband. In these circumstances, managing their responsibilities for provisioning the household is very difficult. While the real value of their existing debts is falling, they may be forced to take new consumption loans. More research is needed to understand this relationship. Of course, very low levels of inflation will also have adverse impacts on employment and earnings available to poor women. These may be worse than those for poor men, depending on the gender structure of the labor market (see the chapter by Braunstein and Heintz). Moreover, inflation may not be driven by domestic policy – it may be imported via increases in the prices of imports, as were the rises in the world market prices of food and fuel in 2007. Reducing public expenditure will not reduce imported inflation.

Similarly, one could consider the differential impacts of insufficient foreign exchange reserves to smooth out volatility in foreign exchange receipts. In so far as poor women are the ones who have to provide the ultimate safety net in volatile conditions, they may be more adversely impacted than men by volatility in the ability to fund imports. Yet, as mentioned above, the level of foreign exchange reserves required is not independent of the extent of capital account liberalization. It is better to tackle the sources of volatility directly by placing controls on capital inflows and outflows.

An emphasis on low inflation and building up reserves is likely to lead to constraints on the expansion of public expenditure. The implications of this may be different for women and girls compared to men and boys. If services and infrastructure that are particularly beneficial to women and girls are considered of marginal importance, then the failure to expand public expenditure will hit women and girls harder than men and boys.

However, the problem is not just one of incorporating gender analysis into PSIAs; it is also that the IMF does not take PSIAs seriously. An examination of IMF staff reports for ten different African countries revealed that the majority focuses on poverty and social impacts only cursorily, in special topic boxes added to the main text (Robb 2003).[2] These boxes analyze the poverty and social impacts of some of the policies being recommended in those countries, but there is little to no discussion of policy alternatives or assessment of whether the selected policies are the best ones in terms of poverty reduction and equitable outcomes. Moreover, the policies considered are generally meso-level policies (such as abolition of fuel subsidies, or privatization of the water sector), not macro-level policies (like those embodied in rules about when aid can be spent).

According to an IMF factsheet "PSIA would *ideally* be based on a comprehensive analysis of policies and public actions (like public spending programs), including direct and indirect effects [...but] *in practice*, because of data and other limitations, a more limited analysis of the immediate social impact of alternative policies may have to be utilized" (IMF 2010: 1, italics added). However, there is a strong perception among many non-governmental organizations (NGOs) that PSIAs are just window dressing. The basic problem is that the IMF does not take seriously the costs of shrinking public expenditure, because they are not conceived to be short-run financial costs.

The unfavorable impression held by NGOs regarding IMF commitment to PSIAs seems to be confirmed by the IMF itself: "The Fund has always relied, in the first instance, on PSIA done by the World Bank and other institutions to build PSIA into its program advice. As part of refocusing in a reduced budget environment, the Fund will have more limited capacity for original PSIA work" (IMF 2010: 2). This document also mentions that poverty and social impact issues will be addressed by area department teams in the course of their regular work (which implies that impact analyses will not be conducted by PSIA specialists).

Gender dimensions of fiscal space

Underlying the policy rules of the IMF is a very constrained view of the amount of fiscal space (i.e. the space for expanding public expenditure) that developing countries have. The IMF definition of fiscal space is the "room in a government's budget that allows it to provide resources for a desired purpose without jeopardizing the sustainability of its financial stability or the stability of the economy" (Heller 2005). To further clarify:

> When the IMF evaluates a country's macroeconomic situation, it is open to the creation of fiscal space through higher foreign grant inflows for spending on infrastructure or social programs. But the IMF would flag a concern if the higher spending jeopardized macroeconomic stability or debt sustainability. Such caution particularly extends to the use of central bank credit, given the IMF's concern with inflation and its damaging effects on growth and poverty.
>
> (*ibid*)

In assessing a country's fiscal space, no attention is given to the positive impact that public expenditure can have on the supply side of the economy (and the subsequent potential increases in tax revenue generated by increases in output). As pointed out by David Goldsborough, the lead author of the CGD study referred to earlier:

> The main issue is the implicit assumptions that the IMF makes – often without much supporting evidence – about how the real economy will respond to changes in fiscal deficits and public spending. The longer-term supply-side effects of higher public spending are, with some commendable recent exceptions, largely ignored in many macroeconomic frameworks. The main IMF focus is on the shorter term; programmes frequently lack concrete medium-term expenditure plans whose longer-term effects can be analysed. Yet, assessing the appropriate medium term fiscal path requires some judgment on the likely impact of higher public spending.
>
> (*Goldsborough 2007: 1*)

The IMF fails to recognize that the inflationary potential of increased public spending depends on the composition of expenditure. We emphasize that expenditure that fairly rapidly increases productivity – or brings into use underutilized resources – will not have an inflationary impact, while expenditure that does not weaken supply constraints – or does not bring into use underutilized resources – will more likely have an inflationary impact. While policies restricting public spending today may succeed in lowering inflation in the short run, they may lead to future increases in inflation if productivity-promoting public spending is lowered (Ismihan and Ozkan 2004). A similar point is made by Roy *et al.*:

> [U]sing fiscal space for increasing military spending will have a significantly different impact from investing in rural roads in the long run, but the standard analytical framework cannot distinguish between the fiduciary outcomes (not to mention developmental outcomes) of these very different spending decisions (2006: 15).

The discussion of fiscal space to date has not considered that the supply response to expansion of public expenditure is structured by the gender order, which shapes the utilization and productivity of men's and women's time. Both the market economy, with which the IMF is concerned, and the non-market, unpaid domestic economy, are shaped by a gendered division of labor that tends to segregate women and men into different tasks and occupations. For instance, women and girls do most of the unpaid work of caring for family and friends. On the one hand, this unpaid work provides a substitute for public services and infrastructure (Floro 1995; Warnecke 2006); on the other hand, it constrains the utilization and productivity of female labor in market-based production (Blackden and Wodon 2006; Chen *et al.* 2005). The gendered obligation to undertake unpaid work may lead to both an overutilization of women's time and an underutilization of men's time. A quick-acting package of public expenditure that both reduces the amount of unpaid domestic work that women have to do (by both reducing the total amount of such work and by redistributing some of it to men) and increases the productivity of their paid work has the potential to contain the inflationary impact of extra public spending. Aid spent in this way should be quite compatible with macroeconomic sustainability and stability over the medium term.

We illustrate this with respect to sub-Saharan Africa. The significant role that women in this region play in the agricultural sector has been noted by many researchers (Bryson 1981; Cleaver and Schreiber 1994; Kisamba-Mugerwa 2001). In low-income agriculture-based countries (which include nearly all of sub-Saharan Africa), agriculture accounts for approximately 32 percent of the growth in GDP and women constitute a substantial majority of the agricultural workforce (Ashby *et al.* 2009; World Bank 2007a).

The *Gender in Agriculture Sourcebook* (World Bank 2009) – a collaboration of the World Bank (Agriculture and Rural Development Department), the UN Food and Agriculture Organization (FAO), and the International Fund for Agricultural Development (IFAD) – highlights some examples of how the lack of equal access to resources constrains women farmers:

- In Ghana, if women and men had equal land rights and tenure security, women's use of fertilizer and profits per hectare would nearly double.
- In Zambia, if women and men enjoyed the same overall degree of capital investment in agricultural inputs, including land, output in the country could increase by up to 15 percent.
- In Kenya, providing female farmers with the same farm inputs, education, and experience as male farmers would increase yields for cowpeas, maize, and beans by as much as 22 percent. According to the World Bank (2007b), this would have increased Kenya's GDP growth rate in 2004 from 4.3 percent to 8.3 percent (a one-time increase).
- In Burkina Faso, shifting labor and fertilizer between men's and women's plots could increase output by 10 to 20 percent.

Lack of secure land rights is one major impediment to women's productivity. Another is women farmers' lack of access to inputs such as credit, fertilizer, and extension services, all of which could be addressed by more and better public expenditure (Doss 1999).

At the same time as they are farming, women are responsible for most of the unpaid care work, and unpaid subsistence work (e.g. the collection of water and fuel) that provision of care requires in many rural areas. Moreover, the amount of care women provide has increased with the high prevalence of HIV/AIDS. According to the Joint United Nations Programme on HIV/AIDS (UNAIDS), in 2007 nearly one-third of all new HIV infections and AIDS-related deaths in the world occurred in sub-Saharan Africa (UNAIDS 2008). As this continues, more demands are made on women farmers to care for family and community members who are living with HIV/AIDS. As noted by Akram-Lodhi (2007), this is likely to reduce the productivity of women farmers and exacerbate the imbalance between aggregate demand and supply of food. Johnston makes a similar point, citing micro-level evidence for Burkina Faso, Swaziland, and East Africa (2008: 103). This is relevant to macroeconomic stability because if domestic food supplies do not grow at a rate commensurate with food demand, food price increases will trigger inflation. As Akram-Lodhi puts it, "macro supply and demand dynamics may thus be a function of gender relations" (2007).

His argument can be criticized for implicitly assuming a closed economy. It might be argued that imports of food can bridge the gap between domestic demand and supply. Yet, with international food prices rising rapidly, importing more food is both importing inflation and putting pressure on foreign exchange reserves. In the current context, there are strong arguments for a program of public expenditure designed to increase productivity of women farmers. As Seguino argues, "by increasing agricultural productivity, governments help to raise output and lower food prices. This reduces inflationary pressures and the demand for imports" (2009: 5). Reducing imports would be very helpful for the balance of payments in African countries, since the continent "spends billions of dollars each year importing food, including 45 percent of its rice and 85 percent of its wheat" (Somma 2008: 9). Another long-run benefit of this type of expenditure is that, by raising income, tax revenues will be generated to cover the cost of government spending (Seguino 2009). Unfortunately, in 2007, agricultural programs and projects accounted for only 4 percent of official development assistance (ODA) in sub-Saharan Africa, and less than 10 percent of ODA efforts to target agriculture explicitly considered gender issues (Ashby *et al.* 2009; World Bank 2007a).

Many ways to support poor women farmers to rapidly improve their productivity have been identified by researchers at the International Food Policy Research Center (Quisumbing and Pandolfelli 2008). They include:

- Increasing women's security of tenure through low-cost, rapid, and transparent community land registration.
- Strengthening and increasing women's knowledge of their land rights;

- Equipping women with fertilizer and improving seeds through targeted fertilizer and seed vouchers.
- Improving women's access to organic methods of replenishing soil fertility.
- Developing new varieties of crops with the participation of women farmers.
- Training male extension workers to meet the specific needs of women farmers and recruiting and training more female extension workers, so that women farmers can get access to the new knowledge provided by extension workers.
- Introducing culturally appropriate labor-saving technologies.

Public investment in such initiatives would improve the food security of poor households and enable women farmers to provide a surplus for sale in local markets. But programs to increase productivity of women farmers need to be coupled with programs of public expenditure aiming to reduce their care burdens. As pointed out by Holmes and Slater (2007), this is not sufficiently recognized. For instance, the World Bank *2008 World Development Report* on Agriculture and Economic Development still treats women farmers as if they have lots of spare time, assuming that "they can absorb increased responsibilities infinitely" and treating their reproductive work "as having little or no economic value" (Holmes and Slater 2007: 2). Public investment should focus on infrastructure (especially investment in energy, water and sanitation) and on the provision of additional caregivers in order to reduce necessary care time. Quick-impact investments in off-grid electricity and alternative fuels are viable (Grown 2006). Additional public expenditure might be able to mobilize additional caregivers in various ways: for instance, by increasing the retention of trained medical personnel working in a given country's public health system and by bringing more men into voluntary sector home-based care programs. One of the reasons why so much unpaid care has to be provided is the shortage of staff in the public health system. A key reason for this shortage is the low pay and poor working conditions that drive nurses to emigrate. Increasing the health sector wage bill might well have the effect of increasing the capacity of the public health system by reducing the migration of nurses. It is surprising that there has not been more discussion of the migration of skilled staff in analyses of the public sector wage ceilings that have been imposed by the IMF.

One response to the shortage of professional staff has been the development of volunteer community-based programs, very often organized through the church (Akintola 2004). In many cases the volunteers are given small stipends. In some cases, men comprise a substantial minority of these volunteers (Kgware 2006). Volunteer programs would be more effective if linked to public provision and supported by the government budget (Ogden *et al.* 2006). One study in South Africa found that stipends are important in attracting male volunteers to care-giving (Kgware 2006). Time-use studies show that it tends to be men who have more spare time in many African countries (Blackden and Wodon 2006; Lloyd *et al.* 2008). If payments to non-professional community-based volunteers can tap the under-utilized resource of male time, this would be another way of spending public money to enhance supply as well as demand.

To summarize the argument, if sub-Saharan African countries were to spend more of their additional aid on support for women farmers to increase their productivity in farming and reduce their care burdens, there would likely be a rapid pay-off in terms of growth in food supply and reductions in poverty. There would be less imported inflation and less need to build up foreign exchange reserves to cover the risks associated with a rising import bill for food. In assessing the extent of fiscal space, it is important to consider the payback from these gender-sensitive and productivity-enhancing uses of aid.

Of course, relaxing conditions to allow governments to spend increased aid flows does not guarantee that aid will be used for the kind of complementary development-promoting package of public expenditure outlined above. This needs to be coupled with reforms of the budgeting process to ensure that money is spent more effectively toward the achievement of development goals. One important aspect of such reforms is the introduction of gender-responsive budgeting, in which governments address the implications of patterns of public expenditure for women and girls as compared to men and boys (Budlender and Hewitt 2002; Guha and Goswami 2006; UNIFEM 2001). Another important reform is providing access to information to civil society groups that act as budget watchdogs, analyzing government budgets and actual spending for the impact on poverty reduction, gender equality, and other important social goals. An example is the Forum for Women and Democracy (FOWODE) in Uganda, which scrutinizes the government budget and provides detailed analysis to enable Members of Parliament to understand the gender dimensions of the budget. They have produced a critique of public expenditure on agriculture in Uganda, calling for more support for women farmers (FOWODE 1999). Their analysis of the 2008/09 Ugandan Budget welcomes an increase in public expenditure on agriculture, but with the critique that much more attention has been paid to export crops than food for local consumption. They also note a failure to address "the time poverty suffered by the women who constitute the majority of farmers" (FOWODE 2008: 3). The growth of organizations such as FOWODE gives some grounds for hope that governments will begin to use the fiscal space that they do have in more effective ways.

The inscription of the gender order in policy rules

As is evident, the IMF policy rules have no explicit mention of gender, and the impact analysis carried out to date by the IMF does not focus heavily on gender. Nevertheless, the gender order is inscribed within the policy rules as a *strategic silence* (Bakker 1994). As noted above, the stated aim of the rules is to safeguard the sustainability of the financial position of a government and the stability of the economy it is governing (Heller 2005). Attention is paid neither to the sustainability and stability of the society and the people that live in it, nor to the negative impacts that their absence would have on financial sustainability and economic stability. In effect, it is assumed that the impact of the macroeconomic rules on social sustainability and stability can safely be ignored, and that social reproduction will carry on in much the same way irrespective of macroeconomic policy rules. People will go on being available to produce goods and services at the same levels of productivity. People will accept these forms of economic and social governance without disruptive protest.

The prevailing gender order in most parts of the world often renders this a plausible assumption. Norms, values, and laws continue to assign to women the obligation to sustain social reproduction through their unpaid work and to punish them through social disapproval, and even violence, if they do not carry out this obligation in a satisfactory way. This gender order supports the assumption that women are "able to compensate fully for any shortfall in the state provision of social reproductive services" (Warnecke 2006: 181).

Nevertheless, the gender order is not an unbreakable straitjacket. If the economic conditions of everyday life deteriorate sharply, there will be some women who either cannot or will not sustain the forms of social reproduction that underpin fiscal sustainability and macroeconomic stability. This was demonstrated in responses to structural adjustment policies in the 1980s and 1990s (Elson 1995). The same is true of the responses in 2008 to the rapid increases in food prices in sub-Saharan Africa. There have been food riots in a number of countries, including Burkina Faso, Cameroon, Côte d'Ivoire, Niger, and Senegal, in which women were the majority of the protestors. According to a report in early 2009:

> [w]omen were in the streets to voice their concerns not only about price inflation, but also about the heavy burden of their reproductive roles. In all the countries where the riots took place, women said they can no longer cope with high prices and poor wages; that the food crisis is too much for them to take; and that they are fed up and tired.
>
> (*UNDP 2009: 17*)

The food price crisis has now been compounded by the growing impact of the global economic crisis, which will further call into question the ability and willingness of women to sustain social reproduction.

IMF policy rules and the economic crisis

The financial crisis that began in 2008 on Wall Street has had an impact throughout the world, leading to a slowdown in economic growth or outright recession in most countries, including the poorest. The IMF has projected that "the 22 most vulnerable low-income countries – many of which are in Africa – will require at least $25 billion in additional concessional financing [in 2009] alone to keep their foreign reserves at safe levels" (IMF 2009a). New, more flexible, conditions were announced in late March 2009 for "precautionary loans" but these are designated for hard-hit rich and middle-income countries (such as Iceland and the Baltic countries), and only a few low-income countries will qualify. Moreover, the economic crisis has led to IMF support for expansionary fiscal and monetary policies in those rich countries that do not need IMF loans. Yet, Third World Network claims that major new IMF loans, made since the onset of the financial crisis in autumn 2008, require fiscal and monetary policy to remain "as tight and restrictive now as they have been in previous years" (Third World Network 2009).[3]

The IMF claims that it did revise inflation targets upwards in poor countries that were hard hit by price increases for imported fuel and food in 2007/8, immediately preceding the global economic crisis (IMF 2009b). In addition, the so-called structural conditions attached to the PRGF (e.g. those relating to privatization, deregulation, and removal of subsidies on fuel) have been reduced in number and given less prominence: they have become benchmarks rather than performance criteria (IMF 2009b: 24).[4] The IMF also claims that "ceilings on public sector wage bills [...] have virtually disappeared. Today, none of the 37 Fund-supported programs in LICs contains a wage bill ceiling as a performance criteria, and only three have indicative targets – a non-binding condition – on the wage bill" (IMF 2009b: 8). But critics argue that there is still pressure to reduce public sector wage bills (Weisbrot *et al.* 2009).

Critics claim that speedy reduction of budget deficits is still given too much importance, as these are often based on over-optimistic growth projections. Weisbrot *et al.* (2009) argue that PRGF agreements in 2008/9 called for reductions in the budget deficit and ceilings on the public sector wage bill in Burundi, Central African Republic, Republic of Congo, Djibouti, Ghana, and Sierra Leone. A reduction of the budget deficit was called for in Burkina Faso, the Gambia, Mali, and Senegal. In contrast, more expansionary counter-cyclical policies were permitted by PRGF conditions in Liberia, Niger, and Zambia. The IMF has been keen to publicize that Tanzania was permitted to widen the fiscal deficit,[5] but Tanzania does not have a PRGF loan; instead, it has a less onerous Extended Structural Facility. Tanzania has experienced GDP growth of about 7 percent a year since 2000 and it had already reduced its debt to GDP ratio to what the IMF considers sustainable levels. It is not typical of sub-Saharan African countries.

The IMF claims that as the recession has deepened, the budget reduction conditions attached to PRGF loans have been eased (IMF 2009b). Yet, the rules embodied in Ghana's PRGF – agreed upon in July 2009 – require a reduction in the budget deficit from 9.4 percent of GDP in 2009 to 6 percent of GDP in 2010 (Weisbrot *et al.* 2009: 33). This is to be achieved through cuts in public expenditure, especially a selective hiring freeze and lower-than-planned salary increases. An Oxfam senior policy advisor has been quoted as saying that "The IMF is too brutal [... and] the only way to make such a deep cut is in social spending [...] teachers' salaries are the main item" (Toynbee 2009). At the same time, people in Ghana are arguing that the problem is not too many public sector workers but too few. It is claimed, for instance, departments that such as the Veterinary Department and the Extension Services of the Ministry of Agriculture are short of staff, but are unable to employ the graduates of their training schools until a vacancy is created by the retirement of existing staff.[6] Still, the IMF persists in seeing public expenditure as something that hampers, rather than promotes, increases in output. The Director of the IMF Africa Department, visiting Ghana in 2009, commented that there is a "need for further fiscal consolidation to stem Ghana's rising public debt ratio and to reduce the crowding out of private sector credit which can result from domestic financing of the budget" (IMF 2009c).

Regardless of the changes that took place to somewhat loosen the policy rules attached to PRGF loans, there has been no attention given to the gender dimension of the rules – despite concerns that low-income women in low-income countries may be particularly adversely affected by the crisis. Therefore, we may see a growing tension in sub-Saharan African and other low-income countries, between a fracturing gender order and the policy rules of the IMF, with women breaking through the strategic silence to voice their discontent and their inability and unwillingness to sustain social reproduction. A rewriting of national and international macroeconomic policy rules is needed to engender a more egalitarian gender order, encompassing both production and social reproduction (Elson 2002; Warnecke 2006), but currently the prospects do not look bright.

Notes

1 The IMF announced in July 2009 that the PRGF will be replaced by a new Extended Credit Facility (ECF) (www.imf.org/external/np/exr/facts/pgrf.htm). It appears that this will not differ substantially from the PRGF in terms of policy rules, although it will not require the prior preparation of a PRSP (www.brettonwoodsproject.org/art-565313; www.fpif.org/fpiftxt/6422).
2 This report was written by IMF staff member Caroline Robb.
3 This report covers all IMF facilities (not only the PRGF), and includes loans to middle-income countries in Eastern Europe and the Baltic region.
4 Focus on structural reforms has not, however, disappeared completely. As the IMF puts it: "Use of structural performance criteria was discontinued on May 1, 2009 in all fund-supported programs ... and specific structural conditions that are monitored under reviews will take the form of structural benchmarks. The aim is to provide countries with more flexibility in achieving their reform goals, putting more focus on the goals themselves and less on specific time-bound measures, thereby enhancing ownership and the likelihood of improving results" (IMF 2009b: 24). So while structural performance criteria have disappeared, structural benchmarks remain.
5 See IMF press conference (www.imf.org/external/np/tr/2009/tr060109.htm).
6 See http://crossedcrocodiles.wordpress.com/2009/07/20.

Bibliography

ActionAid International (2005) *Changing Course: Alternative Approaches to Achieve the Millennium Development Goals and Fight HIV/AIDS*, Washington DC: ActionAid International.

Aizenman, J. and Lee, J. (2005) "International Reserves: Precautionary Versus Mercantilist Views, Theory and Evidence," NBER Working Paper Series, No. 11366: 1–28.

Akintola, O. (2004) "The Gendered Burden of Home-Based Care Giving," Policy Brief, Durban: Health Economics and HIV/AIDS Research Division, University of KwaZulu Natal.

Akram-Lodhi, A.H. (2007) "HIV/AIDS and human development: rethinking the economics using gender," powerpoint presentation to UNDP Expert Group Meeting on Gender Equality, Economic Growth and Poverty Reduction.

Ashby, J., Hartl, M., Lambrou, Y., Larson, G., Lubbock, A., Pehu, E. and Ragasa, C. (2009) "Investing in women as drivers of agricultural growth," International Fund for Agricultural Development. Online. Available at: http://www.ifad.org/gender/pub/sourcebook/flyer.pdf (accessed March 12, 2009).

Bakker, I. (1994) "Introduction: Engendering Macro-Economic Policy Reform in the Era of Global Restructuring and Adjustment," in I. Bakker (ed.) *The Strategic Silence: Gender and Economic Policy*, London: Zed Books.

Berndt, M., Dudine, P., Martijn, J.K. and Shonchoy, A. (2008) "The Spending and Absorption of Aid in PRGF Supported Programs," Working Paper No. 238, Washington DC: International Monetary Fund.

Bird, G. and Rajan, R. (2003) "Too Much of a Good Thing? The Adequacy of International Reserves in the Aftermath of Crises," *World Economy*, 26(6): 873–91.

Bird, K., Curran, Z., Evans, A. and Plagerson, S. (2005) "What has DFID Learned from the PSIA Process?" Poverty and Public Policy Group. London: Overseas Development Institute.

Blackden, C.M. and Wodon, Q. (eds) (2006) *Gender, Time Use, and Poverty in Sub-Saharan Africa*, Washington DC: The World Bank.

Bryson, J.C. (1981) "Women and Agriculture in Sub-Saharan Africa: An Exploratory Study," *Journal of Development Studies*, 17(3): 29–46.

Budlender, D. and Hewitt, G. (eds) (2002) *Gender Budgets Make More Cents*, London: Commonwealth Secretariat.

Center for Global Development (2007) *Does the IMF Constrain Health Spending in Poor Countries? Evidence and an Agenda for Action*, Washington DC: Center for Global Development.

Chen, M., J. Vanek, F. Lund, J. Heintz with R. Jhabvala and C. Bonner (2005) *Progress of the World's Women 2005*, New York: United Nations Development Fund for Women (UNIFEM).

Cleaver, K. and Schreiber, G. (1994) *Reversing the Spiral: The Population, Agriculture and Environment Nexus in Sub-Saharan Africa*, Directions in Development Series, Washington DC: World Bank.

Cruz, M. and B. Walters (2008) "Is the Accumulation of International Reserves Good for Development?" *Cambridge Journal of Economics*, 32: 665–681.

Doss, C. (1999) "Twenty-Five Years of Research on Women Farmers in Africa: Lessons and Implications for Agricultural Research Institutions." CIMMYT Economics Program Paper No. 99-02. MEXICO D.F.: CIMMYT.

Elson, D. (1991) "Male Bias in Macro-Economics: The Case of Structural Adjustment," in D. Elson (ed.) *Male Bias in the Development Process*, Manchester: Manchester University Press.

——— (1994) "Micro–Meso–Macro: Gender and Economic Analysis in the Context of Policy Reform," in I. Bakker (ed.) *The Strategic Silence: Gender and Economic Policy*, London: Zed Books.

——— (1995) "Household Responses to Stabilisation and Structural Adjustment: Male Bias at the Micro Level," in D. Elson (ed.) *Male Bias in the Development Process*, Second edition, Manchester: Manchester University Press.

——— (2002) "The International Financial Architecture – A View From the Kitchen," *Femina Politica*, 11(1): 26–37.

Fedelino, A. and Zakharova, D. (2006) "Reflections on Quantitative Fiscal Conditionality in African PRGF-Supported Programs," IMF Working Paper No. 118, Washington DC: International Monetary Fund.

Floro, M.S. (1995) "Economic Restructuring, Gender and the Allocation of Time," *World Development*, 23(11): 1913–1929.

Fontana, M. (2003) "Modeling the effects of trade on women, at work and at home: a comparative perspective," Trade and Macroeconomics Division, Discussion Paper No. 10, Washington DC: International Food Policy Research Institute (IFPRI).

——— (2005) "Unpaid household work and CGE models: strengths and limitations," Presentation at Global conference on Unpaid Work and the Economy. Levy Economics Institute of Bard College.

Forum for Women in Democracy (FOWODE) (1999) *Sharing the National Cake*, Kampala: FOWODE.

——— (2008) Gender in the Budget Speech, Kampala: FOWODE.

Gacitua-Mario, E., Gros, C. and Kirsch, R. (2008) "Stakeholder Power and Policy Dialogue: Agricultural Reform Lessons," *Poverty in Focus*, 14, Brasilia: International Poverty Centre.

Gillingham, R. (ed.) (2008) *Poverty and Social Impact Analysis by the IMF: Review of Methodology and Selected Evidence*, Washington DC: International Monetary Fund.

Goldsborough, D. (2007) "The IMF and Constraints on Spending Aid," International Poverty Centre One Pager No. 35, Brasilia: UNDP International Poverty Centre.

Grown, C. (2006) "Quick Impact Initiatives for Gender Equality: A Menu of Options," Working Paper No. 462, Annandale-on-Hudson: Levy Economic Institute.

Guha, S. and Goswami, S. (2006) "Impact of Gender Budgeting on Women's Empowerment." Online. Available at: http://www.gender-budgets.org/content/view/645/153/ (accessed January 29, 2009).

Gupta, S., Powell, R. and Yang, Y. (2006) "Macroeconomic Challenges of Scaling Up Aid to Africa: A Checklist for Practitioners," Washington DC: International Monetary Fund.

Heller, P. (2005) "Back to Basics – Fiscal Space: What Is It and How to Get It," *Finance and Development*, 42(2). Online. Available at: http://www.imf.org/external/pubs/ft/fandd/2005/06/basics.htm (accessed April 3, 2009).

Holmes, R. and Slater, R. (2007) "Realising gender in agricultural policies: The fight for equality is not over," *Opinion 91*, London: Overseas Development Institute.

Independent Evaluation Office (IEO) (2007) *An Evaluation of the IMF and Aid to Sub-Saharan Africa*, Washington DC: International Monetary Fund.

International Monetary Fund (2005) "Monetary and Fiscal Policy Design Issues in Low-Income Countries," Policy Development and Review Department and Fiscal Affairs Department, Washington DC: International Monetary Fund.

——— (2008) "A Factsheet: The Poverty Reduction and Growth Facility (PRGF)." Online. Available at: http://www.imf.org/external/np/exr/facts/prgf.htm (accessed January 28, 2009).

——— (2009a). "Africa Conference: IMF Pledges to help Africa get through global crisis," IMF Survey Magazine 3/10/09. Online. Available at: http://www.imf.org/external/pubs/ft/survey/so/2009/NEW031009A.htm (accessed March 11, 2009).

——— (2009b) "Creating Policy Space – Responsive Design and Streamlined Conditionality in Recent Low-Income Country Programs," Strategy, Policy and Review Department, Washington DC: International Monetary Fund.

——— (2009c) "Statement by IMF African Department Director Antoinette Sayeh at the Conclusion of her Visit to Ghana," Press Release No. 09, November 3, Washington DC: International Monetary Fund.

——— (2010) "Poverty and Social Impact Analysis of Economic Policies." Online. Available at: http://www.imf.org/external/np/exr/facts/pdf/sia.pdf (accessed April 25, 2010).

International Poverty Centre (2007) "Using ODA to Accumulate Foreign Reserves in Sub-Saharan Africa," *One Pager*, 37.

Ismihan, M. and Ozkan, F. (2004) "Does central bank independence lower inflation?" *Economics Letters*, 84(3): 305–309.

Johnston, D. (2008) "Bias, Not Error: Assessments of the Economic Impact of HIV/Aids Using Evidence from Micro Studies in Sub-Saharan Africa," *Feminist Economics*, 14(4): 87–115.

Kgware, M. (2006) "Men as carers: a case study," mimeo. Oxfam Australia.

Kisamba-Mugerwa, M. (2001) "Empowering Low-Income Women for Enhanced Food Security in Sub-Saharan Africa," Presentation at Conference Sustainable Food Security for all by 2020, Bonn: IFPRI's 2020 Vision Initiative.

Lapavitsas, C. (2007) "Using ODA to Accumulate Foreign Reserves in Sub-Saharan Africa," International Poverty Centre One Pager No. 37, Brasilia: UNDP International Poverty Centre.

Lloyd, C.B., Grant, M. and Ritchie, A. (2008) "Gender Differences in Time Use among Adolescents in Developing Countries: Implications of Rising School Enrollment Rates," *Journal of Research on Adolescents*, 18(1): 99–120.

McKinley, T. (2005) "Why is the 'Dutch Disease' Always a Disease? The Macroeconomic Consequences of Scaling Up ODA," International Poverty Centre Working Paper No. 10, Brasilia: UNDP International Poverty Centre.

McKinley, T. (2007) "Why is Africa Constrained From Spending ODA?" International Poverty Centre One Pager No. 34, Brasilia: UNDP International Poverty Centre.

McKinley, T. and Hailu, D. (2006) "The Macroeconomic Debate on Scaling Up HIV/AIDS Financing," International Poverty Centre Policy Research Brief No. 1, Brasilia: UNDP International Poverty Centre.

Nayyar, D. (2003) "Why is Macroeconomics Different in Developing Countries?" Initiative for Policy Dialogue Working Paper. Task Force for Macroeconomic Policy, Columbia University.

Ogden, J., Esim, S. and Grown, C. (2006) "Expanding the Care Continuum for HIV/AIDS: Bringing Carers Into Focus," *Health Policy and Planning*, 21(5): 333–342.

Quisumbing, A. and Pandolfelli, L. (2008) "Promising Approaches to Address the Needs of Poor Female Farmers," *IFPRI Note 13*, Washington DC: International Food Policy Research Institute.

Robb, C.M. (2003) "Poverty and Social Impact Analysis – Linking Macroeconomic Policies to Poverty Outcomes: Summary of Early Experiences," IMF Working Paper No. 43, Washington DC: International Monetary Fund.

Rodrik, D. (2006) "The Social Cost of Foreign Exchange Reserves," *International Economic Journal*, 30(3): 253–266.

Roy, R., Heuty, A. and Letouzé, E. (2006) "Fiscal Space for Public Investment: A Human Development Approach." Paper prepared for the G-24 Technical Meeting. Online. Available at: http://www.g24.org/rroy0906.pdf (accessed March 12, 2009).

Schuberth, H. (2004) "Knightian Uncertainty, Accountability and Economic Policy Rules," in: Mooslechner, P., Schuberth, H. and M. Schürz (eds) *Economic Policy Under Uncertainty: The Role of Truth and Accountability in Policy Advice*, Edward Elgar: Cheltenham, UK/ Northhampton, MA, USA.

Seguino, S. (2009) "The Global Economic Crisis and its Gender Implications," Comments prepared for Gender Perspectives on the Financial Crisis Panel at the Fifty-Third Session of the Commission on the Status of Women.

Somma, A. (2008) "The 10 percent that could change Africa," *IFPRI Forum*, Washington DC: International Food Policy Research Institute.

Third World Network (2009) "Statement to the Commission of Experts of the President on the United Nations General Assembly on Reforms of the International Monetary and Financial System." Online. Available at: www.twnside.org.sg/pos.htm (accessed March 20, 2009).

Toynbee, P. (2009) "Wall Street wounded Ghana: IMF tonic could hurt it more," the *Guardian*, April 18, London.
UNAIDS (2008) "2007 Sub-Saharan Africa AIDS epidemic update, regional summary," Geneva: UNAIDS and the World Health Organization.
UNIFEM (2001) *Gender Budget Initiatives: Strategies, Concepts and Experiences*, New York: UNIFEM.
UNDP (2009) "Gender equality and the global food, fuel and financial crises: a perspective from Africa," mimeo.
Warnecke, T. (2006) "A Gender-Aware Approach to International Finance," in B. Clary, W. Dolfsma and D. Figart (eds) *Ethics and the Market – Social Economic Contributions*, New York: Routledge.
Weisbrot, M. (2009) "CEPR Responds to the IMF's Reply and Defence of its Policies in the World Recession," Discussion Paper, Center for Economic and Policy Research, Washington DC.
Weisbrot, M., Ray, R., Johnston, J., Cordero, J.A. and Montecino, J.A. (2009) "IMF Supported Macroeconomic Policies and the World Recession: A Look at Forty-One Borrowing Countries," Discussion Paper, Center for Economic and Policy Research, Washington DC.
World Bank (2001) Engendering Development through Gender Equality in Rights, Resources and Voice, Policy Research Report, Washington DC: World Bank.
——— (2006) *Stakeholders, Power Relations and Policy Dialogue: Social Analysis in Agriculture Sector Poverty and Social Impact Analysis*, Washington DC: World Bank.
——— (2007a) *Agriculture for Development*, The 2008 World Development Report, Washington DC: World Bank.
——— (2007b) *Gender and Economic Growth in Kenya*, Washington DC: World Bank.
——— (2009) *Gender in Agriculture Sourcebook*, The World Bank, the Food and Agriculture Organization, and International Fund for Agricultural Development, Washington DC: International Bank for Reconstruction and Development and the World Bank.

7

THE ROLE OF GENDER IN GOVERNANCE OF THE FINANCIAL SECTOR

Helene Schuberth and Brigitte Young

Introduction

Over ten years ago, Pierre Bourdieu referred to financial capital as the "new Leviathan" (Bourdieu *et al.* 1997). Using the allegorical figure of the fearless sea monster to describe the omnipotence that emanates from financial markets (rather than the state, as Hobbes suggests) he identified the increasing powerlessness and helplessness felt by many ordinary people. The convergence of laissez-faire capitalist values and liberal conceptions of democracy has become a global phenomenon. Today, the destructive effects of self-regulated financial markets have, to paraphrase Alan Greenspan, put "those of us who have looked to the self-interest of lending institutions to protect shareholders' equity, myself included, in a state of shocked disbelief."[1] Years before the present crisis, Bourdieu had pointed out the discrepancy between a global private sector and a public sector that is no longer capable of providing public goods as the necessary basis for social stability and democratic governance. Aspects of human life have increasingly been reduced into objects (commodities) for sale and purchase within economistic systems of market exchange. As a result we witness an emerging global contradiction between the extended power of capital (and the protection by the state) and the increasing human insecurity of a majority of the world's population (Bakker and Gill 2003).

Financial market regulation, by far the most influential and important economic policy field having a sizeable impact on everyday life, is conducted largely behind closed doors, excluding those who are most affected by the spill-over effects of financial governance arrangements into other areas of the "real" economy. Finance is shaped by private-state networks and webs incorporated into multi-level institutional processes and practices. Mechanisms of democratic accountability that typically apply to nation-states are largely missing. Far from assuming that financial governance is reducible to technical fine-tuning, the crisis has demonstrated that different financial governance arrangements have quite different distributional effects. The present market-based financial system has evolved through aggressively implementing regulatory changes that promote a shift to self-regulation and market-based supervision in the governance of global finance which is dominant in Anglo-Saxon countries. These changes have led to increased inequalities in income and wealth by weakening unionized industrial relations, privatizing pension schemes, and making the principle of social solidarity less acceptable in many societies (Mooslechner 2004). Furthermore, financial governance modes have a decisive impact on the degree of financial stability: the Anglo-Saxon regulatory model, which was pushed to the fore by the financial industry with strong support from the vast majority of mainstream economists, has increased the frequency and intensity of financial crises (Reinhard and Rogoff 2009). A certain "groupthink" – a result of decision-making bodies drawn from a narrow social group – has been widely blamed for the financial crisis (Tsingou 2010; Young and Schuberth 2010). Financial crises are thus deeply rooted in a specific regulatory regime and are not the result of accidents, avoidable the next time around by adjusting some minor regulatory screws.

From the perspective of democratic legitimacy, decision making in regard to policies that have distributional effects needs broad-based participation of those affected by it; as such, it requires input legitimacy (Scharpf 1999), the representation of a wider constituency in decision making. One of the most striking features of the prevailing financial governance architecture is the increasingly mitigated role of the state and the shift of regulatory competence to private institutions, what we have termed *financial governance without government*. The prevailing financial system is organized in such a manner as to provide private goods for the benefit of the few (Cerny 2005). But it is widely recognized that financial stability is a global public good (Kaul *et al.* 2003). As a result, the financial sector is thus of strategic public interest.

Given this context, this paper will be looking at one dimension which has not been given sufficient attention, namely the low representation of women in financial markets regulation which we refer to as *financial governance without women*. This issue has – apart from some media attention – met with little interest in academic research.[2] Yet, a gendered analysis of the nature of representation, risk, and regulation is important for a deeper understanding of the finance sector. Whether the crisis could have been avoided if more women had been at the helm of large investment banks is a hotly contested issue, and one that is not the focus of this paper. Nevertheless, this debate, and the crisis more generally, has turned a spot light on the low or even non-existent female representation in top positions of financial institutions, as well as decision-making bodies in key regulatory institutions, central banks, and formal and informal financial networks.

Our interest is in the global regulatory reforms that exclude those who are affected most by the financial crisis: workers, minorities, women, and members of less developed countries. In addressing these exclusions, we call for regulatory reforms that are built on the normative premise that the task of finance is to serve society in terms of growth, efficiency, and equity. A gendered approach is important, since it focuses on factors such as rights, equitable outcomes, and an alternative order that values collective interests over the private. Thus the paper raises questions not just about who sits at the table of financial governance, but rather what are the confines of the reform debates, who benefits and why, what are the social benefits of the present financial system, what are the risks of financial innovations to systemic financial stability, and how could a more humane alternative, one that takes into account social needs of care and reproduction, be envisioned and implemented.

Mooslechner *et al.* (2006) propose an approach that looks at inclusion and exclusion from both a narrow (procedural) perspective and a broader (substantive) perspective. The narrow perspective examines questions of input legitimacy: Who is part of the decision-making bodies? Whose voice is heard? And what are the mechanisms by which female exclusion takes place? From a substantive perspective, these procedural aspects are linked to the economic, social, political, and cultural effects of the prevailing regulatory regime. They are often indirect and invisible, even though they are important. Linking the procedural with the substantive perspective is essential. Strengthening input legitimacy by increasing female representation in decision-making bodies is a necessary but not sufficient precondition for safeguarding specific women's interests. Membership in the notoriously exclusive male clubs of regulatory decision-making bodies often involves the subordination of women's interests to the standards and norms of these epistemic communities – which themselves adhere to rigid disciplinary boundaries (Tsingou 2010). Deviations from these norms are discredited as unscientific, subjective, and irrational and are interpreted as an inappropriate digression from the model-based objective mode of thinking. With this caveat in mind, we argue that female representation only makes a difference if it comes with an alternative conception of financial order.

We proceed as follows in the paper. In the next section we discuss the role of the economics profession in shaping current regulatory arrangements. We argue that the economic orthodoxy and its rules of financial governance carry a set of norms about men and women that in turn shape risk taking and risk sharing. In the third section, we demonstrate the mechanisms of female exclusion in the global financial architecture by highlighting the mechanisms (what we term *financial governance without women*) operating within the global financial architecture to block women from the top decision-making positions in financial governance institutions and networks in the US (Table 7.1) and the European Union (EU) (Table 7.2), in intergovernmental private and global regulatory institutions (Table 7.3), and in regulatory reform initiatives (Table 7.4). In the fourth section, we give an overview of the institutional arrangements and the main driving forces behind the evolution of the prevailing global financial architecture. In the fifth section, we explore the gender impacts of financial governance arrangements and argue that there are at least two channels through which the financial structure impacts on gender: The direct and most dominant channel is corporate governance modes that have an impact on resource allocation among stakeholders and shareholders. The other channel is the method through which financial governance shapes how risks are "down loaded" and individualized. In the final section of this paper, we discuss the extent to which banking stabilization and stimulus packages disproportionally benefit males.

The role of economics in financial governance

The construction of the rational man in finance

Neoclassical economics in general – and financial economics in particular – assumes that markets are populated by disembodied rational actors pursuing profit maximization and contributing to efficiency and overall welfare. In the last decade, finance as an academic discipline and professional practice has increasingly come to be conceptualized as independent from arenas such as society, history, and politics. Efficient market hypothesis has been the key proposition of neoclassical finance for almost 40 years which claims that financial markets price assets precisely at their intrinsic worth given all the publicly available information (Fama 1970). In this view, assets are valued rationally and prices are established on the basis of investors' immediate information. Even if irrational investors enter the market, rational arbitrageurs will be cognizant of the mispricing and bring prices back to equilibrium levels.[3] This doctrine has been politically enforced by strong vested interests that were able to capture the state: Since the 1980s, states have increasingly formed alliances with private actors through financial liberalization (Lütz 2006) and thus have been able to steer global financial markets toward neoliberal outcomes. Accepting the efficient-market-hypothesis also meant a normative shift to "trust the market" promulgated by neoclassical economics turning a blind eye to the limitations of human rationality that can lead to sudden unpredictable boom–bust cycles (Krugman 2009). Understanding the historical evolution of the normative shift from Adam Smith to John Maynard Keynes to a return to neoclassicism is essential for comprehending the gendered nature of the conceptual apparatus of modern finance.

Marieke de Goede (2005) argues that the discourse on finance is based upon a distinctively masculine conception, through which financial crises are relegated to the territory of madness and delusion. With the widespread dissemination of credit and paper money in the eighteenth century, public discussions and literary representations of the new credit embodied negative and stereotypically female qualities such as loose morals, emotional instability, and hysteria. De Goede examines Daniel Defoe's satirical personification, Lady Credit. Lady Credit symbolizes all the irrational and unpredictable aspects that had to be eliminated from financial discourse in order for the latter to be respected as rational, disinterested, and scientific. Scientific respectability could only be achieved through the appropriation of both statistical practices and moral ascetics from the natural sciences. The financial discourse implies that in times of crisis *financial man* loses self-control and is prevented from seeing economic reality by the delusions that Lady Credit generates. The virile mastering of Lady Credit guarantees the smooth and neutral workings of the financial sphere. This conceptualization of a divide between feminine irrationality, on the one hand, which disturbs the smooth and stable functioning of financial markets, and masculine rationality, on the other hand, which generates efficient markets and benefits all, is implicitly inherent in the debates on financial crisis today. This distinction is maintained precisely because finance is male dominated, and the fact that mostly men have been in the driver's seat in the present financial meltdown.

Until autumn 2008, when the world economy came close to a systemic financial meltdown, several crisis explanations were put forward. They hold in common the belief that the crisis was a minor accident that can be avoided by adjusting some of the regulatory screws (i.e. by reforming rating agencies, improving cooperation among regulatory authorities, and increasing transparency). They further hold that the major explanatory factors behind financial bubbles and busts are collective greed and moral indecency that cannot be legislated away. Instead of calling for strict legislation that starts with the assumption that boom and bust cycles are a systemic phenomenon of unregulated markets (Semmler 2006), blame is placed on greedy and boundless human nature, on irrational and boisterous investment decisions.

During episodes of crisis, the conventional wisdom that efficient financial markets stabilize the economy is temporarily modified. Waves of optimistic and pessimistic sentiments come to the fore. All of a sudden, the characteristics of the economic man equipped with all the necessary formal skills of a rational finance investor deviate from virtuous and prudent behavior – the separation of rational man from irrational females is forcefully preserved by using female attributes such as "hysteria" and "delusion" in the description of the financial crisis.

The ideological premise that women deviate from economic rationality, that they are inherently less rational, less proficient in mathematics, formal economics and science[4] serves to justify women's exclusion. This gendered discourse, and the assumptions about gender differences which underpin it, interests us in two respects: first, the socially constructed notion that women are prone to irrationality, delusion, hysteria, etc. functions to legitimate women's exclusion from finance. But research that tests theories of behavioral finance has shown that male financial investors are generally more risk-prone than women and hence less rational (Barber and Odean 2001). Because of their over-confidence, investors will trade too frequently, thereby increasing risk and reducing returns. Moreover, female investors have been found to be more risk-averse and to avoid aggressive competition (Beckmann and Menkhoff 2008; Niederle and Vesterlund 2005). These studies show that women investors are quite rational in their trading practices.

Sociological characteristics of supervisory authorities – networks of epistemic communities

Financial market regulation, a policy field bringing together the concerns of both financial economics and regulation, is significantly influenced by economic science. Regulators, for instance, rely on private sector risk models when defining banks' need for capital reserves (Redak 2006). But despite the sophisticated models, the current crisis took everybody by surprise. The risk models were and still are inherently incapable of identifying systemic risks (Hellwig 2008). Systemic risk is increased by the homogeneity of these models, and the extent to which they disregard both the complex interactions between financial actors and institutions as well as the counterparty risks of insurers to whom the credit risks were transferred.

Deregulation of financial markets, and the global move toward the Anglo-Saxon self-regulatory model, whereby "soft law" (i.e. voluntary rules and standards of good conduct) is applied, can be appropriately described as *financial governance without government*. The main characteristics of the current regulatory regime include a multi-level system of governance, the strong involvement of private sector entities in regulation, and the exclusion of nation-states in favor of private sector entities, experts, and independent authorities. This governance model, based on groupthink, was forcefully advanced by proponents of the efficient market hypothesis (all of whom were white men). They viewed the emergence of new financial instruments and a shadow banking system that evolved outside the scope of existing regulation to be efficiency enhancing, (such as speculative investment vehicles,[5] elements of the originate and distribute securitization process as well as new off-balance sheet financial vehicles established by banks (Tett 2009)).

Liberalized regulatory rules have operated through international networks of state bureaucracies, independent regulatory agencies, representatives of the financial industry, and economic experts. This is part of a more general restructuring of the state–market relationship on a global scale, in which financial market regulation is far less legitimated through political processes of nation-states. Instead, expert knowledge and professional practices have become increasingly important. Parallel to the retreat of the state from financial regulation is the disappearance of political debate on such issues as the importance of regulation on systemic stability, and its relevance for corporate governance and for income and wealth distribution. The emergence of "epistemic communities" (Haas 1992) can be viewed as a characteristic feature of the new forms of global governance. These networks have in many ways facilitated the international diffusion of neoliberal regulatory practices and their coordination around the world.

The various networks of knowledge-based experts are basically exclusive men's clubs, equipped with an authoritative claim to policy-relevant knowledge. Experts hold a common set of central beliefs and standards of validity that are expressed in internally defined criteria for evaluation, common policy objectives, and shared normative commitments. The research and analysis of regulatory bodies and authorities are motivated by the internal logic of self-referential epistemic communities validated by mathematical models rather than by a desire to understand how the financial markets work and their implication for overall welfare, distribution, and security. Alternative approaches that include the insights of other social sciences and heterodox economics are mostly disregarded (Krugman 2009). In the rare cases when women were granted entrance to these clubs, they were compelled to subordinate themselves to the common set of beliefs defined by male economists. Those who try to intervene and offer alternatives to the reductionist understanding of finance are either unemployed, or marginalized and denied career opportunities. This observation is not just based on anecdotal evidence;[6] it is a major systemic characteristic of global financial governance.

In making this argument, we do not subscribe to an essentialist view of gender that regards the crisis as inherently male. Rather, we argue that the knowledge base underpinning the financial sector reinforces class hierarchy and the pursuit of wealth, and that social actors and their interests are denied representation in financial governance. We begin with the premise that there exists a gender order of norms, values, and hierarchies, which is reflected in the different approaches to risk and can be considered as one of the primary factors of the financial crisis.

Delegation to independent agencies

One influential view in economic policy circles and supervisory bodies considers financial governance to be an exclusive expert terrain, in which output legitimacy is achieved to the extent that clear statutory objectives (such as financial stability and transparency requirements) are fulfilled. This kind of legitimacy may suffice if the goal of policy is to find ways of improving the overall well-being of societies. But a policy with redistributive consequences can only be legitimated by voters and their elected representatives (Majone 1997). Hence, any policy with implications for redistribution requires input legitimacy; the incorporation of all groups in the decision-making process that are affected by financial governance. In reality, financial regulation has been increasingly conducted beyond the political sphere and governed by semi-state institutions (such as independent central banks and regulatory authorities) and the financial industry itself. The financial crisis has revealed significant problems of regulatory capture that emerge when regulatory bodies incorporate private interests while excluding the interest of the public. It follows that "state-anchored security is inseparable from democracy" (Dorn 2009). From this perspective, women's lack of representation in financial market regulation is undemocratic, especially given the fact that they are disproportionately affected by financial crises – a truth we witnessed during the Asian Crisis (1997/98) and the Latin American Crisis (2000/2002) (Singh and Zammit 2000; Limm 2000; Young 2003). As these studies have shown, financial governance has a tremendous impact on the everyday life of women (see Chapter 4).

Financial governance without women

Women are under-represented in the top decision-making positions of key regulatory institutions and networks (both formal and informal).[7]

In the US women are better represented than their European counterparts; in the Securities and Exchange Commission (SEC), women make up 60 percent of the five commissioners (one of whom is the first woman to serve as the agency's permanent chair) (Table 7.1). But one has to bear in mind that women's representation in US financial governance institutions improved only after the meltdown in the financial sector.[8]

In contrast to the US, female representation in the supervisory structures of the EU is low.[9] Table 7.2 depicts selective committees of the Lamfalussy architecture, which are comprised of representatives of supervisory bodies of the EU-countries. This committee structure was implemented in 2001 to deal with security issues and

TABLE 7.1 Female representation in financial governance institutions and networks in the US

US institutions	*Female (%)*	*Number of members*	*Chair*
Securities and Exchange Commission (SEC)[a]	60	5	F[b]
The Federal Reserve System (FED)[c]	20	10	M
US Commodity Futures Trading Commission (CFTC)[d]	25[e]	4	M
Federal Deposit Insurance Corporation (FDIC)[f]	20	5	F

Notes

a http://www.sec.gov/about/commissioner.shtml (SEC commissioners).

b Mary L. Schapiro was formally nominated upon Obama's inauguration into office on January 20, 2009 as Chairwoman of the Securities and Exchange Commission.

c http://www.federalreserve.gov/monetarypolicy/fomc.htm (members of the federal open market committee).

d http://www.cftc.gov/aboutthecftc/commissioners/index.htm (CFTC Commissioners).

e The female member of the CFTC is Jill E. Sommers. She was re-nominated by President Obama on July 20, 2009 for a second five-year term.

f http://www.fdic.gov/about/learn/board/index.html (FDIC board of directors).

was extended to banking and insurance in 2004. The Lamfalussy process is supposed to speed up legislation on harmonization, liberalization, and deregulation of financial services in the EU (Financial Services Action Plan) through splitting decisions and implementation measures containing technical details. Legislation on framework principles (Level 1) is determined by the Council and the European Parliament on the basis of Commission proposals. The technical details are delegated to various committees at Level 2. The committee's task at Level 3 is to ensure enhanced cooperation and networking during the transposition of EU measures into national law. Thus the process of rule-making has been Europeanized. This implies strictly limiting the role of the national policy processes, such as national parliaments, since the process is now in the hands of the European policy network. This supranationalization of financial integration is dominated by a very small circle of experts excluding stakeholders who are affected by the finance-led restructuring of the European financial sector. As a result, it is empowering expert committees at the expense of a more democratic legitimate decision-making process (Weber 2006).

Table 7.3 gives an overview of women's representation in select public as well as private global institutions with regulatory competencies. The lack of women in intergovernmental decision-making bodies is well documented (Warnecke 2006), and representation in private sector institutions is equally negligible. Among the latter is the International Accounting Standards Board (IASB), which has adopted fair value accounting in International Financial Reporting Standards (IFRS) (Novoa *et al.* 2009). Another influential global network included in this study is the

TABLE 7.2 Female representation in financial governance institutions and networks in the EU

European committees and institutions	*Female (%)*	*Number of members*	*Chair*
The European Central Bank (ECB)[a]	5	22	M
Lamfalussy Level I			
Economic and Financial Affairs Council (ECOFIN)	11	27	M
Economic and Financial Committee (EFC)	7	67	M
European Commission, DG Internal Market & Services[b]	17	12	M
European Commission, DG Economic & Financial Affairs[c]	18	11	M
Lamfalussy Level II			
European Securities Committee (ESC)[d]	28.5	28	M
Lamfalussy Level III			
Committee of European Banking Supervisors (CEBS)[e]	11	47	M
Committee of European Securities Regulators (CESR)[f]	16.5	30	M
Committee of European Insurance and Occupational Pensions Supervisors (CEIOPS)[g]	0	5[h]	M

Notes

a http://www.ecb.int/ecb/orga/decisions/govc/html/index.en.html (members of the Governing Council).

b http://ec.europa.eu/dgs/internal_market/departments_en.htm (commissioner and directors).

c http://ec.europa.eu/staffdir/plsql/gsys_www.branch?pLang=EN&pId=3&pDisplayAll=1 (commissioner and directors).

d http://ec.europa.eu/internal_market/securities/docs/esc/esc-members_en.pdf (ESC members).

e http://www.c-ebs.org/Aboutus/Organisation/Members.aspx (CEBS members).

f http://www.cesr-eu.org/index.php?page=members_directory&mac=0&id= (CESR members).

g http://www.ceiops.org/content/view/99/122/ (CEIOPS managing board).

h Due to the unavailability of data, the management board instead of the member state representatives has been taken into account. This accounts for the huge difference in numbers of members in CEIOPS and its sister organisations, CESR and CEBS, respectively.

Basel Committee on Banking Supervision, an informal forum of supervisors and central bankers of G10 that formulates broad supervisory standards and guidelines, and recommends statements of best practice in banking supervision.

In a report on reforms of the international monetary and financial system, the Stiglitz Commission concludes that, "those who are affected by the failure of regulation [...] should have a large voice in any regulatory structure" (Stiglitz 2009). This principle was largely disregarded in all of the wise men and expert committees that were set up by the G20 to prepare proposals for regulatory reforms (Table 7.4).

TABLE 7.3 Female representation in intergovernmental, private and global regulatory institutions

Institution	*Female (%)*	*Number of members*	*Chair*
Intergovernmental institutions			
IMF Board of Directors	4.5	24	M
World Bank Board of Directors	12	24	M
Private sector entities			
International Accounting Standards Board (IASB)[a]	7	13	M
International Institute of Finance (IIF)[b]	0	30	M
Global committees			
The International Organization of Securities Commissions (IOSCO)[c]	30	20	F
Basel Committee on Banking Supervision[d]	8	25[e]	M
International Association of Insurance Supervisors (IAIS)[f]	6	17[g]	M

Notes

a http://en.wikipedia.org/wiki/International_Accounting_Standards_Board#IASB_Members (IASB members).

b http://www.iif.com/about/bod/ (IIF board members).

c http://www.iosco.org/lists/display_committees.cfm?cmtid=5 (IOSCO members of the executive committee).

d http://www.bis.org/bcbs/organigram.pdf.

e In contrast to the other intergovernmental, private and global regulatory institutions, female representation in the Basel committee structure has been used instead of member representation due to a lack of public information on membership.

f http://www.iaisweb.org/__temp/2007-2008_Annual_report.pdf.

g In case of the IAIS, only the executive committee has been taken into consideration.

The De Larosière Group, which at the request of President Barroso prepared proposals for EU regulatory reforms and architecture, had only male members. Similarly, the Working Group on the reform of the IMF was exclusively comprised of men, and even the Stiglitz Commission had only two female members.

Global financial architecture – evolution, legitimacy, and representation

Development of the current regulatory regime

Conventional wisdom explains the globalization of finance as an inescapable process brought about by strong market forces. In search of the highest yields, global, fluid, and borderless money bypasses regulation and leaves little policy maneuverability than to lift restrictions on the mobility of capital. While this powerful narrative

TABLE 7.4 Female representation in regulatory reform initiatives

Wise men and expert committees	*Female (%)*	*Number of members*	*Chair*
High Level Expert Group on EU Financial Supervision Larosière Group[a]		8	M
G20 Working Group 1[b] Enhancing Sound Regulation and Strengthening Transparency	7	29	M
G20 Working Group 2[c] Reinforcing International Cooperation and Promoting Integrity in Financial Markets	4	27	M
G20 Working Group 3[d] Reform of the IMF	0	27	M
Stiglitz Commission[e] The Commission of Experts of the President of the UN General Assembly on Reforms of the International Monetary and Financial System	9	22	M

Notes

a http://ec.europa.eu/commission_barroso/president/pdf/statement_20090225_en.pdf (De Larosière Group).

b http://www.g20.org/Documents/g20_wg1_010409.pdf (Working Group 1 members).

c http://www.g20.org/Documents/g20_wg2_010409.pdf (Working Group 2 members and experts).

d http://www.g20.org/Documents/g20_wg3_010409.pdf (Working Group 3 members and participants).

e http://www.un.org/ga/president/63/commission/members.shtml (members of the commission).

has been circulated *ad nauseam*, recent research has shown that financial integration was a deliberate political strategy – one among a set of viable alternatives – that was enforced with strong backing by legal, political, and intellectual elites. With the implementation of the European Financial Services Action Plan (FSAP) in 2000, the EU endeavored to construct a single market for financial services (Weber 2006). This process entailed the integration of financial markets that had been geographically fragmented until then. In this way, the member states of the EU were facilitators of global processes. They increasingly transformed themselves into agents of transnational neoliberalism (Cerny 2002). Countries that insisted on regulation were threatened with capital outflows. In order to pre-empt the ability of the financial sector to impose sanctions, many politicians often accepted the arguments of the financial sector in order to comply with its interests. As a result, the Anglo-Saxon self-regulation model, which was favored by the financial sector, was accepted and diffused globally. The deregulation of financial markets and the further use of innovative financial instruments (such as credit derivatives or the technique of manufacturing safe bonds out of risky ones) were not superseded by efforts to globalize, harmonize, and coordinate financial regulation and supervision. Financial market regulation within the realm of nation-states remained focused on national banking, while financial markets and institutions outside the banking system were subject to weak or no regulation (such as special purpose vehicles, and hedge or private equity funds). The result was a power vacuum in which the private regulatory institutions and networks, along with their self-defined sets of rules and forms of self- and co-regulation, have become dominant. The international diffusion of these regulatory models and practices has been facilitated by knowledge-based experts or groups in international arenas. The low representation of women in such decision-making bodies, regulatory groups, and private sector entities is a constant across time and space.

Multi-level governance of finance

In financial market regulation, competing and overlapping structures have emerged along with networks of formal and informal interrelationships between public and private bodies, which appear to be as complex as those in medieval times (Cerny 2005). Thus, the inherently multi-level nature of finance precipitates multi-level institutional processes and practices that are strongly influenced by private sector interests. This has been associated with a change in the logic of democratic accountability, which historically has been restricted to the nation-state. In key areas of policy making, multi-level governance by supranational, private, technical, and network sources of authority has undermined traditional nation-state mechanisms of democratic accountability (such as elections and legislation), while in procedural terms, the public sector still plays a key role in setting standards (Porter 2001). In global finance, the state has been actively complicit in shifting regulatory competence to private institutions, as indicated by the evolving mechanisms of self-regulation and co-regulation in financial governance.

Private financial market regulation: financial governance without government

The growth of private financial governance is one of the distinctive features of contemporary financial regulation (Mosley 2006). From an institutional perspective, two broad types of private actors can be identified. First, private autonomous authorities and institutions are involved in the establishment and enforcement of rules. For example, Private Credit Rating Agencies (CRA) played an important role at various stages in the subprime crisis (Hellwig 2008). They assigned credit ratings for issuers of certain types of debt obligations as well as for the debt instruments themselves, and developed guidelines to be enforced by portfolio investors or bond issuers (De Larosière 2009; Sinclair 2008). Under the Basel II agreement of the Basel Committee on Banking Supervision (BCBS), banking regulators are empowered to recommend credit ratings from certain approved CRAs (Redak 2006).

Another important private institution with rule-setting authority is the IASB, which develops the IFRS and promotes the use and application of these standards. At a more informal level, the International Institute of Finance (IIF) (the world's only global association of financial institutions with important regulatory proficiencies) is also an important rule setter and rule enforcer. The IIF regularly issues principles of conduct that are supposed to be implemented by its members.[10]

Second, public or semi-state institutions such as independent central banks or supervisory authorities create rules with different degrees of binding. Private actors bear the enforcement responsibilities. The Basel II framework, in which self-regulation of banks is dominant, is a case in point (Redak 2006). In other areas, autonomous private actors are involved in the rule-setting process. In the last decade this kind of governance has gained importance with the establishment of the Financial Stability Forum (FSF), which was set up after the Asian crisis on Germany's initiative. This body is comprised of representatives of the Ministries of Finance, Central Banks, and supervisory bodies of the G7 countries, as well as five other major international finance centers. Private, semi-state, or public international standard-setting bodies and other groupings are also members of the FSF. An example is the IASB, whose representatives sit alongside governments in the Financial Stability Forum session, and jointly develop accounting standards. The FSF develops indicators for early warning systems, conducts studies, and identifies potential dangers for financial market stability. However, the recommendations they make are not binding. In an effort to overhaul the international financial architecture, the 2009 G20 London summit agreed to establish a successor to the FSF, the Financial Stability Board, which will include all G20 countries, FSF members, Spain, and the European Commission.

While state-private arrangements are dominant in the development of financial governance rules, there is one rare example of public rule setting and public enforcement. In 1989 the Financial Action Task Force on Money Laundering (FATF) was founded by the G7 in order to combat money laundering and terrorism financing. It is currently made up of 32 countries and territories and two regional organizations. However, the FATF works only on the basis of recommendations; it has no legal means at its disposal to implement them (Vlcek 2007).

The impact of financial governance arrangements on gender

The gendered implications of the financial structure are two-fold. First, corporate governance modes impact resource allocation among stakeholders and shareholders; second, financial governance affects financial risk sharing in societies differently for men and women discussed later in this section. In regard to the first channel of influence, increased shareholder value restricts the capability to transfer resources from profitable to less profitable sectors. In an established market for corporate governance, the increased focus on short-termism is an attempt to increase returns on equity. This will distribute income from stakeholders to shareholders (De Jong 1997). The transfer of revenues to shareholders and to the growing financial sector has meant that in the US the profit share of the financial sector has increased from

10 percent in the early 1980s to 40 percent in 2007 (Philippon 2008). In recent years the shareholder model has been challenged by the private equity industry. This industry differs in that it is exempt from many of the regulations applying to traditional collective investment schemes. More importantly, it has evolved from a relatively marginal investment class to an alternative stock exchange listing. Private equity firms are thus even more subject to short-termism with slower wage growth than is the private sector as a whole (Evans and Habbard 2008).

The shift to shareholder capitalism, together with global markets and the spread of information technology, has meant that standard employment relationships are on the decline and a dramatic increase in precarious work has occurred. Women are specifically affected by these tendencies, since they make up the majority in part-time employment, self-employment, fixed-term work, temporary work, on-call work and home work (Elson 2000; Bakker 1994). In 2008, 35.2 percent of working women in the EU held part-time jobs, compared with 7.5 percent of working men.[11]

~

In the long history of financial crises, the real economic effects have been long lasting and severe (Reinhard and Rogoff 2008, 2009). Studies analyzing the gendered effects of financial crises, in particular the East Asian crisis in the later 1990s (Singh and Zammit 2000; Limm 2000; Young 2003) have shown that given the concentration of female jobs in exports and tourism in this region, women suffered from higher unemployment, which persisted after recovery (Buvinic 2009). The spill-over of the financial crisis to the real economy was sudden, and the recession reached an unprecedented scale compared with recent decades. In terms of the present financial and economic crisis, early job losses are mostly in sectors with a greater concentration of male workers (for example, in construction and manufacturing). But female unemployment can be expected to rise disproportionally with budgetary consolidation, since women workers are concentrated in education, health, and social services, areas where fiscal retrenchment sets in first. Furthermore, unemployed women face greater risks of immediate poverty, as they are more likely than men to have been employed in low paid work and therefore do not have access to savings (or other forms of income, such as loans) (Trade Union Congress 2009). The degree of affectedness depends on the upcoming shape of the business cycle (whether it will be V-, U-, W- or L-shaped), the fiscal packages established to counter the crises (and the extent to which gender is a factor of consideration in their construction), as well as the fiscal consolidation strategies. In developing countries, job losses for women will be greater, as they are concentrated in export manufacturing industries and in tourism (especially in Asia and Latin America) (Seguino 2009). Irrespective of the economic structure of particular countries, gender norms are often such that women bear the brunt of the crisis because of the male bread-winner paradigm, which prevails across cultures (Elson 2000). In times of rising unemployment, the tendency is to protect men's employment and to sacrifice women's jobs.

While the first channel of the gendered implications of the financial structure highlights the shift from a stakeholder corporate model to a shareholder model with its focus on short-term profits combined with the increase of non-standardized jobs, the second channel demonstrates how financial governance arrangements impact on how risk sharing is organized in society differently for men and women. Having little, if any, savings and limited ownership of financial and real wealth (Deere and Doss 2006), women are particularly affected by the individualization of risk. The subprime crisis in the US is a case in point; there is considerable evidence showing that subprime lending was disproportionally sold to women (particularly minority women) (Fishbein and Woodall 2006). These trends are reflected in mounting debt levels and the crippling costs of servicing these debts, compared to the relatively flat income growth of single mothers throughout the 2000s. Focusing on single mothers, Montgomerie and Young (2010) demonstrate the important gender dimension of the subprime market and the gendered lending techniques that shaped the processes of financial exclusion and inclusion. Single mothers not only experience a gender pay gap, but also are more likely to be part-time or flexible workers with commensurate wage differentials. This is exacerbated by the fact that they are solely responsible for all social reproduction obligations. New access to credit for homeownership was supposed to expand homeownership levels among America's socially marginalized communities. By participating in the credit and housing boom, subprime borrowers could fulfil the American dream and join the asset price regime of residential capitalism (Schwartz 2008). Thus, poor women and minorities became integrated into the asset market through the availability of subprime loans. But the minimal gains in homeownership for single mothers are not sufficient to justify the massive risk of indebtedness that they have incurred in the recent credit and housing booms. Rising household indebtedness is not incidental to America's financial implosion; rather it is indicative of how the individualization of risk affects those who can least afford it.

Moreover, the working poor and single mothers have disproportionately experienced a protracted period of rollbacks in government social services and income transfers, which serve only to compound their financial insecurity. Increased pressure from the financial industry has made fiscal restraint the dominant strategy of many governments. The liberalization policies that underpin global finance have had costly repercussions on public budgets at the national levels. These costs stem from additional spending requirements to adjust societies to fast economic change, and at the same time confront declining resources for public budgets. The result is a "fiscal squeeze" (Grunberg 1998) that increases the pressure to downsize public expenditures through the re-privatization of what was once public (Brodie 1994; Fraser 1989). At the same time, pressure is placed on annual income to service the staggering debt levels. Through this process, financially insecure households are rendered more vulnerable. The intensification of financialization in the economy over the past decade has increased both the financial risk as well as the human insecurities experienced by low-income households. This is especially true for poor women and minority groups (Montgomerie and Young 2010).

Banking stabilization and stimulus packages: The impact on gender

To counter the severe economic contraction, the developed and – to some extent – the middle income countries have engaged in banking stabilization measures, expansionary monetary policies (including non-standard measures), and fiscal stimulus. By the end of February 2009, the financial and banking rescue schemes, which include capital injections, guarantees of issuance of banking securities, bank asset purchases, swaps, and other guarantees amounted to a total government commitment of 22 percent of GDP for the EU and 29 percent of GDP for the US.[12] The fact that banking stabilization is almost exclusively funded by the taxpayer – without contributions from shareholders, managers, or unsecured creditors – has attracted wide criticism from academics and non-governmental organizations. Even mainstream economists have warned that socialization of losses and privatization of profits have occurred at unprecedented levels and that both practices involve moral hazards and set the stage for another crisis (Zingales 2008). Banking packages have stabilized the financial sector, but they have also led to a rise in dividends and higher (executive) wages in the financial industries. These steps are disproportionately favoring men. With the exception of Iceland, which placed women in charge of its newly state-controlled banks, no country placed conditions on public funding in order for financial institutions to increase the female quota of the boards. Gender equality, as a corporate goal, is not part of the political debate on conditionality, which focuses largely on manager compensation and credit availability.

In addition to financial rescue measures, substantial fiscal stimulus packages were enacted to stimulate demand in the economy. As a percentage of GDP, the fiscal stimulus packages for 2009 were predicted to reach a level of 1 percent in the EU[13] and 2.1 percent in the US. In reaction to the malfunctioning of financial intermediation, central banks worldwide have adopted different kinds of quantitative and qualitative easing measures. Some of them – for example the Federal Reserve and the European Central Bank – strongly expanded their balance sheets in order to inject liquidity into the banking system. Some have directly purchased goods or less quality assets in selected distressed segments of private financial instruments. But as Sylvia Walby (2009) observed, the experience of consolidation measures, as a consequence of financial crises, shows a general retrenchment in expenditures for education, childcare, and health programmes.

Conclusion

The conceptualization of women in economics – particularly financial economics – as less rational and less proficient in the formal sciences has contributed to their discrimination in global finance. The excessive reliance on expert knowledge – with its tendency to privilege quantitative modelling – and the delegation of regulatory functions to private actors has led, in the words of Dorn (2009), to a situation where "regulators are captured by their knowledge base." The most striking aspect of the financial system that emerged after the breakdown of the Bretton Woods system is the shift of the regulatory competence to mostly private institutions (*financial governance without government*) combined with the low female representation in financial market decision-making structures (*financial governance without women*). It is therefore not surprising that the ongoing analyses of the origin of the crisis and the discourse and decision making on regulatory reform is solely confined to financial insiders, mostly males, who were the culprits in the financial meltdown in the first place.

Despite the worst financial crisis since the Great Depression in the 1930s, the underlying principles of the efficient market hypothesis remain sacrosanct. As the proposals for the G20 in Pittsburgh (on 25 September 2009) so clearly demonstrated, mostly band-aid solutions in the form of reducing the bonus and manager salary culture, requiring banks to hold higher capital requirements, and establishing stronger supervisory authority over large banks (too big to fail) are advanced. There is little awareness among decision makers that financial crises are a systemic phenomenon of the unregulated markets created and facilitated by states. State actors in combination with private entities have, through legal and political means, reconstituted financial markets without democratic accountability. Financial integration that promotes the Anglo-Saxon governance mode of self-regulation was thus a deliberate political strategy among a set of viable alternatives, backed and supported by the economic, financial, and legal elites across the globe.

Whether the inclusion of women in the decision-making process of financial market regulation would make a difference in terms of stricter regulation and categorical rejection of regulatory capture is a question that this paper cannot answer. However, the mere fact that women are largely absent in any of the top levels of regulatory institutions or formal and informal networks raises democratic issues. *Bringing women into the finance sector* would signal a re-envisioning of finance as a global public good. The prevailing financial system is organized in a manner to provide private goods for the benefit of the few; indeed, while profits are privatized, losses are socialized. Given its systemic impact, financial stability as a global public good needs to be more inclusive in order to create opportunities for all those affected by financial markets. This means to involve the public in decision making, and to make sure that the benefits are equally distributed around the globe (Kaul *et al.* 2003). As this paper has pointed out, the problem is not only that women are absent from financial governance structures, they are nevertheless affected in many crucial ways. The mode of corporate governance has important gendered implications. Since the majority of women are stakeholders, they are impacted by recessions more dramatically than men (who are more likely than women to be shareholders). At the same time, women also seem to bear the brunt of budget consolidations and fiscal retrenchments following severe financial crisis. Moreover, as the present subprime crisis in the US has shown, financial governance plays a crucial role in how risk sharing is organized in society. Low-income women were integrated into the asset regime, but at the cost of mounting debt levels and crippling costs to service these debts.

Essentially the question of women's inclusion as full citizens in the financial arena rests on persistent gender norms. As long as economics is constructed as an abstract science removed from the experiences of people's lives, and as long as women are seen as less rational, less knowledgeable in formal economics and science, the field of neoclassical economics in general, and finance in particular, will be unable to harness its full potential and provide benefits for all social groups globally.

Acknowledgement

We want to thank Isabella Bakker for her insightful comments and helpful suggestions on an earlier draft of this chapter.

Notes

1 *Financial Times*, October 23, 2008.
2 Some of the studies are Lukas and Klatzer (2002), Warnecke (2006), Walby (2009), Antonopoulos (2009), Seguino (2009); Montgomerie/Young (2010); Young (2003, 2010); Bakker (2002); Elson (2002), van Staveren (2002).
3 In response to a growing number of contradictions that could not be explained by the efficient market hypotheses, a new approach to financial markets has emerged – behavioral finance (Thaler 2005). It investigates the impact of human behavior and psychology on financial markets. But it is not a radical deviation from the efficient market hypothesis, but rather a supplement to it. It maintains the strict division of rational and irrational behavior and the premise that human behavior has a distorting influence on economic fundamentals.
4 At a conference convened by the National Bureau for Economic Research in 2005, Lawrence Summers, president of Harvard University at that time, suggested that "innate differences" between men and women help explain the lack of top-level female professionals in science and engineering. But studies show that discrimination against women in the academy is alarmingly widespread, if often unconscious. Bauer and Paludi (1983) conducted a study in which 180 men and 180 women were asked to grade a paper on a five-point scale. Results indicated that the articles were differentially perceived and evaluated according to the name of the author.
5 The general economist's view of regulatory authorities on hedge funds expressed by the Banque de France, is mentioned here in place of many other examples: "In our view, most calls for the regulation of hedge funds are based on a misperception of the effectiveness of financial regulations, perhaps coupled with a lack of understanding of the positive contribution of hedge funds to the financial system ... Hedge funds provide considerable benefits, not only to their investors and advisors, but more importantly to the economy at large by facilitating price discovery, market efficiency, diversification, and by being potentially able to put a floor under a crisis, a function not easily implemented by regulated institutions due to a minimum capital ratio, relative to performance evaluation and other considerations" (Danielsson and Zigrand 2007: 1).
6 The most prominent example is the effort undertaken in the late 1990s by Brooksley Born (who was at the time head of the US Commodity Futures Trading Commission) to regulate derivatives markets. She incited fierce opposition from Alan Greenspan and Robert Rubin (then Treasury Secretary). Michael Greenberger, who was a senior director at the commission, recalls, "Greenspan told Brooksley that she essentially didn't know what she was doing and she'd cause a financial crisis ... Brooksley was this woman who was not playing tennis with these guys and not having lunch with these guys. There was a little bit of the feeling that this woman was not of Wall Street," *New York Times*, October 8, 2008. Born's recommendations were suppressed and she left government.

7 The bodies and committees from Tables 7.1 to 7.4 are – due to informational constraints – selective and not comprehensive.
8 The chairwoman Mary Shapiro was inaugurated by early 2009, after the former SEC president faced strong criticism of regulatory failure. Elisse B. Walter was appointed in July 2008 as commissioner of the SEC.
9 The few women represented in the committees are often from the Nordic EU-countries or from EU-10.
10 See the latest Report of the IIF (2008).
11 Eurostat.
12 ECB-Eurosystem: selected financial indicators, cut-off date February 19, 2009.
13 Including the 1.4 percent estimated impact of automatic stabilizers, the net deficit ratio will increase by 2.4 percent. In addition 0.3 percent of EU GDP will come from the EU's own budget and the European Investment Bank. Source: European Commission Services.

Bibliography

Allen, F. and Douglas, G. (1997) "Financial Markets, Intermediaries, and Intertemporal Smoothing," *Journal of Political Economy*, 105(3): 523–546.

Antonopoulos, R. (2009) "The Current Economic and Financial Crisis: A Gender Perspective," *Economics Working Paper Archive wp_562*, The Levy Economics Institute.

Bakker, I. (1994) "Introduction: Engendering Macro-Economic Policy Reform in the Era of Global Restructuring and Adjustment," in I. Bakker (ed.) *The Strategic Silence. Gender and Economic Policy*, London: Zed Books.

——— (2002) "Who Built the Pyramids? Engendering the New International Economic and Financial Architecture," *femina politica*, 1: 13–25.

——— (2003) "Neo-liberal Governance and the Reprivatization of Social Reproduction: Social Provisioning and Shifting Gender Orders," in I. Bakker and S. Gill (eds) *Power, Production and Social Reproduction*, Houndmills/Basingstoke: Palgrave Macmillan.

Bakker, I and Gill, S. (eds) (2003) *Power, Production and Social Reproduction*, Houndmills/ Basingstoke: Palgrave Macmillan.

Barber, B. M. and Odean, T. (2001) "Boys Will be Boys: Gender, Overconfidence and Common Stock Investment," *Quarterly Journal of Economics*, 116(1): 261–292.

Bauer, W. D. and Paludi, M. A. (1983) "Goldberg Revisited: What's in an Author's Name," *Sex Roles*, 9(3): 387–390.

Beckmann, D. and Menkhoff, L. (2008) "Will Women Be Women? Analyzing the Gender Difference Among Financial Experts," Discussion Paper No. 391.

Bourdieu, P., Barets, Paul and Steinrücke, M. (1997) *Mobilisierungen gegen den Neoliberalismus. Das Tagebuch der Streiks in Frankreich*. November/Dezember 1995, Hamburg: VSA-Verlag.

Brodie, J. (1994) "Shifting the Boundaries: Gender and the Politics of Restructuring," in I. Bakker (ed.) *The Strategic Silence. Gender and Economic Policy*, London: Zed Books.

Buvinic, M. (2009) "The Global Financial Crisis: Assessing Vulnerability for Women and Children, Identifying Policy Responses," Prepared written statement, Division for the Advancement of Women Interactive Expert Panel on Gender Perspectives of the Financial Crisis, March 5. Commission on the Status of Women, Fifty-Third Session, New York.

Cerny, P.G. (2002) "Webs of Governance and the Privatization of Transnational Regulation," in D.M. Andrews, C. Randall Henning and L.W. Pauly (eds) *Governing the World's Money*, Ithaca: Cornell University Press, pp. 194–215.

——— (2005) "Power, Markets and Accountability: The Development of Multi-level Governance in International Finance," in A. Baker, D. Hutson and R. Woodward (eds) *Governing Financial Globalization. International Political Economy and Multi-Level Governance*, London: Routledge, pp. 24–48.

Danielsson, J. and Zigrand, J.-P. (2007) "Regulating Hedge Funds," *Financial Stability Review*, Special Issue on Hedge Funds, 10. Online. Available at: http://www.banque-france.fr/gb/publications/telechar/rsf/2007/etud3_0407.pdf (accessed September 30, 2009).

Deere, C. D. and Doss, C. R. (2006) "The Gender Asset Gap: What Do We Know and Why Does It Matter?" *Feminist Economics*, 12(1–2): 1–50.

De Goede, M. (2005) *Virtue, Fortune and Faith: A Genealogy of Finance*, Minneapolis: University of Minnesota Press.

De Jong, H. W. (1997) "The governance structure and performance of large European corporations," *The Journal of Management and Governance*, 1: 5–27.

De Larosière, J. (2009) Report of the High Level Group of Supervision in the EU, Brussels, 25 February 2009. Online. Available at: http://ec.europa.eu/commission_barroso/president/pdf/statement_20090225_en.pdf (accessed 5 April 2009).

Dorn, N. (2009) "Ponzi Finance, Regulatory Capture and the Credit Crunch," 19 March 2009. Online. Available at: http://ssrn.com/abstract=1365250 (accessed May 5, 2009).

Elson, D. (2000), "Progress of the World's Women 2000," UNIFEM Biennial Report, New York: United Nations Development Fund for Women.

——— (2002) "International Financial Architecture: A View From the Kitchen," *femina politica*, 1: 26–37.

Evans, J. and Habbard, P. (2008) "From Shareholder Value to Private Equity – the Changing Face of Financialisation of the Economy," *Transfer*, 14(1). Online. Available at: www.etui-rehs.org (accessed September 16, 2009).

Fama, E. (1970) "Efficient Capital Markets: A Review of Theory and Empirical Work," *Journal of Finance*, 25: 383–417.

Fishbein, A.J. and Woodall, P. (2006) "Women are Prime Targets for Subprime Lending: Women are Disproportionately Represented in High-Cost Mortgage Market," Washington DC: The Consumer Federation of America.

Fraser, N. (1989) *Unruly Practices: Power, Discourse and Gender in Contemporary Social Theory*, Minneapolis: University of Minnesota Press.

Fukuda-Parr, S. (2008) "The Human Impact of the Financial Crisis on Poor and Disempowered People and Countries," UN General Assembly: Interactive Panel on the Global Financial Crisis. Online. Available at: http://www.un.org/ga/president/63/interactive/gfc/sakiko_p.pdf (accessed March 24, 2009).

——— (2009) "The Gender Perspectives of the Financial Crisis," United Nations Commission on the Status of Women, New York, March 2–13, 2009.

Gerding, E. F. (2009) "The Outsourcing of Financial Regulation to Risk Models and the Global Financial Crisis: Code, Crash, and Open Source (March 01, 2009)," Washington Law Review, forthcoming. Online. Available at: http://ssrn.com/abstract=1273467 (accessed November 28, 2009).

Gill, S. (2003) *Power and Resistance in the New World Order*, Houndmills/Basingstoke: Palgrave Macmillan.

Ginn, J. (2004) "European Pension Privatisation: Taking Account of Gender," *Social Policy and Society*, 3(2): 123–134.

Ginther, D. and Kahn, S. (2004) "Women in Economics: Moving Up or Falling Off the Academic Career Ladder?" *Journal of Economic Perspectives*, 18(3): 193–214.

Grunberg, I. (1998) "Double Jeopardy: Globalization, Liberalization and the Fiscal Squeeze," *World Development*, 26(4): 591–605.

Haas, P. M. (1992) "Introduction: Epistemic Communities and International Policy Coordination," *International Organisation*, 46 (2: Special Issue on Knowledge, Power and International Policy Coordination): 1–36.

Hall, P. A. and Soskice, D. W. (eds) (2001) *Varieties of Capitalism. The Institutional Foundations of Comparative Advantage*, Oxford: Oxford University Press.

Hardy, D. C. (2006) "Regulatory Capture in Banking," IMF Working Paper 06/34.

Hellwig, M. (2008) "Systemic Risk in the Financial Sector: An Analysis of the Subprime-Mortgage Financial Crisis,"Working Paper Series of the Max Planck Institute for Research on Collective Goods, 43, Max Planck Institute for Research on Collective Goods.

Hermann, C. and Mahnkopf, B. (2009) "The Past and Future of the European Social Model," Paper prepared for the 9th European Sociological Association Conference, Lisbon September 2–5, 2009.

International Institute of Finance (IIF) (2008) Final Report of the IIF Committee on Market Best Practices: Principles of Conduct and Best Practice Recommendations, July 17, 2008.

Kaul, I., Connceição, P., Le Goulven, K. and Mendoza, R. U. (2003) *Providing Global Public Goods. Managing Globalization*, Oxford: Oxford University Press.

Krugman, P. (2009) "How did economists get it so wrong?" The *New York Times*, 6 September 2009. Online. Available at: www.nytimes.com/2009/09/06/magazine/06Economic-t.html? (accessed November 3, 2009).

Limm, Joseph Y. (2000) "The Effects of the East Asian Crisis on the Employment of Women and Men: The Philippine Case," *World Development*, 28(7): 1285–1306.

Lukas, K. and Klatzer, E. (2002) "Ein feministischer Blick auf die Finanzmärkte, *Kurswechsel*, 3/2002.

Lütz, S. (2006) "Political Economy Approach to Financial Reform," in P. Mooslechner, H. Schuberth and B. Weber (eds) *The Political Economy of Financial Market Regulation. The Dynamics of Inclusion and Exclusion*, Edward Elgar: Cheltenham, UK/Northampton/MA, USA.

Majone, G. (1997) "Independent Agencies and the Delegation Problem: Theoretical and Normative Dimensions," in B. Steunenberg and F. van Vught (eds) *Political Institutions and Public Policy. Perspectives on European Decision Making*, Dordrecht: Kluwer Academic Publishers: 139–156.

Montgomerie, J. and Young, B. (2010) "Home is Where the Hardship is: Homeownership, Social Reproduction, and Financial (In)security," (under review).

Mooslechner, P. (2004) "The Transformation of the European Financial System – A Brief Introduction to Issues and Literature," Proceedings of OeNB Workshops, No.1, 7–22.

Mooslechner, P., Schuberth, H. and Weber, B. (2006) *The Political Economy of Financial Market Regulation. The Dynamics of Inclusion and Exclusion*, Edward Elgar: Cheltanham, UK/Northampton/MA, USA.

Mosley, L. (2006) "Privatising Global Governance? Dilemmas in International Financial Regulation," GARNET Conference on Global Financial and Monetary Governance, the EU, and Emerging Market Economies, Amsterdam, September 27–29, 2006. Online. Available at: http://www.unc.edu/~lmosley/MosleyFinRegulationMay2005.pdf (accessed July 3, 2008).

Niederle, M. and Vesterlund, L. (2005) "Do Women Shy Away From Competition? Do Men Compete Too Much?" NBER Working Paper No. 11474.

Novoa, A., Scarlata, J. and Solé, J. (2009) "Procyclicality and Fair Value Accounting," IMF Working Paper No. 39.

Philippon, T. (2008) "The Evolution of the US Financial Industry from 1860 to 2007: Theory and Evidence," New York University, Working Paper, November 2008.

Online. Available at: http://pages.stern.nyu.edu/~tphilipp/papers/finsize.pdf (accessed December 15, 2009).

Porter, T. (2001) "The Democratic Deficit in the Institutional Arrangements for Regulating Global Finance," *Global Governance*, 7: 427–439.

Redak, V. (2006) "Risks, Ratings and Regulation: Toward a Reorganization of Credit via Basel II?" in P. Mooslechner, H. Schuberth and B. Weber (eds) *The Political Economy of Financial Market Regulation. The Dynamics of Inclusion and Exclusion*, Edward Elgar: Cheltenham, UK/Northampton, MA, USA.

Reinhard, C. M. and Rogoff, K.S. (2008) "This Time is Different: A Panoramic View of Eight Centuries of Financial Crises," NBER Working Paper No. 13882. Online. Available at: http://www.nber.org/papers/w13882 (accessed March 13, 2009).

——— (2009) "The Aftermath of Financial Crises," Paper prepared for presentation at the American Economic Association meetings in San Francisco, January 3, 2009.

Saha, D. and von Weizäcker, J. (2009) "EU Stimulus Packages. Estimating the size of the European stimulus packages for 2009: An update," Bruegel Policy Contribution, Issue 2009/02, April.

Salacuse, J. W. (2002) "European Corporations American Style? Governance, Culture and Convergence," Paper presented at a conference hosted by the John F. Kennedy School of Government, April, 11–12.

Scharpf, F. (1999) *Governing in Europe: Effective and Democratic*? Oxford. Oxford University Press.

Schwartz, H. (2008) "Housing, Global Finance, and American Hegemony: Building Conservative Politics One Brick at a Time," *Comparative European Politics*, 6(2): 262–284.

Seguino, S. (2009) "The Global Economic Crisis, its Gender Implications, and Policy Responses," Paper prepared for *Gender Perspectives on the Financial Crisis*, Panel at the 53rd Session of the Commission on the Status of Women, United Nations, March 5.

Semmler, W. (2006) *Asset Prices, Booms and Recessions: Financial Economics from a Dynamic Perspective*, 2nd edn, Heidelberg/New York: Springer Pub.

Sinclair, T. J. (2008) *The New Masters of Capital. American Bond Rating Agencies and the Politics of Creditworthiness*. Cornell Studies in Political Economy, Cornell University Press.

Singh, A. and Zammit, A. (2000) "International Capital Flows: Identifying the Gender Dimensions," *World Development*, 28(7): 1249–1268.

Stiglitz, J. (2009) "Principles for a New Financial Architecture, The Commission of Experts of the President of the UN General Assembly on Reforms of the International Monetary and Financial System." Online. Available at: http://www.un-ngls.org/docs/ga/cfr/newfinancialarchitecture.pdf (accessed May 15, 2009).

Tett, G. (2009) *Fool's Gold. How Unrestrained Greed Corrupted a Dream, Shattered Global Markets and Unleashed a Catastrophe*, London: Little, Brown Book Group.

Thaler, R. (ed.) (2005) *Advances in Behavioural Finance, Vol. II*, Princeton, NJ: Princeton University Press.

Trade Union Congress (TUC) (2009) "Women and the Recession." Online. Available at: http://www.tuc.org.uk/extras/womenandrecession.pdf (accessed December 12, 2009).

Tsingou, Eleni (2010) "Regulatory Reactions to the Global Credit Crisis: Analyzing a Policy Community Under Stress," in E. Helleiner, S. Pagliari and H. Zimmermann (eds) *Global Finance in Crisis. The Politics of International Regulatory Change*, London/New York: Routledge.

Van Staveren, I. (2002) "Global Finance and Gender," in J. A. Scholte and A. Schnabel (eds) *Civil Society and Global Finance*, London: Routledge.

Vlcek, W. (2007) "Surveillance to Combat Terrorist Financing in Europe: Whose Liberty, Whose Security?" *European Security*, 16(1): 99–119. http://www.informaworld.com/smpp/title~content=t713635117~db=all~tab=issueslist~branches=16 - v16.

Walby, S. (2009) "Gender and the Financial Crisis," Paper for UNESCO, 6 April.

Warnecke, T. L. (2006) "A gender-aware approach to international finance," in B.J. Clary, W. Dolfsma and D.M Figart (eds) *Ethics and the Market Insights From Social Economics*, New York: Routledge: 175–190. http://www.informaworld.com/smpp/title~content=t754161867~db=all~tab=issueslist~branches=1 - v1.

Weber, B. (2006) "The Construction of the Single Market in Financial Services and the Politics of Inclusion and Exclusion," in P. Mooslechner, H. Schuberth and B. Weber (eds) *The Political Economy of Financial Market Regulation. The Dynamics of Inclusion and Exclusion*, Edward Elgar: Cheltenham, UK/Northampton, MA, USA.

Young, B. (2003) "Financial Crisis and Social Reproduction: Asia, Argentina and Brazil," in I. Bakker and S. Gill (eds) *Power, Production and Social Reproduction*, Houndmills/Basingstoke: Palgrave Macmillan.

——— (2010) "From Microcredit to Microfinance to Inclusive Finance: A Response to Global Financial Openness," in G.R.D. Underhill, J. Blom, D. Muegge (eds) *Global Financial Integration Thirty Years On*, Cambridge: Cambridge University Press.

Young, B. and Schuberth, H. (2010) "The Global Financial Meltdown and the Impact of Financial Governance on Gender," GARNET-Policy Brief, January 2010. Paris: CERI/Science-Po.

Zingales, L. (2008) "Greenspan roundtable: the wrong prescription," *The Economist*, Online. Available at: http://www.economist.com/blogs/freeexchange/2008/12/greenspan_roundtable_the_wrong.cfm (accessed February 2, 2009).

8

MACROECONOMIC GOVERNANCE, GENDERED INEQUALITY, AND GLOBAL CRISES[1]

Stephen Gill and Adrienne Roberts

Introduction: global financial crisis and neoliberal governance

This chapter attempts to draw links between macroeconomics and the operation of global financial markets with their particular abstractions and generic, technical language. We explore the range of social forces associated with macroeconomic governance and finance, and their effects at the level of the everyday lives of the poor, where the nature of global inequalities becomes clearer. We seek to draw attention to the class, gendered, and racialized inequalities that are reproduced by disciplinary neoliberalism and how women and other social groups have been integrated hierarchically into the new regime of market citizenship through welfare, social services and subprime mortgages. The context for our discussion is the cascading global financial and economic crisis that has emerged since 2007 and on a scale comparable to the Great Depression of the 1930s.

Beginning with falling real wages of American workers, and their subsequent inability to service their ongoing levels of consumption and debts, the global financial crisis was specifically triggered by arrears and defaults on home mortgages and by falling house prices in the United States (US). Since mortgages were packaged and resold as financial derivatives, when the subprime mortgage crisis intensified, this triggered a financial collapse on Wall Street. The crisis spread throughout the US and global financial sectors. In the US and western Europe, concerns over the solvency of key financial firms set off a series of bankruptcies, forced mergers, and in response, the injection of unprecedented amounts of public money into the financial systems of the world's wealthiest countries. In the US, efforts to save the collapsing financial system have involved the investment of trillions of dollars of taxpayers' money. As of November 2009, the financial rescue packages had involved the investment of an estimated $3 trillion.[2]

At the global level, by 2009 the International Monetary Fund (IMF) estimated the total global cost of the crisis to be $11.9 trillion, with developed countries having invested $10.2 trillion and developing countries, $1.7 trillion (Conway 2009). The international financial institutions (IFIs) have also dramatically increased lending, delivering over $850 billion in additional resources to combat the crisis. Much of this new lending has been aimed at financial stabilization in Europe and certain emerging markets, bypassing many of the poorest countries most in need of assistance (UNESCO 2010: 34).

At the time of writing, it is not at all clear that the massive bailouts and financial stimulus packages will curb the deepening global crisis. Rather, despite assurances from the IFIs and G8/G20 that the global economy is recovering and that governments should begin to phase out temporary stimulus measures (what they refer to as 'exit strategies'), recent events, such as those that have occurred in Greece, point to the ongoing instability of the international financial system.

Indeed, while sovereign debt crisis has been a feature of the global South over the past 30 years, it is now migrating to much of the global North. Much of this is because the bailouts have resulted in very high levels of public debt for a number of countries, e.g. in Greece and other parts of southern Europe. At the same time the IMF has said that it will take 10 to 20 years of austerity measures, involving cuts in public sector wages and public services, and increased privatization of public assets to pay for "future" bailouts, and to pay back government debts. In May 2010 the European Union – or specifically the eurozone economies – created an initiative, a kind of European Monetary Fund, with new bailout funds of €1 trillion in an attempt to "stabilize the financial markets" and bail out Greece. Much of the debt of countries such as Greece is owed to private banks in Germany, France and the US, so the Greek bailout is as much a bailout of these banks as it is for Greece as a country. Greece has been forced to make draconian cuts in social benefits, public sector wages, and pensions, which reverse approximately 30 years of workers' gains – a continuation of the type of structural adjustment and stabilization policies long favored by the Washington-based international financial institutions. Of course the Greek fiscal crisis has also been caused by poor tax collection (allowing wealthy people and professionals to evade paying taxes and to get their money out of the country) as well as by previous governments manipulating statistics, in effect cooking the books with the help of big private banks such as Goldman Sachs, to hide the size of the fiscal shortfalls.

Regardless of the specific outcomes which will vary according to location, what *is* clear is that the rescue packages, which have generally not be been accompanied by any significant changes to the regulation of global finance, ultimately amount to a massive socialization of the private debts of many of the largest financial houses and insurance firms in the US and elsewhere, the cost of which will be borne by taxpayers if their governments succeed in sustaining their planned austerity measures over the coming decades along the lines suggested by the IMF and adopted by the G20.[3]

This is part of a broader trend under neoliberal governance whereby, since the 1970s and 1980s, risk for the majority is increasingly privatized as the market becomes the primary means through which individuals secure their livelihoods and protect themselves from economic and health risks (e.g. through private pensions and private health care). In contrast, the global response to the financial crisis has drawn attention to the long-standing practice of corporate welfare by G20 political leaders who have socialized risk for the very affluent and for many corporations.[4]

The investment of trillions of dollars of public money to socialize the risks of capital stands in stark contrast to the systematic cutting of services aimed at helping the poor and marginalized sectors of the population. Given that black women are disproportionately represented among welfare recipients and that white men dominate the financial sector, the unequal allocation of risk has important gender and racial implications. A further contrast appears in the heightened surveillance and disciplining of those who rely on social and welfare services and the relaxed or, indeed, non-existent surveillance of the financial sector. That is, whereas recipients of social and welfare services have been subjected to intensified forms of surveillance and discipline in order to ensure that they do not misuse funds and that they do indeed constitute the "deserving poor," the financial sector has undergone successive processes of deregulation; surveillance of its risky and highly leveraged investment practices and the exotic financial derivatives that are traded by private insurers and investment houses has been notable by its absence.

As the contemporary financial crisis has made clear, however, the self-regulation of markets generates a number of contradictions and paradoxes that challenge the very reproduction of the capitalist system itself as well as the social reproduction of large segments of the human population.[5] For instance, according to projections made by the World Bank and the IMF, as a result of the financial crisis, up to 227 million more people will be living in absolute poverty by 2020; 1.2 million more children under the age of five will die between 2009 and 2015 and over 100 million more people will remain without access to clean water (WB/IMF 2010).

Though the implications of the crisis for gender relations continues to be debated (largely among various UN agencies and civil society organizations), there is much evidence to suggest that women will be particularly negatively affected by the crisis. For instance, while at the global level, the projected increases for unemployment as a result of the crisis are similar for women and men, women begin from a higher level of unemployment than men.[6] In addition, it has been argued that in the contemporary context, women are more likely to abandon the job search and to concentrate on household duties, thus disappearing from official unemployment statistics. Analyses of past crises have further found that women who have lost their jobs tend to return to work at a slower pace as economic recovery sets in (ILO 2010; Smith 2009). These trends are then compounded by a range of other developments that disproportionately affect the global poor, particularly poor women. According to the UN Special Adviser on Gender Issues and the Advancement of Women:

> the confluence of the global financial crisis – including a projected global economic slowdown, the food and energy crises, the rise in unemployment,

> instability and hostilities, and violence against women and environmental deterioration – had already seriously impacted progress towards achieving gender equality and women's empowerment.
>
> (*Deen 2009*)

These simultaneous crises have the potential to erode some of the gains in gender equality that were achieved in periods of economic growth and to reverse the progress made since the 1995 Fourth World Conference on Women in Beijing. Indeed, despite huge financial bailouts, there has been a notable absence of political and economic commitments to securing gender equity or more broadly, to securing the social reproduction of the global population: "[t]he four largest asset insurance programmes for commercial banks obliged the governments of the United Kingdom and the United States to take on US$786 billion in potential liabilities" which amounts to "over seven times the amount allocated to total international development assistance flows" (UNESCO 2010: 28).

Thus under disciplinary neoliberalism, the majority are made to conform to the dictates of self-help – an individualized and punitive system of surveillance, incarceration, and market discipline. In contrast, the interests of the wealthy few are protected by the use of state action to socialize their risks in a class-based, highly racialized and gendered politico-economic project. This is because the market that has increasingly come to govern and discipline the lives of individuals (e.g. through wage labor, privatized social services and debt) is not, as economic liberals would suggest, a neutral sphere within which all individuals – understood abstractly as *homo economicus* – interact as equals. Rather, the actual operation of markets departs radically from this image of impersonal exchanges taking place between abstract rational actors; class, gender and race continue to influence the terms of one's integration into markets.

For instance, as feminist political economists have extensively argued, the post-war male-breadwinner gender order, which idealized men's participation in the labor market and women's economic dependence on men, has increasingly given way to a new dual-earner model, premised on both men and women's labor force participation (see for instance, Bakker in this volume). While this shift has created new opportunities for some women, labor markets (which have become increasingly precarious for all workers) continue to be gender segmented, and women continue to face discrimination when it comes to pay, working conditions, and upward mobility. Similarly, over the past decade and a half, the number of women who have purchased homes and been integrated into financial (mortgage) markets has grown dramatically. While this decrease in the historical gender gap in home ownership has some progressive appeal, women and racialized minorities are significantly more likely to receive high interest rate loans than white men. Thus, shifting gender orders and women's integration into various markets have not eliminated, but rather reproduced gender-based inequalities. Racial inequalities have also been reproduced in similar ways.

Theorizing global economic governance and crisis: the 'usual suspects' and beyond

The mainstream theorizations of and responses to the contemporary financial crisis offered by the 'usual suspects' tend to fall somewhere within the broad spectrum of liberal economic thought. These "usual suspects," who dominate the IFIs, the US Treasury and Federal Reserve, Wall Street, Ivy League universities, liberal and conservative think tanks, large corporations and the governments of the G8 countries, claim the ability to explain and master crises and in so doing, reinforce the notion that there is no real alternative to the capitalist market system as the supreme mechanism of governance (Gill 1999). While the severity of the crisis has led many of the usual suspects to support the massive injection of public funds into the economy, the capitalist market continues to be presented as the most efficient allocator of global resources.

For instance, in its recent *World Economic Outlook* and *Global Financial Stability* reports, the IMF cautioned against the "rush to regulate," insisting that the market remains the most efficient coordinating mechanism. While the IMF recognized a need for some regulation of the financial sector, its ideal would be to erect the structures necessary for the improved self-regulation of finance (i.e. through increased transparency). The Fund also argued that public assistance should only be considered in cases where the collapse of an institution poses a "systemic threat" and only when there is an "unambiguous plan for exit by the public sector" (IMF 2008b: 38). Ultimately, the institution saw the roots of the crisis lying in a lack of adequate transference of information (i.e. about risks, about the nature of new complex investment structures, and about the role of credit rating agencies who rate only default risk, not downgrades or market-to-market losses).

The G20 consensus (sometimes known in its more global form as the "post-Washington Consensus") draws upon the idea, popularized by Frederich A. Hayek in *The Road to Serfdom* (1944), that a truly liberal capitalism has never really been tried and that more liberalization is needed. In order to fully flourish, capitalism requires the complete abandonment of any form of planning that is not market supporting; other forms of government regulation or intervention in the so-called free market would continue to create contradictions for capital accumulation and undermine the legitimacy of the capitalist system. This theorization is linked to the so-called "efficient markets hypothesis". Here, the basic idea – which has taken an enormous battering as the financial crisis has unfolded – is that the system of free markets is the most efficient means of allocating resources and, indirectly, of organizing and governing society. The case is made that markets provide an epistemological as well as logistical solution to the problems of economic decision making. Markets are said to provide clear and decentralized flows of information to market participants, allowing them to respond to the forces of supply and demand and thus to structure their economic expectations to the incentives provided in the market.

The problem for the pure liberals is that there have never truly been free markets since governments (and to a lesser extent, private monopolies and cartels) have created obstructions to the proper functioning of markets. In many respects, the IFIs see such obstructions as having caused – or having helped cause – many of the recent problems that have produced turmoil on Wall Street and subsequently, a full-blown global financial crisis.

By the same token, such obstructions are viewed as having compounded the problems of global food and energy markets. These "market imperfections" have had devastating consequences for the livelihood of billions of people. Some of the obstructions that the IMF recently described as contributing to rising food costs are "unfavorable weather conditions, rising fuel costs, rising biofuels production, and, more recently, trade restrictions" (IMF 2008a: 7). The IMF argues that in order to ensure that the market in food is able to function properly, governments should pass high food costs on to consumers which will both encourage the production of food and compel citizens to reduce their demand (i.e. by eating less) (IMF 2008a: 23). In a similar manner, the World Bank has argued that the completion of the Doha Round trade talks, which would entail the further liberalization of trade in agriculture and services, is the best and most efficient means of addressing rising levels of poverty in the context of the financial crisis (WB/IMF 2010).[7] The human costs of re-aligning the forces of supply and demand are, of course, never considered paramount. Nor are the ways in which these costs are unevenly borne. For instance, the IMF's insistence on the need to pass on high food prices ignores more than 15 years of extensive research on gender and intra-household resource allocation, which suggests that men and women, as both producers and consumers, will be affected differently by the global food crisis, with women and girls shouldering more of the costs (IFPRI 2008; Macan-Markar 2008; UNPFA 2005).

Essentially, an analysis of recent IFI documents reveals the premise that, as in the past, the roots of crises are located *externally* to the system of liberalized trade and finance, giving the illusion that this system is an efficient, coherent, and rational whole. The sustainability of a system based on so-called free markets is never challenged. Rather, for the IFIs, the problem is that the proper functioning of capitalism is constantly being hindered by political and other extra-economic forces. Very little systematic concern is given to the unequal consequences and effects of the functioning of capitalism, and of market discipline, such as those referred to above with respect to global food prices.

A more compensatory neo-Keynesian approach to crises has been offered by economists such as Nobel Prizewinners Paul Krugman and Joseph Stiglitz who, among others, argue for a restoration of something such as the financial regulatory framework established in the 1930s to prevent repeats of the Great Depression – a framework that needs to be extended to cover a wider range of non-traditional banking institutions. As with the more free-market oriented analyses, the basic structure of the capitalist system is not questioned, and only the degree to which it should be regulated is considered. Other voices that might argue for a full-blown socialization of capital are, of course, never referred to as being credible in the mainstream media.

We might contrast these views with the central idea propounded by Karl Polanyi in *The Great Transformation*, which was published in 1944, the same year as Hayek's *Road to Serfdom*.[8] Polanyi argued that trends toward the emergence of a self-regulating capitalist market system are not the result of a long evolutionary process of trial and error that proves its mettle relative to socialist alternatives (the Hayekian view). Rather, it is the work of the conscious agency of the state, acting on behalf of definite social forces to instantiate an historically unprecedented social experiment, whereby society is subordinated to economic forces – that a self-regulating market system requires the authoritarian and wide-ranging application of state power (i.e. to separate economics from politics in order to allow "free" markets to function). As feminist scholars have pointed out, Polanyi's argument that markets have been socially constructed has important gender-related implications as men and women have historically had different relations to the market (Benería 2003: 122). For instance, a large proportion of women in the world engage in unpaid relations of production and social reproduction such as unpaid agricultural work, volunteer work, and domestic labor. As much of this work is only indirectly linked to the market and not equally subjected to the pressures of competition and profit maximization, it often responds to norms and motivations such as love, nurture, altruism, or other socially constructed norms of behavior (Benería 2003: 122–3; Folbre and Nelson 2000). In other words, while market society gives ontological primacy to the individual, understood analytically to be rational economic man – or *homo economicus* – this view ignores socially and historically constructed gender variations in norms, values, and behavior. Further, as we will argue in the following section in relation to the allocation of mortgage loans in the US, the actual operation of the market departs radically from this image of impersonal exchanges taking place between abstract utility-maximizing individuals.

Polanyi further pointed out that a fully self-regulating market system is both a utopian/dystopian project and, in his view, is effectively unattainable. The reason is because of the stresses and dislocations it tends to engender, thus provoking a disparate but politically significant counter-movement of those elements of capital and labor, as well as producers on the land, who are subjected to its crises, to social atomization and to the attempts to render labor and land or wider spheres of life and nature into commodities, or more precisely, what Polanyi called "fictitious commodities" (Polanyi 1944: 71). In other words, Polanyi challenged the ability of society's new form of market-driven governance to adequately ensure the social reproduction of the labor force and the ecological framework (Brodie 2003: 52–53). He also challenged its ability to ensure the reproduction of capitalism itself. With respect to the nineteenth century, Polanyi noted: "*Paradoxically enough, not human beings and natural resources only but also the organization of capitalistic production itself had to be sheltered from the devastating effects of a self-regulating market*" (Polanyi 1944: 132, our emphasis). Recent crises have once again drawn attention to these fundamental tensions and contradictions generated by attempts to organize society around a self-regulating market.

Disciplinary neoliberalism and gender orders

Dominant interpretations of the financial, food, and fuel crises leave out a number of important issues. They ignore how capital has greatly expanded its scope and has come to mediate ever more aspects of our daily lives and relations of social reproduction. As men and women have had different relations to the market, there are a number of distinctly gendered dimensions to this process that have thus far been largely invisible in mainstream analyses, which also ignore how the disciplinary power of capital is unequally and selectively deployed, thus reproducing class, racial and gender hierarchies at various sites and scales, as well as creating hierarchies between states. Mainstream analyses further fail to recognize the ways in which the structural and disciplinary power of capital has increasingly been expanded and institutionalized through a variety of mechanisms including international organizations (e.g. the IFIs and the World Trade Organization), international trade and investment legislation, and regulation governing private and public debt obligations (e.g. mortgage and national debt). In this section we draw on the concept of disciplinary neoliberalism in order to offer a different way of theorizing and historicizing crises and to begin to address some of the limitations identified above.

Disciplinary neoliberalism

Disciplinary neoliberalism is a concrete form of structural and behavioral power that combines the structural power of capital with more diffuse and capillary forms of what Foucault termed "disciplinary power."[9] It involves both a discourse of political economy and a relatively punitive program of social reform. It is also a conscious and specific political project involving the restructuring of the state and public policy in order to deepen, extend, and secure capitalist markets. The concept of disciplinary neoliberalism describes a global socioeconomic order characterized by the growing power of capital and the intensification of its discipline on society.

Neoliberal forms of discipline are institutionalized and operate at various degrees of intensity across a range of public and private spheres and in various state and civil society complexes (Gill 2008: 137–38). Despite the illusion that such disciplinary power is formally egalitarian, disciplinary neoliberalism is a highly unequal and hierarchical form of power. In the rest of this section we will draw attention to several aspects of disciplinary neoliberalism and the social relations it (re)produces. Specifically, we will focus on disciplinary fiscal and monetary policy, the disciplining of the poor, the reprivatization of social reproduction and the disciplinary relations involved in home ownership and financing.

Fiscal "prudence" and "sound" money

Under previously "normal" conditions, surveillance of governments, e.g. by the IMF, private bond-rating agencies, and by private investors was intended to make them conform to neoliberal policies, euphemistically called "fiscal prudence" and "sound money" – at least until the financial crisis caused their abandonment in the state of a global economic "emergency". "Normality" meant limiting monetary and fiscal policy space, with institutional arrangements such as independent central banks ensuring that the private interests of capital were protected from democratic accountability. Of course, the prevailing argument justifying such independence is that such sound policies were needed to maintain low inflation. On the other hand, when capital is threatened, as in the current crisis, this independence allows central banks to step in with public funds to bail out the private banks.

In practice what this stance has meant, leading up to the financial collapse, was that the US federal government practiced very lax monetary and fiscal policies, allowing for a glut of cheap credit to be available, mainly to US firms and consumers, while poorer nations (and many US states which are legally prohibited from running fiscal deficits) have been tied to the mast of fiscal and monetary rectitude, bound by conditionality associated with IMF and World Bank loans, as well as loans from wealthier creditors. Indeed, insofar as the IMF and the World Bank adopted more flexible approaches to fiscal deficits and inflation between 2007–2010, new evidence suggests a return to their traditional principles of macroeconomic governance, with conditionalities requiring recipient countries to reduce public spending and increase interest rates in order to avoid inflation (UNCTAD 2009; UNESCO 2010). Loan conditionalities that compel governments with limited fiscal policy space to impose procyclical policies and macroeconomic tightening stand in stark contrast to the countercyclical policies and large stimulus packages that were being used to stimulate the economy in most developed countries in 2007–2010 (UNCTAD 2009).

Such variation in the enforcement of sound monetary and fiscal policies reproduces unequal power relations between states, while at the same time constraining the ability of many governments, particularly those in the underdeveloped world, to adequately address poverty (i.e. through taxation and spending). Neoliberal fiscal and monetary policies that subordinate the needs of citizens to the attraction of foreign capital (such as low inflation, low public debt and expenditure, low taxation, and low budget deficits) also have implications for domestic social relations, as advocates for gender equity and other equity-seeking groups lose some of their room to maneuver when making claims on the state (Elson 2004).

As noted above, there is also a disjuncture between the intensive surveillance and disciplining of governments to conform to neoliberal macroeconomic policies and the general lack of surveillance of capital itself (reflected in events leading up to the credit crunch and subsequent financial collapse in the US). Further, there is a notable lack of surveillance and enforcement of many global political obligations, particularly those relating to issues of gender equity, poverty alleviation, official development assistance (ODA), and the environment. Such a lack of political commitment, budgetary resources, and surveillance/monitoring capabilities threatens to undermine important commitments made to supporting more equitable and sustainable relations of social reproduction.

Disciplining the poor versus the socialization of risk

At the meso level, and in stark contrast to the socialization of risk for the wealthy financiers, disciplinary neoliberalism is operationalized by compelling the majority of the population to conform to the dictates of self-help and market discipline, and thus to privatize their risk. With the rise of disciplinary neoliberalism, the post-1945 approach to the governance of poverty, which was grounded in a commitment to social citizenship and the maintenance of the well-being of citizens, has given way to a new regime of market citizenship whereby the market is materially and discursively constructed as the best, if not the only, means of assuring one's well-being (Bakker 2003, 2007). Under disciplinary neoliberalism, poverty is individualized and the poor are viewed as lazy and irresponsible individuals whose condition is enabled through their dependence on the state. Discipline is further instilled through the extensive surveillance and even criminalization of those who have to rely on the state for social assistance and by the replacement of welfare with "workfare," which links welfare benefits to work requirements (Peck 2001).

So whereas the lack of surveillance of the financial sector has potentially put taxpayers on the hook for trillions of dollars, finance has rarely been identified in the mainstream media – at least up until the recent eruption of populist rhetoric – as a significant threat to social order. Rather, the label of the "threatening other" has been reserved for the poor – particularly the non-white poor – who, with the retreat of the welfare state, have increasingly come to be governed by the law, the police, and various penal institutions (Parenti 1999; Wacquant 2001).[10] Thus the norms and rules governing the financial sector and the social sector are fundamentally different: the former relies on self-regulation while the latter is based on surveillance and the disciplining effects of low wages, unemployment, an eroding social safety net, as well as the law, the police and prisons. Indeed, in the aftermath of the Enron scandal, and in light of the massive losses cascading through the US economy, it remains to be seen whether those Wall Street titans who racked up losses worth hundreds of billions of dollars will face conviction or imprisonment for their financial crimes and wanton neglect of their fiduciary responsibilities. So far there is little evidence that this is happening.

The reprivatization of social reproduction and the emergence of a new gender order

The shift to increasingly market-governed social policy under disciplinary neoliberalism also has distinctly gendered dimensions. As feminists have extensively documented, the social citizenship regime that characterized Keynesian forms of provisioning was based on an idealized gender order that viewed men as the breadwinners and privileged them in the economic and political spheres while women were assigned the responsibilities of care and domestic labor (Bakker 2007; Elson and Cagatay 2000).[11] Here, provisioning tended to be based on a two-tier system whereby social assistance programs that served primarily a female clientele (such as welfare or Aid to Families with Dependent Children) were politically less legitimate and less well funded than were the social insurance programs (such as social security and various forms of disability and unemployment insurance) that were primarily accessed by men (O'Connor *et al.* 1999; Orloff 1993: 315). This idealized gender order gave rise to gendered forms of surveillance and discipline; the social assistance programs accessed primarily by women were more oriented toward the monitoring and disciplining of clients' behavior than those programs accessed by men (Orloff 1993: 315). That is, as the state took on some of the costs associated with social reproduction, it also deepened its control over these processes, thus entrenching its influence over women and mothers, and through them, the family as a whole.

With the adoption by numerous governments of increasingly restrictive fiscal and monetary policies, there have been significant cuts in budgetary expenditures in most countries, including in the areas of social assistance, health, and education (Bakker 2003: 76). Many of these changes have been institutionalized and locked-in at the macro level through new constitutionalist mechanisms (see Chapter 3 in this volume). The reduction of public expenditures, combined with the declining power of many unions to compel capital to assume some of the costs associated with social reproduction, has led to the increasing "reprivatization of social reproduction" as much of this work has shifted onto families and/or the market. This process has had particularly negative effects for women who tend to perform the majority of social reproductive labor. For example, as public support for health care services has declined, the responsibility of caring for the ill and the elderly has been shifted onto households, and particularly onto women (Bezanson 2006; Morris *et al.* 1999). While some middle- and upper-class women have been able to pay for private health care and child care, others have not. In this way, the impact of the reprivatization of social reproduction has had differential effects on women, largely based on their class, race, sexuality, and citizenship (Bakker 2003: 76).

Such forms of privatized provisioning are informed by and serve to reproduce the assumption that the gender order that characterized the era of the Welfare State has largely given way to a new gender order whereby women and men both participate in full-time, permanent paid employment. Here, governments increasingly assume that women, as workers, are not dependent on men and they design access to social programs accordingly. While the male breadwinner model had numerous disadvantages for women, the new dual earner model is also highly disadvantageous, particularly since the trend is movement away from this type of work and toward part-time and precarious forms of employment for both women and men (Cohen 2007: 30).

In certain respects, the emergence of a new gender order has benefited some (but by no means all) women: gender attitudes have shifted, many women have increased their participation in the paid labor market, some of these women have entered into powerful and highly paid positions (though these remain a minority) and some women have gained various degrees of financial independence from both men and the state. However, the loosening of women's dependence on men and the state has been met with an increasing dependence on the market: a market that is itself shaped by gendered assumptions, meanings, and allocations of risk. That is, the gendered disciplinary relations that exist between women and men in the household and women and the state as social provider are increasingly being joined to, or in some cases replaced by, gendered relations of disciplinary neoliberalism. This point is clearly evidenced in the unequal distribution of subprime mortgage loan products in the US, where the working-class, women, and racialized minorities have been deemed "riskier" borrowers and thus charged significantly higher interest rates.

There's no place like home

In the past decade and a half, the US has witnessed a dramatic increase in the number of women who have purchased their own homes, with the number doubling from one in ten in 1990 to over one in five in 2003. However, rather than serving to decrease gendered inequalities in wealth, women have been disproportionately targeted for subprime loans, preventing them from using their homes as wealth-building assets to the same extent as men with similar levels of income. According to a report released by the Consumer Federation of America, whereas around 24 percent of male borrowers receive subprime mortgages, for women this number is approximately 32 percent. With subprime borrowers paying between $85,000 and $186,000 more in interest than average borrowers over the amortization period of a typical mortgage, this difference has clear financial implications for women and their families (Fishbein and Woodall 2006b: 3).

Although there has been astonishingly little research and commentary on the gendered nature of risk assessment in the US mortgage industry, studies that do exist have shown that a gender bias is clearly present. For instance, while women make up 30 percent of borrowers for all mortgages, they make up 38.8 percent of subprime borrowers, bringing the rate of over-representation to 29.1 percent. Though it is the case in the US that women working full time, year round earn almost 25 percent less than their male counterparts and that women are 42 percent more likely to live in poverty than men, such disparities do not account for the over-representation of women in the pool of subprime mortgages. Rather, gender disparities in all mortgage products (including home purchase, refinance, and home improvement loans) exist across all income levels and actually increase as levels of income rise. That is, whereas women earning below the median income are 3.3 percent more likely to receive subprime mortgages than men with similar incomes, women who earn double the median income are almost 50 percent more likely to receive such mortgages than men (Fishbein and Woodall 2006b: 3–4).

Financial risk assessment in the US is not only highly gendered, but also highly racialized. Based on information collected under the recent Home Mortgage

Disclosure Act (HMDA), one study found that African-American and Latino borrowers received a significantly disproportionate share of higher-rate subprime loans than their white counterparts. The study found that borrowers of color were more than 30 percent more likely to receive a higher-rate loan than white borrowers. This was the case even when risk factors such as income and property location were taken into account (Gruenstein *et al.* 2006). A separate study found that whereas around 20 percent of white borrowers and 13.5 percent of Asian borrowers received subprime loans in 2005, these loans were given to almost 40 percent of Latino borrowers and over 50 percent of African-American borrowers (Fishbein and Woodall 2006a). The latter study also found that in predominantly black neighborhoods, borrowers are five times more likely to receive a subprime loan than borrowers living in predominantly white neighborhoods. Bringing the class and racial nature of lending into even sharper relief, it has been found that homeowners living in high-income black neighborhoods are twice as likely as homeowners living in low-income white neighborhoods to have subprime loans (HUD 2000).

Given the significant lending biases against women and racialized minorities in the US, it is perhaps unsurprising that women of color face some of the highest levels of discrimination and have the highest rates of subprime lending. For instance, whereas an African-American woman is 5.7 percent more likely to receive a subprime mortgage than an African-American man, she is 256.1 percent more likely to receive one than a white man. Again, this disparity is not linked directly to income levels, but rather exists at every level of income and grows as income rises (Fishbein and Woodall 2006b: 3–4).

These studies, therefore, draw attention to the ways in which individuals are drawn into market relationships on unequal terrain and reveal the highly class-based, gendered, and racialized nature of disciplinary neoliberalism. These dimensions are not considered by the advocates of the neoliberal political and economic project (i.e. most mainstream economists, central governments, and the major international financial institutions) and the solutions they have proposed to the contemporary crises will only serve to reproduce gender-based inequalities in financial markets and the unequal distribution of risk associated with financial and other crises. Furthermore, given that many of the proposed solutions to the global financial crisis are based on the assumption that while there may be a need for some increased regulation of finance, the capitalist market system remains the best and most efficient allocator of global resources, they fail to address the inherent contradictions of capitalism and the contemporary disciplinary neoliberal project.

Conclusion

The contemporary global financial, food, and fuel crises have brought to light numerous tensions and contradictions generated by the governance of society along disciplinary neoliberal lines. As Polanyi argued over a half a century ago, the attempt to create a self-regulating market system poses threats to our basic conditions of existence: to relations of social reproduction, the environment, and ultimately, to the reproduction of capitalism itself. Throughout this chapter, we have pointed to a number of tensions and contradictions generated by the disciplinary neoliberal project.

A central contradiction is generated by the socialization of risk for the wealthy few and the individualization and privatization of risk for the majority of the world's population. In addition, the financial sector and the social sector are governed in contradictory ways. The financial sector – directly responsible for the near-collapse of the global economic system – largely relies on self-regulation. In contrast, the social sector has become increasingly punitive, and disciplinary and carceral institutions have come to play an increasingly important role in the governance of poverty, particularly among the non-white population.

There is a further tension between liberal economic discourse and policies based on the assumption that the market serves to coordinate exchanges between abstract individuals (*homo economicus*) and the everyday experiences of those who come into contact with the market. As the example of subprime mortgage lending in the US reveals, gender and race continue to influence the terms under which one is integrated into markets and the disciplinary neoliberal project. As such, the rise of the dual-earner gender order and the increasing integration of women into increasingly insecure and precarious labor, financial and other markets may serve to reproduce rather than eliminate gender-based inequality.

Additional tensions and insecurities are created by the extension of market relations to govern essential aspects of social reproduction such as access to food, fuel, health, and welfare services. Past and present crises have made apparent the ways in which the governance of these necessities through precarious markets has the potential to create crises of social reproduction. Given the unequal distribution of resources and unpaid labor in many households, such crises may also exacerbate existing gender inequalities.

The political sustainability of neoliberal governance has become increasingly questionable in a world characterized by growing inequalities, cascading crises and dislocations, as well as cumulative threats to the biosphere and challenges to basic livelihood. Such developments may be giving rise to a new form of what Polanyi called the "double movement," which in a slightly different political language means a counter-hegemonic movement of political forces at both national and global levels across the political spectrum to counter the attempt to instantiate a self-regulating market order, and to ensure social protection of not only labor, land, and basic livelihood, but also of capital against the atomization and dislocations engendered by a market imperative fully subordinated to financial greed.

Today's new double movement – embodied in the dialectic of market versus social protection – therefore involves a wide-ranging form of progressive internationalism. Of course, it also includes many reactionary, hyper-nationalist forces opposed to disciplinary neoliberalism, as was the case when global liberalism collapsed during the aftermath of the Great Depression of the 1930s.

The problematic of the future of global economic governance in general, and of macroeconomic governance in particular, will therefore rest on political struggle, and the degree to which such forces can mount an organized challenge, based on a new social ethic and grounded in effective policies to regulate and democratize capital, and ultimately to create an alternative and hopefully new and forward-looking form of hegemony that will be embodied in more ecologically sustainable and socially responsive forms of governance.

Notes

1 This is an updated version of the paper we presented at the September 2008 New School Conference. We thank Isabella Bakker for comments.

2 CNN's bailout tracker offers a breakdown of funds committed to and invested in the financial rescue plan. The bailout tracker is available on-line at: http://money.cnn.com/news/storysupplement/economy/bailouttracker/index.html#STIMULUS (accessed June 3, 2010).

3 Chris Giles and Christian Oliver, 'G20 drops support for fiscal stimulus' *Financial Times*, June 5, 2010.

4 As Joseph Stiglitz, the former chief economist of the World Bank argued, when the bail-out was announced in September 2008 celebration erupted on Wall Street as "the banks realized that they were about to get a free ride at taxpayers' expense. No private firm was willing to buy these toxic mortgages at what the seller thought was a reasonable price; they finally had found a sucker who would take them off their hands – called the American taxpayer" (Stiglitz 2008).

5 Social reproduction refers to the processes that encompass the biological reproduction of the species (and its ecological framework) and the ongoing reproduction of the commodity of labor power. Social reproduction also involves institutions, processes, and social relations associated with the creation and maintenance of communities – upon which, ultimately, all production and exchange rests. Access to the basic necessities for social reproduction is shaped by various overlapping hierarchies built along the lines of gender, race, ethnicity, class, and citizenship. For instance, women – who tend to take on the majority of the work associated with child rearing and care, which are key components of social reproduction and of a healthy and a well functioning society – make up the majority of the world's poor and illiterate (Bakker and Gill 2006: 36–37).

6 See ILO (2010) for further discussion of the effect of the crisis on women's unemployment in different countries and different sectors of the economy.

7 Specifically, in the *Global Monitoring Report 2010*, written by staff at the World Bank and the IMF, it is argued that: "[a]s the global economy gradually recovers, governments must ensure that the long-run benefits of an open and transparent multilateral trading system are not compromised by short-run pressures to protect domestic markets. Concluding the Doha Round would not only improve market access. It would also strengthen the international trading system, constrain future increases in tariffs and subsidies, help governments resist protectionist pressures as they unwind current expansionary policies, and provide a much needed boost to keep markets open" (WB/IMF 2010: 125).

8 A new edition of Polanyi's book has been published with an approving preface by Stiglitz.

9 In *Discipline and Punish*, Foucault (1995) argues that in eighteenth-century Europe, sovereign forms of power that were aimed at controlling the body of subjects (e.g. through physical violence and torture) were eventually superceded by more "disciplinary" forms of power that aimed to control the consciousness and subjectivity of the individual in order to foster processes of self-regulation, and to produce docile bodies. Disciplinary institutions such as the military, the school, and the prison exert a *productive*

power that seeks to construct a particular sort of individual – one who is responsibilized, normalized, and docile. For Foucault, the transition to disciplinary power is related to the rise of capitalism and the need for capital to exert a more constant and totalizing exploitation of bodies (1995: 221).

10 Bringing this trend into stark relief, in 2008, just fewer than 1 in 100 adults were incarcerated in federal prisons and local jails and the inmate population is expected to continue to grow at a rate that triples the growth of the general US population (The Pew Centre on the States 2008: 5).

11 We refer to an *idealized* gender order here in order to draw attention to the fact that this did not reflect the everyday experiences of many women. Racialized, colonized, and immigrant women were particularly likely to diverge from this idealized gender order as social and economic discrimination often made it impossible for them to assume this role in the household. They were also much less likely to turn to the state for protection or economic relief.

Bibliography

Bakker, I. (2003) "Neoliberal Governance and the Reprivatization of Social Reproduction," in I. Bakker and S. Gill (eds) *Power, Production, and Social Reproduction*, New York: Palgrave Macmillan.

——— (2007) "Social Reproduction and the Constitution of a Gendered Political Economy," *New Political Economy*, 12(4): 541–556.

Bakker, I. and Gill, S. (2006) "New Constitutionalism and the Social Reproduction of Caring Institutions," *Theoretical Medicine and Bioethics*, 27(1): 35–57.

Benería, L. (2003) "Economic Rationality and Globalization: A Feminist Perspective," in M. Ferber and J. Nelson (eds) *Feminist Economics Today: Beyond Economic Man*, London and Chicago: University of Chicago Press.

Bezanson, K. (2006) "The Neo-liberal State and Social Reproduction: Gender and Household Insecurity in the Late 1990s," in K. Bezanson and M. Luxton (eds) *Social Reproduction: Feminist Political Economy Challenges Neo-liberalism*, Montreal and Kingston: McGill-Queen's University Press.

Brodie, J. (2003) "Globalization, In/Security, and the Paradoxes of the Social," in I. Bakker and S. Gill (eds) *Power, Production and Social Reproduction*, New York: Palgrave Macmillan.

Cohen, M.G. (2007) "The Shifts in Gender Norms Through Globalization: Gender on the Semi-periphery of Power," in M.G. Cohen and J. Brodie (eds) *Remapping Gender in the New Global Order*, Abingdon and New York: Routledge.

Conway, E. (2009) "IMF puts total cost of crisis at £7.1 trillion," *Telegraph*, August 8, 2009.

Deen, T. (2009) "Financial Crisis Threatens Women's Meager Gains," *Inter Press Service*, March 4, 2009.

Elson, D. (2004) "Engendering Government Budgets in the Context of Globalization(s)," *International Feminist Journal of Politics*, 6(4): 623–642.

Elson, D. and Cagatay, N. (2000) "The Social Content of Macroeconomic Policies," *World Development*, 28(7): 1347–1364.

Fishbein, A.J. and Woodall, P. (2006a) "Subprime locations: patterns of geographic disparity in subprime lending," Washington, DC: The Consumer Federation of America.

——— (2006b) "Women are prime targets for subprime lending: women are disproportionately represented in high-cost mortgage market," Washington, DC: The Consumer Federation of America.

Floro, M.S. and Dymski, D.A. (2000) "Financial Crisis, Gender, and Power: An Analytical Framework," *World Development*, 28(7): 1269–1283.

Folbre, N. and Nelson, J.A. (2000) "For Love or Money – or Both?" *Journal of Economic Perspectives*, 12(2): 123–140.

Foucault, M. (1995) *Discipline and Punish: The Birth of the Prison*, New York: Vintage Books.

Gill, S. (1999) "The Geopolitics of the Asian Crisis," *Monthly Review*, 50(10): 1–10.

——— (2008) *Power and Resistance in the New World Order*, 2nd edn, New York: Palgrave Macmillan.

Gruenstein, D.B., Ernst, K.S. and Li, W. (2006) "Unfair lending: the effects of ethnicity on the price of subprime mortgages," Centre for Responsible Lending.

Hayek, F.A. (1944) *The Road to Serfdom*, Chicago: The University of Chicago Press.

HUD (2000) *Unequal Burden: Income and Racial Disparities in Subprime Lending in America*, US Department of Housing and Urban Development.

IFPRI (2008) *Helping Women Respond to the Global Food Price Crisis*, Washington, DC: International Food Policy Research Institute.

ILO (2010) *Women in Labour Markets: Measuring Progress and Identifying Challenges*, Geneva: International Labour Office.

IMF (2008a) *Food and Fuel Prices – Recent Developments, Macroeconomic Impact, and Policy Responses*, Washington, DC: International Monetary Fund.

——— (2008b) *Global Financial Stability Report: Containing Systemic Risks and Restoring Financial Soundness*, Washington, DC: International Monetary Fund.

Katz, C. (2001) "Vagabond Capitalism and the Necessity of Social Reproduction," *Antipode*, 33(4): 709–728.

Macan-Markar, M. (2008) "ASIA: food crisis adds to women's burden," *Inter Press Service (IPS) News Agency*. Online. Available at: http://ipsnews.net/news.asp?idnews=42162 (accessed November 4, 2008).

Morris, M., Robinson, J. and Simpson, J. (1999) *The Changing Nature of Home Care and its Impact on Women's Vulnerability to Poverty*, Ottawa: Status of Women Canada.

O'Connor, J., Orloff, A. and Shaver, S. (1999) *States, Markets, and Families: Gender, Liberalism and Social Policy in Australia, Canada, Great Britain, and the United States*, New York: Cambridge University Press.

Orloff, A. (1993) "Gender and the Social Rights of Citizenship: The Comparative Analysis of Gender Relations and Welfare States." *American Sociological Review* 58(3): 303–328.

Parenti, C. (1999) *Lockdown America: Police and Prisons in the Age of Crisis*, London and New York: Verso.

Peck, J. (2001) *Workfare States*, New York: Guilford.

Polanyi, K. (1944) *The Great Transformation: The Political and Economic Origins of Our Time*, Boston: Beacon Press. Reprint, 1957.

Smith, M. (2009) "Analysis Note: Gender Equality and Recession," European Commission's Network of Experts on Employment and Gender Equality Issues. Online. Available at: http://grenoble-em.academia.edu/marksmith/Papers.

Stiglitz, J. (2008) "A better bailout," *The Nation*, September 27, 2008.

The Pew Centre on the States (2008) *One in 100: Behind Bars in America 2009*, Washington, DC: The Pew Charitable Trusts.

UNCTAD (2009) *Trade and Development Report*, New York and Geneva: United Nations.

UNESCO (2010) *EFA Global Monitoring Report 2010: Reaching the Marginalized*, Paris and Oxford: UNESCO Publishing and Oxford University Press.

UNPFA (2005) "Niger food crisis especially dangerous for pregnant women," Press Release, Dakar, Senegal: United Nations Population Fund. Online. Available at: http://www.unfpa.org/news/news.cfm?ID=660 (accessed November 15, 2008).

van Staveren, I. (2001) "Gender biases in finance," *Gender and Development*, 9(1): 9–17.
Wacquant, L. (2001) "The Penalisation of Poverty and the Rise of Neo-liberalism," *European Journal on Criminal Policy and Research*, 9(4): 401–12.
WB/IMF (2010) "Global Monitoring Report 2010: The MDGs After the Crisis," Washington, DC: The International Bank for Reconstruction and Development/The World Bank.
Young, B. (2003) "Financial Crises and Social Reproduction: Asia, Argentina and Brazil," in I. Bakker and S. Gill (eds) *Power, Production and Social Reproduction*, New York: Palgrave Macmillan.

INDEX